DESIS IN THE HOUSE

For the brave women of Apna Ghar,

Sunaina Maira

April 25, 2002

In the series

Asian American History and Culture

edited by Sucheng Chan, David Palumbo-Liu, and Michael Omi

DESIS IN THE HOUSE

INDIAN AMERICAN

YOUTH CULTURE

IN NEW YORK CITY

Sunaina Marr Maira

Temple University Press

PHILADELPHIA

Temple University Press, Philadelphia 19122
Copyright © 2002 by Temple University
Published 2002
Printed in the United States of America

⊖The paper used in this publication meets the requirements of
the American National Standard for Information Sciences—Permanence
of Paper for Printed Library Materials, ANSI Z39.48-1984

Library of Congress Cataloging-in-Publication Data

Maira, Sunaina, 1969–
    Desis in the house: Indian American youth culture in New York City /
    Sunaina Marr Maira.
        p.   cm. — (Asian American history and culture)
    Includes bibliographical references and index.
    ISBN 1-56639-926-2 (cloth: alk. paper) — ISBN 1-56639-927-0 (pbk: alk. paper)
        1. East Indian Americans—New York (State)—New York—Ethnic identity.   2. East
Indian Americans—New York (State)—New York—Social conditions.   3. East Indian
Americans—New York (State)—New York—Social life and customs.   4. Youth—New
York (State)—New York—Social life and customs.   5. Children of immigrants—New
York (State)—New York—Social life and customs.   6. Youth—New York (State)—New
York—Social conditions.   7. Children of immigrants—New York (State)—New York—
Social conditions.   8. New York (N.Y.)—Social life and customs.   9. New York
(N.Y.)—Social conditions.   10. Subculture—New York (State)—New York.   I. Title.
II. Series.

F128.9.E2 M35 2002
305.89140747—dc21

                                                                                    2001034071

**For my parents,
and the desi youth who lent
their stories to this book**

Contents

Acknowledgments

ere you meet the people whose ideas, advice, caring, work, and support made this book possible, and who are present in some way on the pages that follow. I am sure to leave out some names in this genealogy of time and advice shared, and I can in no way do justice to the generosity of those whose contributions I allude to here.

I am deeply indebted to my mentors for their unflagging support and thoughtful advice: Robert LeVine, who introduced me to anthropology and the uses of rigorous scholarship in the public world and whose kindness made graduate school life bearable; Marcelo Suárez-Orozco, for working me with closely on this project at so many different stages, for his incredible acumen, for his advocacy on behalf of immigrants, and for believing in me always; and Tom Shaw, for his incisive and insightful critique and for coming to New York to go to a desi party—so he could see firsthand the questions with which I was grappling! Thank you to Gary Okihiro and Sucheta Mazumdar for their support, their inspiring work, and their progressive vision of Asian American studies.

I also want to thank the friends and comrades whose work has shaped my own in different ways, and who have shown me the social and political uses of theory: Vijay Prashad, who has been a clear-headed interlocutor and wise friend from the earliest moments of this work, and whose comments on the manuscript were instrumental in reshaping the book; Somini Sengupta, whose writing and ideas are always a step ahead of the journals; Rajini Srikanth, for being such a generous and thoughtful friend and collaborator; Naresh Fernandes, for his wonderful writing and ongoing support; Sangeeta Kamat and Biju Mathew, for their inspiring activism wherever they happen to be; Amitava Kumar, for setting an example of elegant Marxist critique; and Sonia Arora and Raju Rajan, for proving me wrong on at least one hypothesis! And thank you to the participants and organizers of Youth Solidarity Summer for giving me a reason to do this work and for continuing to remind me why I do it.

A big thanks to the students and the deejays in New York, and earlier in Boston, who shared their time and thoughts with me. Meg McLagan and Mun-Hou Lo have provided encouragement, insight, and sane advice in New York and in Cambridge. The cultural producers and community activists who poured so much of their time into creating the Diasporadics festival with me in New York deserve mention for demonstrating the ways in which the arts can challenge confining understandings of diasporic lives. I also want to thank Connie Sutton, Department of Anthropology, New York University; Jack Tchen and the Asian/Pacific/American Studies Program and Institute at New York University; Tim Taylor, Department of Ethnomusicology, Columbia University; and Philip Kassinitz and the Center for Urban Research, City University of New York, for helping me feel connected to an academic community in New York.

Thanks to the visionary supporters of Asian American studies who have blazed a trail at the University of Massachusetts, Amherst—faculty, staff, and graduate and undergraduate students including: Lucy Burns, Nina Ha, Sally Habana-Hafner, Jim Hafner, Margo Culley, Michael Elgarico, and Molly Agarwal. There were also many colleagues in English and other departments at the university who helped create a space for me to develop these ideas in different settings and who provided inspiration along the way; thanks especially to Sarah Babb, Randall Knoper, Christine Cooper, R. Radhakrishnan, Arlene Avakian, Robbie Schwarzwald, Bill Strickland, and Martin Espada.

Janet Francendese has been the most supportive, sound editor I could have hoped for; thank you for working with me as this became a book. Thanks also to Jennifer French and Shamell Roberts at Temple University Press, to Anita Mannur for her timely help in the final stages, and to Naren Gupte at P. M. Gordon Associates for his always thoughtful advice, patience, and understanding during the production process. A huge shout out to Srinivas Kuruganti for letting me use his gorgeous photographs; they convey visually all of what I hope to say about the desi party culture.

A million thanks to Miguel for his patience and faith as this project has developed over the years, and for the incredible culinary works as I ran between classroom and computer.

1

Introduction

Countries have no sympathy; only praises
amplified like distances for the newer
land: the housing gauntlets we had to enter,
stripped but with freedom!
Standards change like faith in a foreign country:

. . .

Did you pledge allegiance to lawns and fences,
better lives for us; the best western education?
Neighbors take the place of extended families,
freedom expires

From "A Better Life," by Diane Mehta (1996)[1]

New York City is laid out on a grid not just of cross-cutting streets and avenues but of intersecting stories of migration and cultural re-creation. The city has historically been a node of multiple diasporas, and today immigrants from South Asia[2] are increasingly visible on its streets, on its campuses, and in the drivers' seats of its taxicabs. While the wave of Indian immigrants who arrived in the late 1960s and 1970s and spread out to the suburbs of America were mainly professionals and graduate students, many of those who came to New York and New Jersey in the 1980s and 1990s tend to be less affluent and not so highly educated. Newsstand workers from Gujarat, India, who run kiosks on sidewalks or in subways are now part of Manhattan's daily landscape, as are the men from North India and Pakistan who drive yellow cabs or the Bangladeshi waiters who work in Indian restaurants. South Asian immigrant labor has become a visible and integral part of New York City at the turn of the new century.

Less visible in the media, not to mention academic literature, are the children of these immigrants and of their more well-to-do compatriots who work in technology, finance, health, education, and other professions. The second generation of post-1965 Indian immigration began to come of age and to enter colleges and the workforce during the late 1980s and 1990s, but the stories of these Indian American adolescents and young adults have not yet been etched into the larger narratives of immigration, ethnicity, racialization, and youth cultures in the United States. These second-generation youth have collectively created a new popular culture, based on dance parties and music mixes, that is as much a part of New York—and also global—club culture as it is of a transnational South Asian public culture. They have crossed national boundaries to identify collectively as "desi," a colloquial term for someone "native" to South Asia and one that has taken hold among many second-generation youth in the diaspora of Indian, Pakistani, Bangladeshi, Sri Lankan, or even Indo-Caribbean, descent.

In the portrait of one young Indian American woman that follows, I begin to grapple with some of the questions raised by the experiences of second-generation youth in the 1990s and to explore what constitutes the "authentic" ethnic subject, subcultural codes of belonging and exclusion, and the resources that popular culture offers to second-generation youth. Layered into this discussion of the different social spaces that this young woman travels through—"Indian," "American," "local," "foreign," "college," "home"—is the dimension of time, for these experiences emerge at a particular historical moment and are linked to previous moments in the histories of Indian Americans. The temporal element cannot be separated from the spatial map that emerges in this story. A discussion of the historical contexts of Indian immigration to the United States is thus embedded in the narrative at points of intersection between individual and collective experiences, deliberately highlighting the dynamic meaning of history in self-making rather than separately presenting a "grand historical narrative" of Indian immigrant experiences (Marcus 1998, p. 14).

Radhika: Reflections of a "Fake Indian"

Radhika, a twenty-two-year-old woman who was studying at Hunter College when I met her in 1997, grew up in Jackson Heights, Queens. Hunter is a public institution that is part of the City University of New York (CUNY) system, and its extremely diverse student body traditionally draws the children of immigrant and working-class families— a tradition invoked during the heated debates and student protests over changes in CUNY's admission policy in the late 1990s. I met Radhika through a friend who was invited to speak in a course on multicultural literature that Radhika was taking at the time. Sitting in the bustling college cafeteria suffused with warm light and the noisy hum of conversations in several different languages, Radhika said, "When I first came to Hunter, I didn't identify myself as Indian, so [I felt] don't call me an Indian, don't associate me with an Indian, uh-uh, that just won't work!" Later, she remarked, "Today, I define myself as an American with an Indian cultural background, but don't ever call me [Indian] because I'm not Indian." Her insistence on positioning herself within the nation-state, as an "American," and her uneasiness about claiming an unqualified "Indian" identity, were strikingly different from the stance taken by most of the other youth I spoke to, who embraced the label "Indian" more eagerly than even a hyphenated "Indian American" identification. My conversation with Radhika coincided with a moment in her life when she was reframing her definition of what it meant to identify ethnically, as she remarked:

> When I took the . . . multicultural literature course with Professor J., that was the first course I'd taken in the college on any cultural environment and basically discussed the whole concept of identity and ethnicity . . . that's when it really hit me that so many people are really proud of who they are, and where they come from, if you look at the Spanish-speaking people, Latinos or however they really want to be defined, these people are very proud . . . and they have, the African Americans with their slavery, and the Latinos with being discriminated. . . . I mean, they have all that.

Two striking issues emerge from Radhika's reappraisal of ethnic identification. One is that the intellectual frameworks the course provided had helped her place her reluctance to identify as Indian within a comparative analysis of race politics and had encouraged her to reflect critically on the meaning of being Indian American. She had come to a realization that ethnic identity need not be a totalizing identity and could be critically and selectively reconstructed: "The course basically helped me understand that there's no reason for me to be totally estranged from [my ethnic identity]. I may not like every aspect of it, and I don't have to like every aspect of it." This self-conscious, intellectual exploration of ethnic identity among college-age youth leads to what some call an "ethnic revival" in the second generation (Gans 1979; Roosens 1989). This revival is often spurred by formal programs of study, and it was an experience shared by most, if not all, of the Indian American youth to whom I spoke.

The second dimension of ethnic identity that Radhika pondered in the multicultural literature course, as if from a distance, was collective pride not just in one's "roots" but in a history of resistance to oppression centered on ethnicity. In pointing to the race consciousness of Latinos and African Americans, she was not simply turning to textbook portraits or political rhetoric about other communities of color, for she lived in a predominantly Latino area of Jackson Heights and had a multiethnic circle of friends. In Radhika's reflection lies almost a tinge of envy of—or a longing for—an ethnic identity that is associated with political defiance. In many ways, Radhika resonated with this view of ethnicity as a source of pride and resistance in the face of discrimination, perhaps because of the harassment and censure she associated with her own ethnic identity as a person of color *and* as an "unorthodox" Indian American. She was singled out for being Indian by her non-Indian peers as a child and criticized for being not Indian enough by her Indian American peers in college. Radhika was ambivalent about her Indian ancestry, and about ethnic labels in general if they served only as a mark of identity, for her experience underscored that these identities are often situationally constructed and unstable.

"Hindoos" and Early Labor Migration to the United States

Radhika's refusal to automatically adopt an ethnic label in part stemmed from the racial harassment she experienced as a child in a predominantly White school in Queens. She commented that "little kid jokes . . . can have a great impact on you as an individual," recalling that she was, and sometimes still is, "insulted . . . for the color of [her] skin": "When I walked on the streets and stuff like that, kids in school buses—and even now I get that sometimes, not as much though as before—'Oh, Hindu! Hindus!' They only used to call me Hindu, and what really ticked me off is first, I'm not Hindu! I am *not* Hindu, I am a Christian."

Radhika's family are, in fact, Protestant Christians from the state of Maharashtra in western India, but the children Radhika remembers used "Hindu" as a derogatory word for someone who might well have been Catholic, Muslim, Jain, Buddhist, or Zoroastrian, given the diversity of religions practiced in India. Radhika pointed out, "So I'm not Hindu, that was number one. Second of all, even if I was Hindu, what makes me really . . . Hindu became sort of a negative connotation. . . . [I]t started from when I was growing up, and how I was treated in school, and although you're just being teased and stuff like that, it can have a really great influence on you."

The use of "Hindu" as a pejorative label for Indian Americans has historical antecedents in the United States and Canada and can be traced to the arrival of the first wave of Indian immigrants in Washington and, later, California in the early twentieth century. Those agricultural workers generally emigrated from rural areas in the Punjab, a region in North India and what is now Pakistan, and to a lesser extent from the United Provinces (now the state of Uttar Pradesh in North India), Bengal (East India), and Gujarat (West India) (Hess 1976). Many were initially lured by the advertisements of Canadian employers, particularly those in the railroads; recruiters were especially successful in attracting Punjabi Sikhs, a group that accounted for almost 90 percent of the pre-1920 emigrants to North America (Leonard 1992).[3] Their arrival evoked an ambivalent, if not racist response, and Sikh as well as Muslim labor migrants were caricatured as "Hindoos" by an ignorant public and media.

According to some historians, Indian laborers initially came as "sojourners" rather than as settlers; they lived frugally, their sole object being to return to India with their savings (Hess 1976; Leonard 1992). They were, however, met with hostility by Canadian residents who held "the tide of turbans" responsible for depressed wages. In 1907, a mob of white Canadians assaulted Indian immigrants in the town of Bellingham, Washington, beating them on the streets and dragging them out of streetcars. The eruption set off a series of anti-Indian riots in other towns; seven hundred Sikhs were driven out of Washington into British Columbia and California as fear of the "Hindoo invasion" and new labor competition mounted among local residents (Daniels 1989; Takaki 1989b). Indians began moving to the United States after Canada legislated measures restricting Indian immigration; between 1907 and 1920, approximately sixty-four hundred Indian immigrants, primarily agricultural workers and a few small entrepreneurs, were admitted to the United States and settled on the West Coast (Hess 1976).

In the United States, however, Indian Americans soon became the newest Asian immigrant group to be targeted by the Asiatic Exclusion League, a San Francisco-based group that successfully pressured immigration officials to deny admission to Indian immigrants and that described "Hindus" as "enslaved, effeminate, caste-ridden and degraded" (Hess 1976, p. 162). In 1911, the U.S. Immigration Commission survey of Indian immigrants in California explicitly reflected this racist attitude in its statement that "the East Indians on the Pacific Coast are almost universally regarded as the least desirable race of immigrants thus far admitted to the United States" (Daniels 1989). In response to the pressures of the Asiatic Exclusion League to keep out this "new menace," an immigration restriction law in 1917 designated India one of the countries in the "Asiatic barred zone" from which immigration to the U.S. was prohibited. Between 1911 and 1920, the United States deported some seventeen hundred Indians, and fourteen hundred left voluntarily (Hing 1993), as hysteria over the "new Yellow Peril" mounted (Hess 1976; Takaki 1989a). Over the next twenty years, three thousand Indians returned to the subcontinent, including deportees; however, an equal number are estimated to have entered illegally through Mexico (Hess 1976).

I link Radhika's story to this historical context of migration and racial formation because the children who taunted her, like those who harassed other Indian American youth who grew up in the New York City area, were probably unaware of the long and problematic genealogy of the epithets they used. Obviously, the political and economic circumstances of Indian immigration have changed since the early twentieth-century Punjabi labor migration to the West Coast (although anti-immigrant sentiment has resurfaced there since Proposition 187 and subsequent restrictive measures passed in the 1990s). Nevertheless, for Radhika and others, these labels still convey a racially coded message to the new brown kids on the block that makes them feel unwelcome and leads them to devise ways to strategically manage their stigmatized ethnic identity in childhood, a move that has important implications later in their lives and shapes the youth culture that is the focus of this book.

Post-1965 Immigration and Class Mobility

Radhika's parents were part of the late-1960s migration of technically skilled professionals and students from India that was propelled by the Immigration Act of 1965; her father was a computer programmer and her mother the supervisor of a word-processing pool. It was not until 1965, often considered a watershed year in U.S. immigration studies, that U.S. law revised the half-century-old policy of discrimination against Asian immigrants. The number of new immigrants from Asia, including from India and Pakistan, increased dramatically, giving rise to the second major wave of Indian immigration to the U.S.; the Indian American community expanded from approximately 50,000 before 1965 to 815,500 by 1990, and by 2000 had reached 1,687,765 (Fisher 1980; Hing 1993; U.S. Census Bureau, 2000 Census). Moreover, new criteria for visas shaped the characteristics of post-1965 Indian immigrants and thus the socioeconomic background of many second-generation Indian Americans. The new immigration laws gave preferential treatment to professionals; hence the early wave of post-1965 Indian immigrants consisted of highly educated, skilled professionals who, in a relatively short time, acquired middle- to upper-middle-class status (Agarwal 1991; Helweg and Helweg 1990). On average, these "new immigrants" have had a relatively high median income (figures drawn from the 1990 U.S. Census range from $44,696 in 1989 to $49,309 in 1990, and recent reports suggest that the amount continues to rise) and are fluent in English, the result of their training in a postcolonial nation that has made English-language education available to the middle classes (Agarwal 1991; Hing 1993; Khagram, Desai, and Varughese 2001; Mazumdar 1995; Min 1995).

The image of Indian Americans—and of other Asian American groups—as a "model minority," however, is contingent on the class status and educational achievements of a privileged cohort of the overall immigrant group. The model minority image also may exacerbate the threat of competition in employment and education to older residents or citizens who may perceive resources in this country as "limited goods" (Suárez-Orozco 1995, p. 22). In a brutal example, economic frustration among unemployed laborers fanned racial antagonism and

South Asian–owned businesses in the "Little India" area of Lexington Avenue, Manhattan. (All photos not otherwise attributed are courtesy of the author.)

led to violent assaults against Indian Americans in Jersey City in 1987 (Misir 1996). The self-named "Dotbusters" gang went on a rampage against "dotheads," a derogatory term for Indians alluding to the bindi, an ornamental mark worn by some Indian women on their foreheads, pulling women's saris and leaving one man comatose and another beaten to death.[4] Radhika's parents, who are well-educated middle-class professionals, had fortunately never experienced such brutal racism which is often directed against those perceived as most vulnerable or those most visibly "in the line of fire," such as small business owners or service workers, particularly during an economic recession.

How the public imagines particular immigrant groups depends on particular struggles over class and constructions of race and citizenship that shape and sometimes constrain, the identity strategies that individual immigrants choose—strategies that are dialectically related to histories of arrival, entry, or exclusion. Notions of ethnic authenticity and performances of nostalgia, such as those that emerge in Radhika's narrative, always relate to the material experiences of immigrant communities at particular moments in time.

Interestingly, though Radhika was labeled "Hindu" on the streets of New York City, when she visited her parents' hometown in India she was identified as "American." Distinctions of style were used to mark her as a diasporic Indian, as Radhika observed: "Someone walking on the street with jeans and a T-shirt, I think you can automatically recognize it is an American!" Radhika acknowledged that some young people in her family's hometown, Poona (now called Pune), also wore jeans and T-shirts, but she commented: "They didn't dress the way I dressed, I mean, walking on the street with a men's T-shirt is [we both laugh], you know that person is not from India!" These stylistic markers and subtle gendered performances conveyed her national location without even the tell-tale signs of accent: "They didn't dress the way I dressed, I mean, walking on the street with a men's T-shirt is [we both laugh], you know that person is not from India!" (When I met her, Radhika was wearing an androgynous-looking T-shirt, jeans, and a baseball cap over her short, dark hair.) It is worth pondering that visual cues sufficiently coded to elicit the label "Hindu" in New York suggested "American" in Poona.

In addition to Radhika's early experience of racial harassment was a critique of certain social inequities that she associated with "Indian culture," both in the United States and in India, that contributed to her ambivalence about identifying as Indian. She was explicitly critical of Indian immigrants who emphasized upward social mobility, remarking that many seemed seduced by the "so-called American Dream." As a peer counselor at Hunter, Radhika saw the ways in which this ideology is negotiated daily in the decisions that Indian American youth struggle with in college as they try to enter fields that will realize their immigrant parents' aspirations to secure their foothold in the middle class. Most of these youth, according to Radhika, majored in biology, chemistry, math, and nursing, and some who came to her admitted that their parents' wishes heavily shaped their academic choices.

The second generation's attempts to work out their aspirations for social mobility are intertwined with the bifurcated economic trajectories of Indian immigrants entering the U.S. economy in the 1980s and 1990s. The entry of highly-educated, professional Indian immigrants has continued, but changes in immigration laws after 1965 also brought a third major wave of Indian immigrants that includes a substantial working- and lower-middle-class population as well as relatives of earlier immigrants who enter with family reunification visas, changing the presumed "model minority" profile of the Indian American community. Since 1983, more than twenty-five thousand Indian immigrants have entered the United States annually; in 1989, 85 percent of Indian immigrants entered under family reunification categories, while only 1 percent came with occupation-based visas (down from 18 percent in 1969) (Hing 1993). Together with Indian professionals who have turned to entrepreneurship, these later immigrants have created an Indian business community that owns motels and retail establishments (Khandelwal 1995). The material struggles of these often invisible Indian American challenge the model minority caricature: the 1990 U.S. Census found that 7.4 percent of Indian American families fall below the poverty line, slightly more than White American families (7 percent) (Hing 1993). The economic resources, class aspirations, and financial anxieties that second-generation youth inherit from their parents significantly influence their reworking of racial, ethnic, and gender ideologies as they move through adolescence.

Radhika did not seem to have a conflict with her parents over career choices and financial security; in contrast to the stereotypical Indian American career path of medicine or computer science, she was determined to be a "case social worker." Unlike some of her Indian American friends who were contemplating marriages and introductions to prospective spouses, Radhika was resolutely not interested in planning a domestic family life. She criticized what she saw as oppressive gender roles and double standards operating for men and women in Indian families, such as the practice of arranged marriage, as well as the class-based social divisions she perceived in middle-class households in India. Radhika's family, however, had a rather unconventional migration history, for her mother came to the United States before her father— a reversal of the usual gendered migration trajectory. Radhika's grandfather had migrated to the United States and was followed by his daughter, who then went back to India and got married. Technically,

this made Radhika a third-generation Indian American, a rare generational status in the relatively recent Indian American community on
the East Coast.

For Radhika, this immigration history did not seem particularly remarkable, and she recounted the details of her family's journey rather
vaguely, with broad temporal and spatial strokes. Of more interest to
her were contemporary practices of parent-child relationships or em-
ployer–domestic servant interactions in Indian families. Some of her
social critique may have been based on her exposure, on visits to India,
to a particular slice of Indian middle-class life and may draw on the assumptions of a liberal "American" framework of social difference that
leaves inequities of gender and labor in the United States unexposed.
Radhika, however, was one of the few youth to whom I spoke who focused explicitly on political and economic issues and on social hierarchies in contemporary Indian society, rather than solely on traditional
rituals and on cultural and linguistic competencies that were often
viewed as signs of ethnic allegiance.

Ethnic Authenticity and Remix Youth Culture

Radhika's critical social perspective was another reason for her sense of
alienation from Indian American youth who espoused a narrowly, if
clearly, defined ethnic identity that was based on an uncritically
bounded notion of Indian culture. An "authentic Indian" American, for
her peers, was "someone who's proud of being Indian, who goes to all
these Maharashtra Mandal [regional ethnic association] programs . . .
hangs out with all these Indians"—all things Radhika did not do. She
recalled, "Basically these couple of people that I've encountered have
told me, 'Fake Indian! Why don't you be proud of your culture? You've
got to be proud of your culture, why don't you watch Hindi movies and
all this stuff?' It's like, it doesn't *interest* me, you know. They can't comprehend it, because what they've been told, what they've been brought
up with . . . [is] if you have to be Indian, you gotta be proud of your culture."

Radhika's reflections point to a politics of ethnic authenticity that I
found common among Indian American youth who assess "true"
Indianness according to specific social and cultural criteria: watching
Hindi films; speaking Indian languages, which Radhika did not do because she spoke only English at home; or going to "Indian parties" and

socializing with other Indian Americans, whereas Radhika's friends came from diverse ethnic and racial backgrounds. Underlying these cultural practices of second-generation youth was a collective nostalgia for India as a site of revered "tradition" and authentic identity.

One element of Indian American popular culture that did resonate with Radhika was bhangra remix music: Indian folk music mixed with American dance music and produced by Indian American deejays for dance parties held at clubs, restaurants, or college campuses. Radhika enjoyed bhangra remix because of its hybrid sensibility, although she had never attended any of the parties at which this music was played. The "Indian party scene" is a major component of Indian American youth culture in New York City and a significant context in which social networks are created and ethnic as well as racial and gender ideologies are produced and refashioned. Every weekend several parties are staged on college campuses and, more often, at clubs or restaurants in Manhattan rented by Indian party promoters and filled with droves of young South Asian Americans. Youth move to the beat of the latest remix—of bhangra but also Hindi film music—spun by Indian American deejays; they gather in cliques and couples, the women attired in slinky club wear (tight-fitting shirts and hip-hugger pants or miniskirts) and the men in hip-hop-inspired urban street fashion (the signature Tommy Hilfiger shirts and baggy pants), or in jackets and slacks if required. Many in the crowd are regulars on the party circuit, while others make occasional appearances.

These social events are almost exclusively attended by Indian and South Asian youth; a full-page article on this remix youth culture in the *New York Times* in 1996 noted that often "the only Black people are the security guards" (Sengupta 1996). This ethnically exclusive space reflects the social networks and college cliques among youth who participate in this "desi scene," and who belong to campus communities where those who are identified as "truly" Indian or South Asian are those who fraternize only with other South Asians. This subculture helps produce a notion of what it means to be "cool," for a young person in New York, that is (re)worked into the nostalgia for India yet not seamless with it. The role of remix music in the subculture of Indian parties is a critical site for analysis, opening up debates about reinventing ethnicities, performing gender roles, and enacting class aspirations.

Radhika's critique of ethnic authenticity rested partly on her reading national identity from style, as other youth do, and was not without its

Getting down on the dance floor at a "desi party." (Courtesy of
Srinivas Kuruganti)

own contradictions and assessments of acceptable performances of
"Indian" or "American" identity. Style, for her as for many youth, was
a primary marker of gender-inflected nationality or ethnicity, as was
social behavior. Her response to the "real Indians" was "Look at the
way you act, the girls with all the makeup and jewelry, the way they
wear their dresses, the short miniskirts and all of that, and what are
they doing? They're just being American." In a sense, Radhika was
countering others' critique of her inadequate Indianness with her own
gendered and sexually coded notion of cultural authenticity. Radhika
herself did not wear traditional Indian clothing; in fact, she refused to
wear a sari despite her father's wish to photograph her in Indian garb.
Yet she found problematic Indian American women's display of a sexually provocative style and feminine appearance that she viewed as

symbolically "American." Radhika's reflections on style and ethnicity are interesting for they demonstrate how female bodies are often used to represent national identity or ethnic loyalty, a gendered ideology that emerged in many of the narratives in this study and that powerfully conjoins notions of chastity and authenticity.

Radhika's story speaks eloquently to the role of boundaries marking insiders and outsiders in Indian American youth subcultures, and of the ways in which being Indian has always been defined against those who are not, ostensibly, truly Indian. She also noted the boundaries visible in campus social life *between* ethnic groups; for instance, even the cafeteria at Hunter College where we sat and talked was divided into ethnically specific clusters of students at different tables. This self-segregation along ethnic lines, with its underlying assumptions of ethnic belonging, made Radhika uneasy. She recalled her shock when a high school friend, on going to college, developed "a thick Indian accent" that Radhika had never heard her use before. Her friend, an Indian American woman, was now socializing only with other Indian Americans; when Radhika asked why, her friend explained that she felt "more comfortable" doing so and had "always been Indian." Radhika exclaimed, "I think she's not always been Indian, she didn't really focus on her Indian ethnicity." Her rejoinder points to the constructedness and dynamism of ethnic identity but also suggests that Indian American youth use certain markers of what it means to be Indian in order to contest one another's performances and narrations of ethnicity and to assert their own. The key questions that I address in this book are why the turn to ethnic identity and the emphasis on certain ideologies of Indianness become a common strategy for Indian American youth in the context of American college life, and, ultimately, how postmodern notions of shifting identifications are complicated by everyday practices of essentialization and boundary marking.

Radhika continued to resist ideologies of ethnic authenticity in college, despite her social isolation from her Indian American peers. She expressed pride in her marginalization rather than in ethnic solidarity through participation in popular culture practices and collective nostalgia: "All of them basically go to these Indian parties, watch Indian movies, all that stuff, I don't do any of that stuff! So to them, I'm abnormal, to them, I'm weird, to them, I'm an outsider. And I say, hey, I'm proud to be an outsider." Radhika is able to project a moment when she will arrive at a different articulation of her ethnic identity, for she is "struggling" to reach a point when she will not want not to "diss" (disrespect) her "culture" and has already come "far" from a time when she refused to "be identified as an Indian or with an Indian background."

In addition to pointing to dynamic and conflictual discourses and practices of gender, racialization, and class and to the micropolitics of this Indian American youth subculture (Thornton 1996), Radhika's reflections raise a salient question: Why are possession of Indian language skills, socialization with other Indian Americans, and interest in Indian films considered *more* Indian than engagement with social and political issues relevant to contemporary India and to Indians in the diaspora? What are the social processes that enable a generational cohort of youth to view the desire for social change in India as a betrayal of identification as ethnic subjects, even as they participate daily in mainstream American social and economic life? Ideas of nation and ethnicity in this youth subculture are infused with nostalgia but also with complex and contradictory understandings of culture and power that are worked out through the discourse of ethnic identity as it has been shaped by 1990s multiculturalism. These rhetorical gestures—of ethnic authenticity, of gendered innocence or sexual waywardness, of ritualized coolness—are linked to the particular insertion of Indian Americans into the racial and class structures of the nation-state and into the transnational flows of labor, capital, and media images in the late twentieth century. It is this process, the negotiation of racial ideology and material dilemmas through gendered performances of "nostalgia" and "cool," that this book addresses.

The Study: An Indian American Youthscape

Radhika's story emerged from a study of second-generation Indian American adolescents that I conducted in New York City in 1996–1997. The aim of the project was to learn how second-generation youth negotiate the politics of ethnicity, race, and gender and recreate cultural beliefs and practices in their daily lives, using the resources of youth popular culture and of campus life. (See Appendix for details about the research methods.) The questions I ask here are: What are the meanings of this youth culture in the lives of Indian American youth? How do Indian American youth negotiate simultaneously the collective nostalgia for India (re)created by their parents and the coming-of-age rituals of American youth culture? The book demonstrates that Indian American youth culture is a site where the vibes of "cool" are mixed with the strains of collective nostalgia, and where second-generation youth perform a deep ambivalence toward ethnicity and nationality, a tension that has often been downplayed in readings of youth subcultures and popular "resistance." The space this youth culture offers is not a purely hybrid or "third" space (Lavie and Swedenburg 1996; Bhabha 1990; 1994, p. 38) but is always embedded in the dialectic between the presumably divergent pathways of assimilation and ethnic authenticity. I found that this tension between coolness and nostalgia was most visibly enacted through paradoxes in the discourse and practice of ethnic authenticity, particularly those imbricated with ideologies of gender. The performance of authentic Indianness reveals the ways in which the surveillance of ethnic purity is inherently about the social control of purportedly transgressive sexualities.

This book focuses on a rapidly growing Asian immigrant community at a moment when it attained a significant presence in New York City. The most sizable wave of Indian immigrants, except for the pioneering agricultural communities established in the early twentieth century by Punjabi Sikhs[5] in California (Gibson 1988; Leonard 1992), came to the United States beginning in the mid-1960s. The Immigration Act of 1965 increased the visa quotas for Asian immigrants, particularly for technically skilled professionals and, in lesser numbers, for relatives of immigrants. Indian immigration increased rapidly in the 1980s and 1990s, with 1996 marking the second highest level in U.S. history, making India at the time the country with the third largest number of new immigrants after Mexico and the Philippines (*Little India Business Directory* 1997, p. 62).

The children of post-1965 Indian (or, for that matter, South Asian) immigrants have hardly been studied; while some studies have focused on older second-generation Indian Americans—for instance, in California and the Chicago area (Agarwal 1991; Gibson 1988)—and others have looked broadly at the Indian immigrant community in New York City (Fisher 1980; Lessinger 1995; Mukhi 2000), no research has focused on Indian American or South Asian American youth in New York City. Yet New York is home to the largest Indian American population of any city in the United States and, according to the 1990 census, had 94,590 Indian residents—a conservative estimate, according to some—out of a total population of 815,447 Indian Americans (Khandelwal 1995, p. 181; Lessinger 1995, p. 17); in the year 2000, the Indian population in New York City had officially reached 170,899, making it the second largest Asian American group in the city after Chinese Americans (U.S. Census Bureau, 2000 Census). In 1995, the year before I did this study, New York City was still the most popular destination for Indian immigrants, with 3,638 out of 34,748 documented new immigrants choosing to settle in the Big Apple that year, according to the Immigration and Naturalization Service. The experiences of Indian American youth are inadequately represented not only in academic research but also in popular literature and the mass media. Nevertheless, a specifically youth-focused Indian American popular culture in New York and in urban areas across the United States slowly began to take its place in the repertoire of youth culture practices in the late 1990s mediascape, or perhaps even "youthscape," to bowdlerize a term coined by Arjun Appadurai (1996). Indian American youth culture brings to light the often hidden contradictions of citizenship and belonging, work and leisure, multiculturalism and education, that second-generation youth manage daily, and it points to a larger, material and historical context that structures this youthscape.

I use the term *second generation* to refer to the children of immigrants who were born in the United States or who arrived here before the age of seven or eight.[6] This cutoff age may seem somewhat arbitrary, for identification as "immigrant" or "second-generation" involves subjective dimensions of belonging and displacement; however, the rationale for such a categorization is that second-generation Americans "come of age" in the United States, that is, share in the rites of passage of American high school and have socialization experiences very different from those who come here as young adults.[7] As the Indian American population becomes older and sees the emergence of growing third and later generations, an emphasis on generational categories will likely give way to emphases on how different communities are positioned in, and reconstituted by, local cultural and political contexts. While undoubtedly important in shaping very different kinds of experiences within the community and nation, generational boundaries are often overdrawn in the immigrant and mainstream media as well as in community forums, particularly in belabored discussions of the "generation gap," which recycle familiar tropes of conflicts between immigrant parents and their children. As Lisa Lowe (1996, p. 63) points out,

"The reduction of cultural politics of racialized ethnic groups . . . to first-generation/second-generation struggles displaces social differences into a privatized familial opposition, . . . denying . . . immigrant histories of material exclusion and differentiation." While the family context is an important crucible for shaping future choices (Agarwal 1991; Kibria 1993; Rumbaut 1994; Serafica 1990), it is also important to pay attention to the cultural forms and narratives that youth create in order to make meaning of their worlds. This study deliberately highlights the experiences of youth themselves, rather than their relationships with their parents, in order to move away from this often pathologized focus on "intergenerational conflict" in immigrant families and popular psychology and to give long overdue attention to the subjectivities and cultural practices of second-generation youth.

"Stripped but with Freedom!": Citizenship, Pan-Ethnicity, and Class Mobility

In general, not enough critical attention has been paid to Asian American youth, and when they do surface in the mass media, it is often as either "nerdy" model minority students or dangerous gang-bangers. Indian American youth have tended to be subsumed under the former caricature, but the economic shifts in the national and global economy during the last two decades of the twentieth century, together with an increase in "knowledge-intensive," highly skilled professional and service jobs that require specialized training and educational credentials, have produced an hourglass labor market in the United States that is divided between high-paying, white-collar jobs and low-wage, often part-time, low-skill jobs. Second-generation youth can no longer expect to follow the socioeconomic trajectories of previous generations of immigrant families, who entered the middle class by building on their parents' financial capital (Zhou and Bankston 1998; Perlman and Waldinger 1997). The future lives of Indian American youth will likely take different routes than those of earlier second-generation Americans, not just because of the conditions created by the post-Fordist economy but also because Indian Americans and other immigrant communities of color experience different struggles over race and citizenship from those of their White predecessors.

Indian Americans are the fourth largest ethnic community in the Asian American population, comprising 11.8 percent of the total Asian immigrant population in 1990 (U.S. Census Bureau 1993). Yet the re-lationship of Indian Americans and South Asian Americans to the pan-Asian umbrella is sometimes marked by an ambivalence—among other Asian Americans but also among Indian Americans themselves—about their place in this coalition (Dave et al. 2000; Shankar and Srikanth, 1998). Like other South and Southeast Asian communities, such as Fil-ipino and Vietnamese Americans, Indian Americans' entry into Asian American ethnic identity politics in the 1990s differed from that of Chinese, Japanese, and Korean Americans during the Civil Rights movement of the 1960s and 1970s, the groups who have long been most closely identified with the pan-Asian category forged by the Asian American movement of that era. Some of this dissonance in the exper-iences of Asian immigrant groups, as well as strategic alliance building among them, is enacted in community organizations, in advocacy groups, and on college campuses, where Asian American youth con-front head on, and also intervene in, institutional ethnic identity politics.

A focus on second-generation Indian Americans is crucial to under-standing how Indian Americans and other new immigrant communi-ties will be inserted into the economic and social fabric of the nation-state. Will these young people fulfill their immigrant parents' class aspirations and "pledge allegiance to lawns and fences," or will they come to see themselves as "stripped but with freedom," as Diane Mehta (in Maira and Srikanth 1996) poetically comments on the ironies of upward mobility and cultural displacement? The paths fol-lowed by individuals in the second generation who are on the thresh-old of "adulthood"—a cultural formation associated with occupa-tional/career decisions, creation of some sort of family unit or independent household, political participation, and involvement in civic institutions—will clearly have an impact on the future of the larger ethnic and pan-ethnic community. As Alejandro Portes (1997, p. 814) observes in his call for research focusing on second-generation ex-periences:

> The case for the second generation as a "strategic research site" is based on two features. First, the long-term effects of immigration for the host society depend less on the fate of first generation immigrants than on their descen-dants. Patterns of adaptation of the first generation set the stage for what is to come, but issues such as the continuing dominance of English, the growth of a welfare dependent population, the resilience or disappearance of cultur-

ally distinct ethnic enclaves, and the decline or growth of ethnic intermarriages will be decided among its children or grandchildren.

This research is crucial in an era in which the decline of the welfare state and dependence on cheap immigrant and female labor lurk behind the rhetoric of the unassimilability of the new, nonwhite immigrants (Suárez-Orozco 1995). The experiences of second-generation youth—their educational trajectories, leisure practices, and language choices—were often a lightning rod in the charged immigration debates sparked by the nativist resurgence during the 1980s and 1990s, arising, for example, in confrontations over bilingual education and in moral panics about youth violence.

In the turn-of-the-millennium era of late capitalism, the intensified global circulation of people and goods gives a new edge to U.S. debates about national identity and national "character" that has pressing political and economic implications for immigrant communities. Much of the nativist anxiety about immigration has centered on heightened fear of labor competition in a post-Fordist economy marked by a shrinking number of stable blue-collar jobs and by increased reliance on "flexible" immigrant labor, sometimes undocumented, by corporations and smaller businesses that wish to keep their wage scales at rock bottom (Mollenkopf and Castells 1991; Harvey 1989). The public discourse about domestic labor and cultural cohesion being under siege by a "deluge" of "aliens" often constructs immigrants as threatening "others" and betrays the anxiety about demographic and cultural changes that fueled the anti-immigrant backlash of the 1990s in the United States as well as in Europe (Suárez-Orozco and Suárez-Orozco 1995).

The underlying material context of contemporary immigration, particularly the United States' economic dependence on the "new immigrants" from Asia, Latin America, and the Caribbean, is often ignored in mass media discussions about the newest newcomers, with public debates framing issues in terms of cultural citizenship and national patriotism. Throughout the 1990s, questions about the national—and transnational—allegiances of Asian Americans and debates about their rights and representations repeatedly surfaced in the national media, from the Democratic fundraising campaign involving Asian American lobbyists and donors that plagued Bill Clinton and Al Gore during their respective presidential tenure and campaign, to the infamous indictment of Wen Ho Lee in 2000 on charges of spying for China, despite highly questionable evidence (Scheer 2000). Citizen-

ship has become an uneasy issue for Asian Americans, for these incidents suggest a gap between their constitutionally given legal rights
and their cultural construction as ambiguously nonwhite or "still foreign" Americans (Ong 1999; Lowe 1996; Palumbo-Liu 1999; Tuan
1999). Meanwhile, however, U.S. public culture, particularly youth
culture, has seen a resurgence of interest in Asian and Asian American
popular culture and leisure commodities, from the martial arts films of
Bruce Lee and Japanese *anime* characters to bhangra beats from South
Asia and henna tattoos.

Yet what of Asian American youth themselves, and their understandings of Asian Americanness, nationalism, ethnicity, and citizenship? How do they manage their ambiguous racial construction, especially as they move through institutions of higher education and into
the workforce? What meanings do they make of Asian American cultural production and of the rites of American youth culture in general?
These are the broader questions to which this book speaks, and which
have often been overlooked in research on Asian American youth and
youth culture across the disciplines.

"Countries Have No Sympathy": Transnationalism and Diaspora

As Diane Mehta's evocative poetry suggests in the epigraph, second-
generation youth culture necessarily raises questions about the relationships of immigrant communities to the nation-state in which they
live and the one ostensibly left behind. These social and material relationships are created in the context of global flows of capital, labor,
media images, and ideologies—what Arjun Appadurai calls ethno-
scapes, mediascapes, and ideoscapes (1996). This transnational approach is one of several offered by studies in sociology and anthropology that now emphasize the strategic ways in which immigrant
communities "forge and sustain multi-stranded social relations that
link together their societies of origin and settlement" (Basch, Glick
Schiller, and Szanton Blanc 1994, p. 7, emphasis mine; see also Hannerz 1996; Hastrup and Olwig 1997; Nonini and Ong 1997; Sutton
1992). Transnationalism is intimately associated with the conditions of
late capitalism, or what David Harvey (1989) refers to as globalized
regimes of flexible accumulation that have created a "new international
division of labor" and "new kinds of social organization" that no longer

have to be tied to specific places (Nonini and Ong 1997, p. 10). New forms of immigrant participation and representation in the nation-state across national borders are emerging as a result of these labor migrations and the globalization of media and capital (Basch, Glick Schiller, and Szanton Blanc 1994; Goldring 1996; Grasmuck and Pessar 1991; Mahler 1997; Portes 1995).[8] National identities clearly still arouse fervent loyalties, however, even within the conditions of diaspora, asylum, or exile, and the nation-state continues to play a central role in creating and reinforcing transnational involvements (Basch, Glick Schiller, and Szanton Blanc 1994; Appadurai 1996).

Research on transnationalism in sociology and anthropology extends earlier perspectives on diasporas that have generally focused on the "adaptive constellation of responses to dwelling in displacement" (Clifford 1997, p. 289). Conceptualizations of diaspora have ranged from strict definitions that emphasize preoccupation with a specific origin and a desire, or even a mythology, of return (Safran 1991), to looser notions that encompass the diverse processes of "adaptation to heteroglossia," evident in the South Asian diaspora (Ghosh 1989, p. 75). Anthropology's move toward transnational perspectives addresses the need for a more precise concept than that of diaspora, which has become increasingly amorphous in contemporary usage, and has been prompted in part by the growing acknowledgment that cultures are not discrete, bounded entities fixed to particular localities (Appadurai 1996; Hannerz 1996; Hastrup and Olwig 1997; Lavie and Swedenburg 1996). Some "reterritorialization" of identities does take place (Lavie and Swedenburg 1996), however, for a strong attachment to place often coexists with a global network of relations (Gupta and Ferguson 1997; Maira and Levitt 1997; Olwig 1997). Perhaps where some theorists of transnationalism and diaspora converge is in their acknowledgment of the ways in which locality remains a potent force, but one that does not connote the fixed opposite of "the global" and that is itself "discursively and historically constructed" (Gupta and Ferguson 1997, p. 6). As James Clifford argues, "[T]he term diaspora is a signifier, not simply of transnationality and movement, but of political struggles to define the local . . . in historical contexts of displacement" (1997, p. 287). In a similar vein, Parminder Bhachu, in her study of transnational East African/Indian women in Britain, observes that "the production of new diasporic spaces, of new cultural forms, and new landscapes results in the creation of national and local identities that are increasingly being contested from the margins" (1996, p. 283). This book focuses on the ways in which second-generation youth culture becomes a site of struggles to define notions of authenticity that, while drawing on transnational imaginings of "India," also work to position these youth in relation to hierarchies of race, class, gender, and nationalism that mark them as "local."

One of the most visible—and audible—diasporic cultural forms produced by Indian American youth in New York is the Indian remix music and dance that Radhika found appealing. This second-generation cultural production uses both local and global sounds, borrowing from a vibrant club culture created by British Asian youth that has produced a new "diaspora aesthetic" in music, dance, and style (Hall 1990, p. 236). As Paul Gilroy points out, in Britain this remix music provoked intense "debates about the authenticity of these hybrid cultural forms" (1993, p. 82). In Indian American communities as well, some celebrate the polyphonic qualities of diasporic cultural production while others emphasize the continuity of ancestral traditions. These debates highlight deeper questions of essentialism and hybridity that are bound up with the politics of cultural authenticity, an issue this book takes up as a central problematic. The ways in which the second generation contests and creates local, but also transnational cultural practices reveal how ideologies of gender, class, and nationalism surface in performances of adolescent "cool" and collective nostalgia.

The dialectic between cultural and subcultural nostalgia that runs through this book suggests a rethinking of the notion of hybridity. Focusing only on the "hybridization" of cultural elements, such as music or style, as performed in remix youth culture does not fully capture the complexities of racial ideology and class expectations that Indian American youth negotiate in their daily lives. The limitations in this analytic approach arise in part from shortcomings in conceptualizations of hybridity, particularly as the valorized antithesis of cultural essentialism, which have led other cultural theorists to suggest strategic ways of breaking out of the trap of this binary (essentialist/hybrid) while analyzing the politics of cultural production and consumption. Radhika's story, for example, illustrates the self-consciousness many second-generation youth have about the hybrid nature of their experiences as children of immigrants and the reflexivity inherent in their participation in ethnic studies courses or in performances that showcase cultural nationalism. This self-conscious or reflexive hybridity is analogous to the way in which critical ethnographers produce a metadiscourse highlighting the constructed nature of their own roles and texts. It is possible to conceive of these identity narratives as akin to a "bifocal cultural criticism" that "operates dialectically among possible cultural and ethnic identifications" (Fischer 1986, pp. 232–33).

This reflexivity and bifocality—a lens turned on identifying oneself even as it sees *and* produces the "other"—marked my own relationship to the research project. As a "native ethnographer" constantly questioning my nativeness, and as a recently arrived New Yorker doing research in my own neighborhood among other sites in Manhattan, researcher reflexivity was generative and tantalizing but also complex and sometimes frustrating (Narayan 1993). It became clear to me that research on immigrant or diasporic experiences always holds the potential for dizzying layers of reflexive analyses on dislocation and belonging. Michael Fischer's work on ethnic autobiography reminds us, however, that this "meta"-cultural critique can be a model for innovative ethnographic research on a range of topics, not just on identity and displacement. The coupling of notions of "insider" ethnography and "rescue projects" that correct gaps in the scholarly record leads, according to Virginia Dominguez (2000, p. 363), to a problematic politics of authenticity in knowledge production and academic authority, where "native" ethnographers are presumed to be driven by a "politics of love" and a "politics of correction," both of which are seen as particularly susceptible to subjectivity and identitarianism. I love bhangra remix and dance and grew close to many of the youth involved in the study, but I also want to note that this project was driven not simply by a politics of love but by a sense of frustration with the social exclusions practiced in the name of love for community or country, and with the epistemological and methodological boundaries guarded by disciplinary nationalisms.

A Multisited Research Imaginary

Much research on second-generation youth has tended either to use a decontextualized, psychological approach to ethnic identity or to emphasize quantitative analyses and render the subtlety of individual narratives invisible. This study attempts to take into account both the subjectivity of individual experiences and the implications of collective responses to social and material contexts. In this, it uses the Birmingham school's tripartite framework of youth subcultures examined through "structures, cultures, and biographies": "Biographies cut paths in and through the determined spaces of the structures and cultures in which individuals are located" and are "the means by which individual identities and life-histories are constructed out of collective experiences" (Clarke et al. 1976, p. 57). While positing this framework, John Clarke and his coauthors acknowledged that they were still unable to do justice to individual biographies, and this has in fact been a weakness of much research on youth culture in sociology, anthropology, and cultural studies, even as psychological approaches to adolescence have largely ignored structural contexts and cultural production. My study attempts an ethnography of a spatially dispersed community in an urban context and is grounded in intensive interviews with youth whose lives are shaped by the shared experience of being in college and of living or studying in New York City. These youth traversed the island of Manhattan, which provides the geographic borders of this ethnography, and navigated the city in ways specific to college-age youth, using its nightclubs, bars, college classrooms, and stores as contexts in which to create social networks and express allegiances to particular subcultures.

This book examines an important site that has so far been neglected in Asian American studies and more generally in immigration studies, namely, youth popular culture. Indian American youth have created social spaces where specifically second-generation, not to mention New York-based, racial and class ideologies are expressed through music, style, and dance. The study focuses on young people's negotiation of multiple social identities and structures during their college years, as traditionally defined, because in classic identity development theory, adolescence—and also young adulthood in the contemporary United States—is considered a crucial period for engaging with questions of identity (Erikson 1959). As with other aspects of identity, ethnic identity socialization and development begin in childhood and continue through the life cycle (Allport 1954; De Vos 1982; Matute-Bianchi 1991; Rotheram and Phinney 1987; Waters 1990). However, ethnic identity is often highlighted in adolescence due to transitions into new social contexts that prompt new, or refined, questions regarding one's position in social structures and relationships. Studies of second-generation Indian Americans, and also "later-generation" White Americans, indicate that many individuals experience shifts in their ethnic identifications in late adolescence and young adulthood, partly due to their moving away from families and entering new, sometimes more diverse communities—as occurs, for example, in the "ritualized" migration of moving away to college (Agarwal 1991; Waters 1990).

Discussions of ethnic identity in the United States are often placed within the rubric of identity politics; that is, as Roger Lancaster and Micaela di Leonardo (1997, p. 5) observe, the "modern Western [read: American] tendency to assume that politics derive[s] from the unanimous interests of certain fixed 'identities'—gender, race/ethnicity, sexual preference. Identity politics, very obviously, elides operations of history and political economy, most particularly the workings of class." Lancaster and di Leonardo argue for a theoretical approach that pays attention to social identities and cultural symbols—their construction and politicization—as well as to material contexts, a "robust, many-sided—and politically relevant—form of social constructionism" (1997, p. 4). This synthesis of cultural theory and political economy draws on the strengths of different strands of scholarship that, when used independently, have tended to neglect certain aspects of social and cultural phenomena but, when combined, produce a more rigorous analysis.

Furthermore, Portes contends that studies of immigrant groups thus far have not produced an adequate body of relevant theory but have focused instead on "ground-level studies of particular migrant groups or analysis of official migrant groups" (1997, p. 799). In light of the paucity of frameworks specifically focused on contemporary second-generation experiences, my study uses an eclectic theoretical approach, integrating models and concepts from anthropology, sociology, cultural studies, psychology, and literary criticism that are relevant to the questions at hand. In this, I have been inspired by what George Marcus calls a "multi-sited research imaginary," (1998, p. 20), an approach to fieldwork and theorizing that emphasizes the interrelationships between multiple analytical lenses and that is not theoretically overdetermined or morally "too certain." My study has multiple analytic "sites," for it intervenes in debates about youth subcultures, popular culture, cultural hybridity, second-generation racialization, and the gendering of nationalism by examining the intersections of these issues in cultural practices and personal narratives.

While this study is focused on Indian American adolescents in New York City, their experiences overlap with youth of color from other immigrant groups who share similar class locations and racial positionings, but they are also distinguished by the particular ambiguity of South Asians in relation to Black/White/Asian racial categories. The book is situated in the context of the new wave of research on second-generation experiences in sociology and anthropology that points to the often divergent paths being followed by children of the "new immigrants," particularly in processes of racialization and education (Gans 1992; Portes and Zhou 1992; Perlmann and Waldinger 1997; Roosens 1989; Rumbaut 1994; Suárez-Orozco and Suárez-Orozco 1995; Waters 1994; Zhou 1997; Zhou and Bankston 1998); however, very few of these studies examine youth popular culture or the social spaces created by second-generation or immigrant youth themselves.

Overview

The following chapters build on one another in sequential progression, each addressing a slice of the overarching questions raised in the book. Chapter 2 sets the stage by examining a second-generation Indian American popular culture that draws on diasporic Indian remix music as well as on hip-hop culture. "Indian parties" in Manhattan are the locus for young people's negotiation of a "politics of cool" and a "politics of nostalgia," a dialectical tension that lies beneath the paradoxes of second-generation ethnicity, racialization, and gender ideology. The consumption of hip-hop by desi youth reveals an ambiguous race politics in the second generation—as is the case for some other Asian American youth—that highlights anxieties about class mobility, generational alienation, and a desire to possess "subcultural capital" as defined by youth of color and the culture industries. Chapter 3 traces youth popular culture's insights into everyday experiences, exploring in greater depth the nature of the nostalgia for "India" co-created by Indian American youth, the immigrant generation, and U.S. multiculturalism. These young people use symbolic markers of true Indianness to construct and contest notions of ethnic authenticity, especially in the context of multiculturalism in higher education and of ethnically and racially segregated social lives on college campuses. The ideology of ethnic authenticity is supported by rites of passage, such as journeys "back" to India, and by popular performances that stage particular versions of "true" Indian culture and that coexist uneasily with the hybrid popular culture of remix music and dance. Second-generation youth make a considerable social and material investment in these competing imaginings of Indianness, which are also sites of contradiction and dissent. Chapter 4 analyzes the gendered dimensions of ethnic authenticity that remix youth culture enacts, showing that ideals of femininity and masculinity in the second generation are intertwined with notions of an essential ethnic identity. Female chastity is suggestively linked to the management of hybridity and modernity, as is evident in postcolonial analyses of gender and nationalism. Finally, Chapter 5 weaves together these different strands of analysis, showing the linkages between ethnic authenticity, gender ideology, and youth culture and exploring their implications for the study of social experience and the theoretical and political possibilities of an interdisciplinary cultural studies project.

The study will, I hope, provide stories to which coming generations of Indian American and other second-generation youth can resonate, as well as anyone interested in the often paradoxical politics of cultural production. The layered beats of Indian remix music suggest the mixed desires of Indian American youth, some of whom enact a romance centered on cultural purity while simultaneously reveling in the promiscuity of polycultural rhythms (Kelley 1999). As a young man who was born in the Bronx and grew up in Long Island wrote:

> The discovery of the [Indian party] scene has fundamentally altered my politics. . . . That is why each Friday night I bounce my head to the latest jam, to the latest beat to be found anywhere between New York and D.C. . . . Here is where I find my catharsis. Here is where I suspect many other kids find theirs. . . . Indian Americans have started fusing our own music, producing our own act, and writing our own stories. As with all other Americans, we draw from many traditions—African, Latino, European, Asian—but we do it to our own beats.[9]

2

To Be Young, Brown, and Hip

Race, Gender, and Sexuality in
Indian American Youth Culture

The massive beats of a new sound reverberated in New York City nightlife in the mid-1990s, a mix of Hindi film music and bhangra, a North Indian and Pakistani dance and music, with American rap, techno, jungle, and reggae.[1] The second-generation Indian American youth subculture that introduced this "remix music" has become a recognized part of the city's broader popular culture, heralded to the mainstream by concerts at the Summerstage series in Central Park, articles in the local news media, and documentaries by local independent filmmakers.[2] This chapter explores the tension between the production of cultural nostalgia and the performance of "cool" in this subculture, showing how the dialectic between these structures of feeling reveals the contradictory cultural politics of authenticity for Indian American youth (Williams 1977).

Bhangra remix music constitutes a transnational popular culture in the Indian/South Asian diaspora; it emerged among British-born South Asian youth in the mid-1980s and has since flowed between New York, Delhi, Bombay, Toronto, Port-of-Spain, and other nodes of the South Asian diaspora (Gopinath 1995a). While this "remix youth culture" has emerged in other urban areas in the United States that have large Indian American populations, such as Chicago and the Bay Area, its expressions are shaped by

29

local contexts. There has not as yet been much comparative work on this topic, but it is clear that Manhattan lends this youth culture distinctive features, including particular sonic elements: DJ Tony of TS Soundz in Chicago pointed out to me that while Chicago remixes tend to use house and techno music, New York deejays favor remixes with rap music, and participants in this local subculture tend to adopt a more overtly "hoody," hip-hop-inspired style (see Sengupta 1996).

The New York subculture based on Indian music remixes includes participants whose families originated in other countries of the subcontinent, such as Bangladesh and Pakistan, yet insiders often code events that feature this music as the "Indian party scene" or "desi scene." While participants in the desi scene share certain South Asian cultural codes and common experiences in the United States, aspects of ethnic and national identity play out in particular ways for different national and religious, not to mention regional, groups. The "scene" is a differentiated one: Indian American youth who are not in college also attend these parties, and there are "Indian parties" held outside Manhattan, for instance, on campuses in New Jersey and Long Island that have large South Asian student populations. Manhattan, however, provides a particular context for desi parties because of the presence of city clubs, such as the Madison, the China Club, or S.O.B.'s (Sounds of Brazil), that draw large droves of South Asian American youth who get down to the beats of bhangra. S.O.B.'s, a world music club in downtown Manhattan, has been home to one of the most well known regular "bhangra parties" since March 1997, when DJ Rekha launched "Basement Bhangra," the first Indian remix music night to be featured monthly on the calendar of a Manhattan club—and the first to be hosted by a woman deejay.

The phenomenon of desi parties fits in with the larger structure of clubbing in New York and in other cities, where clubs host different "parties" or nights that are ethnically, racially, and sexually segregated and that feature deejays who can spin the right kind of mix for their target audience, as noted in a special *New York Times Magazine* issue on New York subcultures: "If you club in New York these days, you spend your daylight hours in a living, breathing United Nations and end your nights in an all-but-segregated society. There are the Italian-American jams (where they spin house and hip-hop), Russian-Jewish (hip-hop, R & B), gay (dance, house, disco), black highbrow (hip-hop, R & B, soul), black lowbrow (hip-hop, hip-hop, hip-hop) . . ." (Touré 1997, p. 98).

The association of distinctions such as "lowbrow" and "highbrow" with particular club spaces and music genres illustrates ethnomusicologist Martin Stokes's (1994, p. 3) observation about the production of social spaces *in* music: "The musical event . . . evokes and organizes collective memories and present experiences of place with an intensity, power and simplicity. . . . The 'places' constructed through music involve notions of difference and social boundary. They also organise hierarchies of a moral and political order." It is this power of music and dance to evoke a sense of "place" in a social hierarchy, as well as a spatial location, that makes possible a collective nostalgia for India that combines with the gauging of subcultural status at remix music parties.

The music is remixed, or at least selected, by deejays who perform at parties hosted at local clubs, restaurants, and college campuses by promoters, generally young Indian American men and women, some of whom are college students who do this as a source of part-time income and who have helped create an urban South Asian American youth subculture. Nearly all the deejays that I met or heard about were Indian American, a point that deserves further reflection and that hints at broader questions about social networks within the clubbing industry and the dominance, or at least greater visibility, of Indian Americans within a purportedly pan-ethnic subculture. Information about desi parties circulates in a web of information that, when the scene began to flourish in the mid-1990s, initially could be hard for "outsiders" to break into. As in other dance cultures, remix parties are advertised through word of mouth, mailing lists, Web sites (such as the national www.desiparty.com), and flyers distributed at events, stores, clubs, and other places youth visit on the subcultural circuit. Every weekend, remix parties in Manhattan attract desi youth from New York, New Jersey, Connecticut, and even Pennsylvania, areas that have large concentrations of Indian and other South Asian immigrant families as well as South Asian American student populations. Cover charges are steep but not atypical for New York parties, ranging from ten to twenty dollars, yet the parties draw hordes of youth from a range of class backgrounds who are willing to fork out money for leisure activities. Partygoers are for the most part second-generation, although some first-generation South Asian youth are usually in the crowd as well, participating in the redefinition of desi cool, in its urban, New York/Northeast incarnation, through the creative use of elements of popular culture.

Flyer for Basement Bhangra event at S.O.B.'s in Manhattan.
(Courtesy of DJ Rekha)

In conjunction with the fusion of musical genres, this subculture displays the construction of a culturally hybrid style, such as wearing Indian-style nose rings and bindis[3] with hip-hop clothing and performing ethnic identity through dance, as in the borrowing of folk dance gestures from bhangra while gyrating to club remixes. Indian American women sported bindis long before pop stars Madonna and Gwen Stefani did, but they now do so in the context of commodified ethno-chic; mehndi kits—"Indian body art"—and bindi packets—"body jewels"—have sprouted in clothing stores, pharmacies, street fairs, and fashion magazines in the years since I completed this research (see Durham 1999). The mainstreaming of Indo-chic in the late 1990s is a hotly debated issue, especially among young desi women. It demonstrates the ways in which consumption is used to negotiate ideas of ethnic authenticity, cultural ownership, and race, even as it is made possible by the globalization of American capital and cheap South Asian labor. (See Maira 2000a for a discussion of this new Orientalization of India.) Underlying such debates is always the problematic of consumption and the relationship of youth to the labor market, for there are Indian Americans who are not in college and who attend these parties, as well as young financiers, pre-med students, and aspiring actors; strains of materiality and class mobility mix with the vibes of nostalgia in this subculture.

April 4, 1997. The crowd thickens on the dance floor at S.O.B.'s, the music and darkness effectively blocking out all awareness of the street life just outside on Varick Street, in a largely commercial area of Tribeca in downtown New York. The club's space is small, with a few tables and mock palm trees scattered around the edges of the compact dance floor, in front of a raised stage area where bands occasionally perform. DJ Rekha spins in a tiny loft area that hangs over the bar and watches the crowd below as the insistent beat of the dhol, the percussion base of bhangra music, pounds out over the techno and reggae tracks reverberating amid the tightly packed bodies. Shoulders shrug and arms flail in semblances of bhangra moves, here, far from the wheat fields of the Punjab, far from the Californian orchards where early Punjabi migrants first settled in the early twentieth century.

Tonight, most faces are various shades of South Asian, but a few African Americans and White folks are getting down on the dance floor too, for this is one of the few bhangra club nights that draws a noticeably racially mixed crowd. One of the past Basement Bhangra events featured a booth with mehndi, lacy designs in henna, traced on palms by a young White woman riding the emerging fascination with Indian "body art." This night features an appearance by a live dhol drummer "all the way from Lahore," his yellow turban and sequined kurta presumably authenticating the South Asian elements of this musical fusion. Boota Sheikh has an astonished, if delighted, expression on his face, as if simultaneously bewildered and excited by his performance for a frenzied crowd of young South Asians: women in hip-huggers twisting their arms in movements learned partly from Hindi films and partly from other bhangra nights like this, perhaps in college or at other Indian remix parties. A turbaned Sikh man leaps onto the stage beside the sweating musician, spinning and bouncing with acrobatic, breakdance-like agility. Jumping back into the crowd, he is joined by another young Sikh man, and as the crowd parts in a rapt circle, the two dance around each other in exuberantly coordinated precision. Then three young women who have various degrees of classical dance training step up to the circle, their fluid body movements evoking various genres of Indian dance, "filmi" and folk, and challenging what has been up to now an exclusively male, Punjabi performance. The women's enthusiasm on the dance floor is no less vigorous. The party has most certainly begun.

Indian Remix Music and the Manhattan "Desi Scene"

The emergence of this vibrant Indian American (and South Asian American) youth culture in Manhattan in the mid-1990s was partly due to the presence of the large local Indian immigrant community in the area. New York City is one of the primary receiving areas for Indian immigrants to the United States because of two major factors. First, the local labor market offers a range of employment opportunities, from engineering jobs in industries in nearby New Jersey and Connecticut to employment in hotels, motels, banking, insurance, public health, and garment and jewelry businesses, as well as the import/ export trade (Lessinger 1995). New York City also has traditionally favored small, family-owned retail businesses over national chain stores, which accounts for the increasing number of Indian entrepreneurs, some of whom run the newsstands that dot the city and others of whom own small business that serve the growing South Asian American market—for example, travel agencies and law firms that are advertised in Indian community newspapers and the restaurants and grocery stores in midtown Manhattan and in Jackson Heights, Queens. Working-class Indian immigrants or middle-class Indians who could not find the jobs they had hoped for sometimes find employment in the service sector or unskilled labor market (Lessinger 1995). The taxi industry has absorbed many South Asian immigrant men, particularly from agricultural regions in the Punjab; in 1992, the Taxi and Limousine Commission of New York City reported that 43 percent of Manhattan-based yellow cabs were driven by South Asians, equally represented by Indians, Pakistanis, and Bangladeshis (Advani 1997), and in 1999–2000, that figure was close to 60 percent (Esser et al. 1999–2000). The second factor that has motivated many Indian immigrants to settle in New York City, at least initially, is that many have immigrated through family reunification categories, especially during the 1980s and 1990s. These are immigrants who have chosen to live close to relatives already settled in the area or in localities with a large number of other Indian families, such as Jackson Heights in Queens or Edison in New Jersey (see Kitano and Daniels 1995, pp. 107-109).

The changing spatial concentrations and public culture expressions of Indian immigrant communities in New York City reflect the changing class demographics and immigration patterns of Indian Americans. Until the late 1960s, most Indian immigrants who were students, merchants, and professionals, many from upper-middle-class backgrounds, lived in Manhattan. The community's social and cultural activities were restricted to private spaces and the handful of Indian restaurants and businesses in Manhattan, which were patronized not only by Indians but by New Yorkers from diverse ethnic backgrounds (Khandelwal 1995). Beginning in the late 1960s, however, some Indian professionals moved to Flushing, Queens, or even farther out to predominantly White, affluent suburbs, reflecting their upward economic mobility and the broader pattern, across ethnic groups, of middle- and upper-middle-class relocation to suburbia. More recent arrivals, beginning in the 1980s, settled in receiving areas such as Elmhurst and Flushing, where there continue to be large concentrations of Indian immigrants (Khandelwal 1995). During this period, Indian ethnic activities began to be visible in the public sphere, with Indian-owned business stores and restaurants sprouting in Queens, particularly in the area known as Little India along 74th Street in Jackson Heights. In this neighborhood, immigrants from India as well as from Pakistan and Bangladesh can be seen in traditional clothing as they shop with their families or advertise their goods—a contrast to the generally private display of South Asian ethnicities in Manhattan, where it is rare to see a woman walking down the street in a sari or salwar kameez (a common North Indian and Pakistani women's outfit).

In addition, Khandelwal (1995) points out that while earlier immigrants tended to found pan-Indian organizations and to sponsor public performances of classical Indian arts, later immigrant waves have spawned the growth of regional organizations and sectarian religious institutions that cater to specific subgroups in the Indian American community. At the same time, however, Indian business owners have realized the profitability of gearing their products toward a pan–South Asian market and often emphasize this supranational orientation in signs such as "Indo-Pak-Bangla." While Khandelwal (1995, p. 191) suggests that this pan-ethnic label represents a "new South Asian identity" for immigrants, the pervasiveness and depth of this affiliation is debatable in the first generation, who are generally still rooted in nationalist orientations though they may transcend these for business purposes or for strategic alliance building. Yet I concur with her that Indian "culture" has been broadly popularized; Indian film stars and musicians play to packed stadiums such as the Nassau Coliseum, and spectacular celebrations such as the Gujarati festival of Navratri, accompanied by the traditional dandiya-raas dance, an exuberant group dance performed with sticks, are now organized in towns in New Jersey. Definitions of Indian culture, whether based on classical or popular expressions, exemplify the repertoire of meanings that are attached to "tradition" in diasporic communities and the selective use of cultural production to represent national identity.

This reimagining of "nation" in Indian American communities assumes revealing incarnations at specific historical moments when the need to display a coherent national identity is evoked by acts of commemoration or national pride. One of the years I was doing my fieldwork, 1997, was coincidentally the fiftieth anniversary of India's independence and saw several well-publicized events in New York City that showcased Indian classical music and traditional arts. Concerts featuring lineups of Indian classical music maestros were held at elite arts institutions such as Lincoln Center and Carnegie Hall, and the Asia Society organized several art exhibits on the Upper East Side. Members of the Indian immigrant elite flocked to these and a host of other events that were held throughout the year and that demonstrated the different, sometimes competing, strands of Indian art and culture that Indian immigrants selectively import to define tradition and represent the nation (see Mukhi 2000). It is also worth noting that established arts institutions and the Indian and mainstream American media gave comparatively little attention to the fact that 1997 was also the fiftieth anniversary of Pakistan's creation, highlighting both the reproduction of antagonistic nationalisms in the diaspora and the ongoing Orientalist preoccupation with "India" in the American public imagination (Mehta 1979; Prashad 2000).

The multiculturalism of the 1990s provides the context for officially sanctioned displays of national culture by immigrant communities that coexist with popular re-creations of tradition in youth subcultures. Remix music and dance emblematize performances of what Sunita Sunder Mukhi calls a "vernacular Indianness" (2000, p. 6). The tension between the two versions of nationalism produced on specific occasions highlights the contradictory workings of the politics of nostalgia in youth culture.

My analysis of this youth subculture focuses more on the meanings that remix music, dance, and style have in the lives of desi party participants than an ethnomusicological treatment of the music's sounds and lyrics or a focus on the deejays. This is partly a position arising out of methodological training but partly, too, a position deliberately chosen to build on work in cultural studies that is attempting to engage with "the domestic, the mundane or even the material in subcultural and music writing" (McRobbie 1999, p. 145) rather than analyzing only the media or the producers of expressive culture. The line dividing producers and consumers of remix youth culture is highly permeable; youth shape the popular culture in which they participate, and several deejays are students and participants in the larger youth subculture themselves. My purpose, however, is to move away from the "cult of the deejay" that pervades some of the emerging media representations of this and other dance cultures and to focus instead on understanding how youth make meaning of the popular culture they have co-created. What are produced in this subculture are not just forms of music and dance but ways of being, female or male, an Indian American subject (McRobbie 1999, p. 145). I am primarily interested in the politics of youth subcultures, and my approach draws on a tradition of critical cultural studies that offers feminist and materialist analyses of youth cultural production (Clarke et al. 1976; Cohen 1997; Kelley 1997; Leblanc 1999; McRobbie 1991, 1997; Rose 1994a; Sansone 1995; Willis 1977).

Perhaps one of the most nuanced analyses of contemporary U.S. youth culture, grounded in sociological insights into lived experience, is the work of Juan Flores. In his collection of incisive essays on Latino popular culture and politics, *From Bomba to Hip Hop*, Flores suggests a framework for analyzing popular culture inspired by Johannes Fabian: "He invites us to think of popular culture not so much as an entity comprised of products and processes, or as a bounded social space such as low or marginal, but as a relation or system of relations. Rather than marking off boundaries and defining separate spheres of cultural practice, perhaps popular culture is about the transversing and transgressing of them, and characterized by a dialogic among classes and social sectors, such as the popular and non-popular, high and low, restricted and mass" (Flores 2000, p. 20).[4] In emphasizing a relational and dialogic approach to popular culture, Flores attempts to shift the frame of analysis from a spatial one, where the tension is between "high" or "low" popular culture, to a temporal framework, where popular culture is created in a historical relationship between notions of "tradition" and "modernity" and also between "the 'people' as subject and object of knowledge" (2000, p. 20). Popular culture expresses what Flores calls "the problem of contemporaneity," the simultaneous "coexistence of tradition and modernity" (2000, p. 21), a temporal dialectic that is deeply embedded in second-generation youth cultures, which are always wrestling with notions of purportedly vanishing "traditions" and of the derivative or threatening practices of the present.

This popular culture is a critical site for understanding how second-generation youth are positioning themselves in the landscape of ethnic and racial politics, because it showcases performances of ethnic authenticity, cultural hybridity, racialized gender ideologies, and class contradictions. I argue that in remix youth culture, the politics of nostalgia is infused into the production of "cool," a dialectic that has revealing implications for understanding processes of ethnicization and racialization among second-generation youth in the United States and for notions of essentialism and subversion in cultural theory. The rest of this chapter unfolds in three main sections that are linked in jigsaw-like fashion: The first uses subcultural theory to understand some of the cultural contradictions mediated through remix music and dance; the second explores gendered and sexualized performances of these contradictions as they evoke notions of authenticity, nostalgia, and nationalism; and the third examines constructions of authenticity and subcultural cool in remix youth culture's sampling of hip-hop.

Subcultural Theory and the Politics of Youth Culture

Viewing Indian American youth music and style as products of a subculture draws on the particular tradition of cultural studies associated with neo-Marxist theorists in the United Kingdom, particularly the early emphasis on a materialist ethnography (Kirschner 1998; Turner 1996).[5] According to Stuart Hall and other theorists of the Birmingham school (Clarke et al. 1976, p. 47), individuals belong to a shared subculture when there is "a set of social rituals which underpin their collective identity and define them as a 'group' instead of a mere collection of individuals. They adopt and adapt material objects—goods and possessions—and reorganize them into distinctive 'styles' which express the collectivity . . . [and] become embodied in rituals of relationship and occasion and movement." The term *youth subculture* refers to a social group that is distinguished by age or generation, but theorists of youth subcultures also note that the category "youth" is socially and culturally constructed and has often been the focus of debates over social control, as well as a marketing principle for the music and fashion industries (Clarke et al. 1976). The Birmingham theorists strategically chose the term *subculture* rather than *youth culture* because, they argued, the latter descriptor obscured the links between the cultural construction of youth as a distinct category and the creation of a "teenage [consumer] market"; the concept of a "subculture," in their framework, was embedded in a deeper structural explanation of the dialectic between "youth" and youth industries (Clarke et al. 1976, p. 16).[6]

Understanding a subculture and its rituals, such as those of the desi party scene in New York, helps explain why a popular culture based on music in particular has such strong appeal for youth. Simon Frith (1992, p. 177) has written that "for young people . . . music probably has the most important role in the mapping of social networks, determining how and where they meet and court and party." In other words, in societies with commercialized popular cultures, music has become a ritual that is important in the socialization of youth. Frith argues that by providing a subtle and complex means of individual and collective expression, "[music] is in many respects the model for their involvement in culture, for their ability to see beyond the immediate requirements of work and family and dole" (1992, p. 177). His insight also suggests that subcultures—expressions of distinctive identities organized around particular rituals or commodities—exist in relationship to the broader context of "culture," against which the web of social meanings, relationships, and material experiences of particular subcultures are defined. Popular culture is saturated with ideologies about youth that are racialized, gendered, and classed, but it also offers an arena in which youth may reappropriate or symbolically transgress existing racial, gendered, and class boundaries.

This provides the basis for the Birmingham school's central argument (which has had a significant influence on cultural studies) that youth subcultures are based on rituals that resist the values inherent in the dominant culture. The creation of a subculture is understood as a response to the personal, political, and economic contradictions or crises that youth confront on the brink of adulthood (Clarke et al. 1976). This argument was used to explain the emergence and significance in postwar Britain of youth cultures that were particularly appealing to working-class youth, in the context of a growing leisure industry that targeted youth as important consumers of music, fashion, and mass media. Early subcultural theorists were particularly interested in decoding the political implications of youth style and socialization. Emphasizing the interpretation of rituals and symbols, they drew heavily on structuralist and semiotic approaches (Cohen 1997, p. 157). Dick Hebdige (1979, pp. 2–3), in his heavily semiotic analysis, contended that subcultures which revolve around the use of commodities, such as fashion and music, have a symbolic dimension that is infused with political meanings not always obvious to the outsider or adult observer. He wrote that "the tensions between dominant and subordinate groups can be found reflected in the surfaces of subculture—in the styles made up of mundane objects which have a double meaning." Hebdige suggested that, on the one hand, these signs act as markers of difference for the dominant culture but, "on the other hand, for those who erect them into icons . . . these objects become signs of forbidden identity, sources of value" (1979, pp. 2–3).

This semiotic approach has its problems, particularly in its handling of intentionality and its reading of subcultural politics (Cohen 1997; Frith 1997; Gelder 1997). Cultural studies theorists and sociologists point out that the Birmingham school's early subcultural theory often overinterpreted social action in terms of resistance and symbolic resolution (Cohen 1997; Epstein 1998). Angela McRobbie, while emphasizing the value of the "structural, historical, and ethnographic" approaches of early cultural studies research, cautions against the "dangers of pursuing a kind of cultural populism to a point at which anything which is consumed and is popular is also seen as oppositional" (1994, p. 39). Other contemporary cultural studies theorists have similarly argued that early subcultural studies neglected analyses of the aesthetic aspects of youth culture, privileging politicized interpretations of youth style, and glossed over the contradictions and conflicts within these subcultures (Cohen 1997; Thornton 1997a). Feminist critiques have also noted that this early research deemphasized or even misinterpreted the role of women and girls, focusing instead on male, working-class youth and portraying females as more passive or as identified with the "mainstream" (McRobbie 1991; Pini 1997; Thornton 1997b). Contemporary subcultural theorists and researchers have a more complex vision but acknowledge that the basic tenets of subcultural theory, reaching back to its early Chicago school roots, are still useful (Duncombe 1988; Leblanc 1999; Sardiello 1998). As Sarah Thornton (1997a, p. 201) observes, "Subcultural ideologies are a means by which youth imagine their own and other social groups, assert their distinctive character and affirm that they are not anonymous members of an undifferentiated mass."

A contemporary American youth subculture that has been analyzed through the lens of subcultural theory and that provides an important cultural idiom for Indian American youth in New York is hip-hop. Tricia Rose (1994a; 1994b) views the language, style, and attitude of hip-hop as embodying a critique of the condition of urban youth who face unemployment, racism, and marginalization in a postindustrial economy. She suggests that rituals of clothing and the creation of a distinctive hip-hop style not only show an "explicit focus on consumption" (1994b, p. 82) but offer urban African American and Latino youth who have limited opportunities for social mobility an alternative means of attaining status.[7] Rose describes hip-hop as a hybrid cultural form that relies on Afro-Caribbean and African American musical, oral, visual, and dance practices. Thus it weaves a commentary on existing circumstances with references to ancestral cultures from the Afro-Caribbean diaspora in order to create a "counterdominant narrative." While interpretations of resistance and oppositionality have been problematized in contemporary youth culture studies, the politics of hip-hop as a social movement become apparent when juxtaposing the experiences of the youth Rose describes with those of the Indian American youth in this study. These second-generation youth occupy a very different class and racial location from most Black and Latino youth in New York City, but in fashioning their own second-generation style they have adopted elements of hip-hop, particularly the use of clothing, dialect, and musical bricolage. Hebdige (1979) points out that, as in the case of punk in Britain, the meanings attached to particular styles are often redefined once they are commodified and recuperated by the mainstream. What does this particular performance of ethnic "cool" tell us about the racial and ethnic locations that Indian

American youth are choosing for themselves, and what are the meanings of this consumption of Blackness by desi and other Asian American youth?

By sampling Indian music, second-generation youth draw on sounds from Hindi movies and Indian music that their parents introduced them to when they were children in order to inculcate an "Indian" identity. By remixing these with rap and reggae and by donning hip-hop gear or brand-name clothes, Indian Americans display the markers of ethnicity and material status used in a multiethnic, capitalist society. To understand the collision of racialized, gendered, and ethnicized imaginings with material aspirations in this remix popular culture, I first outline the cultural contradictions facing second-generation youth that are enacted at "desi parties" in Manhattan and that are part of the popular discourse used to explain these events, and then suggest more layered interpretations that reveal gendered tensions and underlying racial and material processes.

Mediating Multiplicity

The early Birmingham theorists viewed youth subcultures as attempts by youth to resolve symbolically the tensions between the larger group culture, or "parent culture," and their own generational concerns. Similarly, in the case of the desi party scene, one can read this diasporic subculture as an attempt to mediate between the expectations of immigrant parents (in this case, literally the parents' culture) and those of mainstream American peer culture by trying to integrate signs of belonging to both worlds. Indian American youth use musical remixes and urban fashion as materials with which to construct and display a seemingly hybrid or "cut 'n' mix" style that symbolically juxtaposes the influences of the varying social and material contexts in which they have come of age. Hebdige writes that "style in subculture" is composed of "gestures, movements . . . which challenges [sic] the principle of unity and cohesion, which contradicts the myth of consensus" (1979, p. 17). The experiences of second-generation and immigrant youth challenge notions of a seamless, embracing American culture, as do the daily realities of youth of color or teenagers struggling to support their families. Postmodernists would argue that cultural dissonance and multiple identities mark all our lives in an era of global capital, media, and migration. The cultural scripts or "schemas" that the children of

Desi youth performing the pleasures of bhangra on the dance floor. (Courtesy of Srinivas Kuruganti)

immigrant parents must juggle daily, however, display a specific character, as suggested by psychological and ethnographic research on Indian immigrant families in the United States and Canada (Agarwal 1991; Bacon 1996; Gibson 1988; Wakil, Siddique, and Wakil, 1981).[8]

One of the themes running through this book is that the immigrant generation's desire to preserve an authentic ethnic identity lingers in the second generation, for whom being Indian becomes a cultural ideology used to calibrate the authenticity, even the goodness, of self and others. Yet Indian American youth are simultaneously positioning themselves in the racial and class hierarchies of the United States and coming of age in contexts shaped by public institutions such as schools, colleges, and the workforce. A uniquely Indian American subculture allows second-generation youth to socialize with ethnic peers while reinterpreting Indian musical and dance traditions through the rituals of American popular culture. As Jean Comaroff suggests, "Syncretistic ritual . . . movements are . . . 'at once both expressive and pragmatic, for they aim to change the real world by inducing transformation in the world of symbol and rite'"—"a world," Nicholas Dirks adds, "in which representation is itself one of the most contested resources" (cited in Dirks 1994, p. 487). For Indian American youth who are in college and who participate in the ethnically demarcated club culture of New York, representation through campus organizations and popular culture rituals becomes a way to stake a claim in local spaces, but it is a claim with limited potential for changing the categories that define them. Some youth culture theorists argue that in presumably "oppositional" subcultures, the "resistance of the subculture is reduced to ritual" and this ritualized "resistance itself becomes an end" (Epstein 1998, p. 11).

The "subcultural solution" as conceptualized by the Birmingham school remains a representational solution to the crises of youth, and one enacted only in the realm of the social and symbolic. Using the notion of ritual as a site for reimagining the social order, however, Phil Cohen argues that such a subculture is seductive to youth because it helps them to ideologically resolve the paradoxes between the different social spheres that they occupy by enacting an option that may not be possible in actuality (in Clarke et al. 1976). The performances that remix youth culture in New York makes possible, while not enabling wider systemic change, fulfill an immediate social and affective need for desi youth and have a pragmatic and not just expressive dimension. Les Back (1994), analyzing the "intermezzo culture produced in the fusion of bhangra and reggae in Britain," argues that in the alternative public sphere of the dance, "liminal ethnicities are produced that link together different social collectivities" (cited in S. Sharma 1996, p. 36). Since this popular culture involves events that are almost exclusively attended by South Asian youth, it is often condoned by parents who would be more hesitant to allow their children to go to regular clubs or parties with non–South Asian friends, especially while youth are still in high school or living at home. Madhu, who grew up in New Jersey and whose parents were actively involved in recreating social networks of immigrants from the region in Gujarat to which they belong, said, "I think for the party scene, overall, I think they like us to go because it keeps you hanging out with the Indians. I think they're realizing that . . . you know, it's not like all these Indians are that good, and that the fights go on, and Indians actually do drink and they do stupid things, a lot of other stuff, but I think they probably figure that stuff goes on in all parties so we might as well have it with other Indians [rather] than with Americans."

Parental approval, at least during the initial years of this desi party scene, seems a largely unintentional benefit for youth seeking to participate in the rituals of American youth popular culture, such as clubbing, dating, and performances of subcultural style. Ravi, who grew up in Orange County, California, and was a veteran of the party scene on both the East and West Coasts, noted the "two sides" that most of his second-generation peers displayed, one for "Indian parents" and the other for public spaces outside parental scrutiny. He laughingly mused about the literal "switching" of these situational identities, symbolized by the practice of layered clothing, "to the point where a couple of girls [going to parties] would change in the car afterwards, which was funny. . . . They would wear a nice long shirt when they went out, but the shirt would come up to the midriff, [a] halter, you know? Or they'd wear it underneath but a sweater over it and the sweater comes off all of a sudden and all of a sudden their pants come off and it's a skirt. So I mean, there's definitely that side."

After the party is over, however, youth must return to the constraints of interacting with their parents, peers, and communities (Cohen 1997; Gelder 1997). Sanjay Sharma points out that the "liminal ethnicities" represented by British Asian dance culture, if created at all, may be limited to the "transitory and contingent spaces of the dance floor" (S. Sharma 1996, p. 36). Hybridity, though fashionable in cultural theory and also, literally, in "ethnic chic," is not always easy to live, for social institutions and networks continue to demand loyalty to sometimes competing cultural ideals that second-generation youth may find difficult to manage. For many, liminality is an ongoing, daily condition of being betwixt and between cultural categories (Turner 1967; 1987, pp. 101, 107) that is symbolically expressed in remix culture. This is, however, only one of several spaces that Indian American youth negotiate, and other contexts elicit a more bounded, fixed notion of Indianness.

The performance of a visibly hybrid ethnicity occurs in specific contexts and is not always optional; it belongs to a range of performances of cultural scripts in everyday life. Indian American youth still switch among multiple identities, as they did when moving between high school and family, only now perhaps they change from the baggy pants and earrings that they wear among peers to conservative attire on the job, or from being in secret relationships at college to acting as dutiful daughters on visits home. These transitions clearly have a gendered dimension, and the negotiation of ethnic identity and national culture is embodied differently by women and men, as is visibly enacted in the remix music subculture.

Hoods and Hoochy Mamas: The Innocence of Tradition

A revealing source of tension within this Indian American world of dance parties and social gatherings is the contestation of sexual and gender roles and of racialized images of desire. Many of the young people I interviewed noted that a "hoody" or streetwise hip-hop image was not considered as appealing for women in this subculture as it was for men, and that the predominant style associated with desirable femininity was designer-inspired urban fashion. Slinky club wear that allows a flash or more of leg or midriff is the style popular among many young women at desi parties; at the time of my study, this meant hip-hugger pants, halter tops, and miniskirts. Some women sport a diamond nose stud or nose ring in a nod to ethnic style. A glamorous femininity is pervasive—kohl-lined eyes, dark lipstick, and arched eyebrows—and an emphasis on slimness, if not sheer thinness. This feminized image had become the look for many hip-hop women artists in the 1990s, some of whom moved away from androgynous rapper style to the "ghetto fabulous" look (George 1998, p. 119). The Indian American remix subculture, however, showed little variation in the coding of female style and, more important, an underlying preoccupation with the stylistic coding and regulation of Indianness, and implicitly of Blackness, especially for women.

At the outset, I should note that while the atmosphere at desi parties is as sexually charged as at most dance clubs, the vibe is generally heterosexist, if not homophobic (which is also generally true of mainstream club culture). There are a few exceptions, and parties that are more queer friendly and attract slightly older crowds include Basement Bhangra, which boasted an occasional drag performance, or the defiantly nonbhangra party Mutiny, which is cohosted by DJ Siraiki and DJ Rekha (launched after I had finished my research in New York and

Flyer for the Mutiny party benefit for the campaign to free Satpal Ram, a British Asian man unjustly imprisoned in the United Kingdom, November 2000. (Courtesy of Vivek Bald)

which has an explicitly progressive mandate that is encapsulated in its name).[9]

There are certainly queer youth in these desi party spaces but, especially at the weekly parties that target college-age youth, they are not visibly "out." The straight remix party scene coexists with a queer desi subculture scene in Manhattan where, arguably, bhangra remix first became a subcultural "staple." Gayatri Gopinath writes of the "strategic appropriation of bhangra by queer South Asians in the West . . . signifying South Asianness to mainstream (white) queer communities, as well as to other queer people of colour" and comments, "We know what a high it can be to walk into a bhangra party and revel in the sight of queer brown folks doing their thing . . . bhangra enacts a subaltern 'counter-public' space, as queer theorist Jose Muñoz terms it" (1995b, pp. 9–10). At parties hosted by the South Asian Lesbian and Gay Association (SALGA) and in their floats for the Gay Pride March in New York, bhangra remix has long been explicitly acknowledged as a signifier of "queer diasporic identity" and hybrid popular style that is linked to queer desi subcultures in other diasporic communities, for instance, in Toronto and London (Gopinath 1995b). Yet, by the late 1990s in New York, the potentially subversive queer bhangra scene existed in counterpoint not only to public spheres in which brown bodies were invisible but also to a parallel, often aggressively heterosexual bhangra remix youth subculture where queerness was invisible.

Notions of style and body image are embedded in deeper contradictions in the gender constructions and heterosexual roles that are played out in remix youth culture and that are contested by some who find this constricting. Often this contestation is enacted not only in gendered but also in racialized terms, with an underlying concern about appropriate femininity and the perils of racial border crossing. Manisha, whose friends were mainly African American and Latino and who often dressed in hip-hop gear—with a gold "Om" pendant dangling around her neck—reflected, "Guys can get away with [the 'hoody' look] but girls who are considered 'cool' dress prettier. I think the guys are intimidated by that [girls with a hip-hop look], it's taken as a sign of being closer to Latinos or Blacks, of being outside of the Indian circle, as I am . . . the guys may think we're rougher, or not as sweet." This "sweet," more conventionally feminine look, often associated with the ethnically and racially coded marker of long, straight hair, is also rife with contradictions; an ambivalence about the appeal of "innocent" femininity creates yet another doubling in these enactments of desire. While most men favor for Indian American women the demure, feminized image over the androgynous hip-hop look, the former presentation is in turn passed over on the dance floor for women who perform a more sexualized style—the "hoochy mamas." Yet these women are considered "loose," that is, not the type of woman an Indian American man would like to marry. Among men, however, a somewhat wider range of images of male desirability seems to apply, although these are no less racialized than for women.

For some women who go to these "Indian parties," what is most frustrating is the discomfort they feel being subjected to aggressive male advances and female heterosexual competitiveness. Reena, for example, said she enjoys the music and socializing, "but it's also a lot of competition, in the sense that you have all these hoochy mamas in there with their tight-fitting dresses and stuff like that and trying to be all up on everyone. I just remember getting into my brother's car and being like, I'm just way too mature for this, because like guys [are] coming up to me, 'Hey, baby, what's your number?'" Reena's comment highlights the problems of heterosexual objectification in club culture, even while young women may take pleasure in vamping it up in their "tight-fitting dresses." Her observations of sexual play in this remix youth culture have to be situated in relation to the contradictory expectations of immigrant families that daughters successfully negotiate mainstream society while simultaneously performing the role of primary bearers of culture (Agarwal 1991). The chastity of daughters becomes emblematic not just of the family's reputation but also, in the context of the diaspora, of the purity of tradition and ethnic identity, a defense against the promiscuity of "American influences" (Bhattarcharjee 1992; Das Dasgupta and Dasgupta 1996; Gibson 1988; Mani 1993), as discussed in greater depth in Chapter 4.

In this subcultural context, the popular image for young women is to wear fashionable and provocative clothing styles; yet, when talking about their peers, both males and females often criticized women for wearing revealing clothes or for trying unduly hard to attract the attention of men. As Lauraine Leblanc (1999, p. 127) demonstrates vividly in her study of punk girls in the United States and Canada, men in male-dominated subcultures have played an "important part in controlling girls' sexuality by setting up paradoxical sets of expectations. They both attempted to engage girls in sexual activity and sanctioned girls who adopted a more liberal, instrumental 'masculine' view of sexual activity"; yet even punk girls "colluded with the males in making sure that all subsequent girls would be subjected to the same tests" of subcultural membership (p. 122). Leblanc argues that subcultural capital is a double-edged sword for girls, for it often requires them to accommodate to a confining gender script if they wish to be accepted. In the case of punk, "gender becomes problematic for punk girls in ways that it is not for their male peers" (p. 141).

In the desi party subculture, a different set of norms for heterosexual appeal operate for young men than for young women, for "doing gender" is more explicitly tied to negotiations of material status for desi males (Leblanc 1999 p. 141). Several youth pointed explicitly to the need for men who belong to this subculture to flaunt brand-name "gear" to signal their buying power and thus their appeal in the heterosexual dating market. The *behavior* of Indian American men, however, is not read as a marker of ethnic authenticity. While the women I spoke to often criticized men who projected a sexualized or promiscuous image in the party scene as unreliable and unappealing for long-term relationships, they did not consider these men "less Indian" for their hypersexuality. Machismo becomes linked to nationalism, however, and in some cases even to specific regional identifications, through practices that are common in club culture generally but are framed within the desi party scene by a discourse of ethnic marginalization and internal differentiation.

Nationalism, Regionalism, and Violence

Different levels of identification operate simultaneously at desi parties in New York and reflect the multiple allegiances created away from the dance floor: the "South Asian" label of many campus student organizations; the exclusively Indian American composition of many social networks among youth; and the regional clustering of community organizations and so-called youth gangs (Melwani 1996; Prashad 2000). The intersection of these different identifications in second-generation youth culture is not always a peaceful coexistence. Desi parties in New York have the reputation of being the scene of regular outbursts of violence among partygoers, both men and women. Some Indian American youth resented what they saw as a negative portrayal of Indian gatherings in the media and complained about club managers refusing to book Indian events for fear of disruption. Yet the same youth acknowledged that these fights were common occurrences that left them feeling frustrated. Sharmila, who had been involved in organizing parties sponsored by the South Asian student organization at New York University, commented that the image of males associated with these parties was "more aggressive. . . . And more fights, always more fights. Now there's fights at every party. It's just like this whole—oh! it's scary to me, because everywhere you go, there's fights."

People pointed to different explanations for the ugly brawls that ensue and that sometimes bring in the police. Some attributed them to an aggressive sensitivity to perceived "disrespect"—macho defenses of slights against girlfriends or, sometimes, women's fury over aspersions on their character—while others chalked up the incidents to drunkenness. DJ Baby Face, who has been spinning at parties and clubs for at least ten years and has been a part of "the scene" since its inception, pointed to another possibility that suggests the troubling side of nationalist solidarity. At a desi party held at The Tunnel, a Chelsea club, on a "regular" night, with a racially and ethnically diverse crowd mingling in the fluorescent passageways, he commented, "Here, it's mixed, they're Indians, but also Whites, Blacks. You don't see Indians creating trouble. But you just get a bunch of Indians in a room all together, they feel powerful, you get fights breaking out. Here, no fights will break out." Some might be tempted to argue that this eruption of male aggressiveness in a space created to bring desi youth together has overtones of a displaced racial or class frustration; as Michael Brake argues of "masculinist subcultures": "They emphasize maleness as a solution to an identity otherwise determined by structural features" (cited in Leblanc 1999, p. 107). Yet, in the case of Indian remix parties, I am less convinced that this violence is an indirect response to deeper social frustrations than that it is a common use of leisure spaces by youth to play out scripts of heterosexual male bravado (not to mention the fact that young desi women at parties are also known to have physical spats).

DJ Baby Face's observation is persuasive, for it seems that the creation of an exclusively Indian or South Asian social space may have provided a popularly used outlet for a macho, nationalist fervor or even for a more particularist, regional jingoism. Commenting on the violence, Sharmila said, "Because people bring it down, like, [she becomes assertive] 'Well, *I'm* Gujarati, we're all Gujaratis,' or we're all this . . . Malayali, and Gujarati, and all of the songs, 'We're Gujaratis!' And people will say, 'Oh, come on, give it up, Gujaratis,' or, 'Come on, give it [up], Pakistanis,' 'Come on—,' and because people are saying that it brings up . . . more division." Other youth also described desi parties as being spaces supporting not just pan-Indian identification but also regional allegiances that extend beyond the party subculture to everyday social life, so that there are regional subcultures nestled within the larger Indian American subculture, as elaborated in the next chapter. For instance, some of the South Asian youth "gangs" in the New York City area are regionally based, as is apparent from their names: for instance, MHS (Malayali Hit Squad) or PBN (Punjabi By Nature).

The invoking of regional identity through particular music mixes is most obvious in the passion that the sound of the dhol drum used in bhangra arouses in many Punjabis and Sikhs, who respond vigorously on the dance floor to deejay shout-outs of "Punjabis in the house!" A flyer for a bhangra remix party hosted by the United Sikh Association announced that the association "proudly presents Mera Desh Punjab," which literally means "my country is Punjab" (although, testifying to

United Sikh Association @ NYU
Proudly Presents

Mera Desh Punjab

Putting Queens on the map
DJ Kucha   DJ Rami
Representing U.K.
Dholi and Experimental Percussionist
Deep Śingh
Friday the third of October, 1997
The Eisner & Lubin Auditiorium in Loeb Student Center
Doors open at 8:00 pm
$3 Members $5 NYU $7 All Others
For More info please contact Jatinder Kaur @ (212) 463-9885
LOEB FRI. & SAT. NIGHT
ENTRANCE POLICY
ADMISSION BY VALID COLLEGE PHOTO ID
ONLY. NON-COLLEGE GUEST MUST BE ACCOM-
PANIED BY AN NYU STUDENT (ONE GUEST PER
STUDENT AND GUEST MUST HAVE VALID PHOTO ID
(DRIVER'S LICENSE, PASSPORT, ETC.). NO NON-
STUDENT UNDER 18 YEARS OF AGE.
METAL DETECTOR IN USE; BAGS CHECKED. NO
RE-ENTRY. DOORS CLOSE AT MIDNIGHT.

"My country is Punjab." Flyer for bhangra party, 1997.

the translocal nature of loyalties in diaspora, the flyer also describes the local deejays as "putting Queens on the map"). At an event at the Smithsonian Institution in Washington, D.C., I witnessed the strong affective investment that some diasporic Punjabis have in bhangra when I gave a talk on the reinvention of bhangra music and dance. My talk followed a series of impressive performances of largely traditional bhangra dance styles, as well as a turntable demonstration by DJ Rekha for a packed audience with many South Asian Americans in the crowd. Immediately after the event, I was accosted by several older South

Asian immigrant men, mostly Punjabis, who fervently insisted that bhangra had unique features, such as its rhythm or its improvisational nature, that I had failed to mention. It was clear to me not just that these men were unsettled by the sight of two young Indian American women discussing—and producing—a remixed version of this folk music associated with club culture, but that an intense regional pride and nostalgia invoked this passionate, if sometimes confrontational, response.

The association of regional pride with bhangra seems to have been socialized in the second generation as well. John, whose family is from the South Indian state of Kerala, said of his Punjabi and Sikh friends:

> So they love it, that's their music, they feel more invigorated by that. And everyone else who prefers the Hindi [film music remixes] to this, you know, but . . . I think Sikh men love Punjabi music, or Punjabis in general love the bhangra, you know, and they want to just get up, which is good, it's good. And when the bhangra comes on, that's my cue to leave, because I don't want to get involved with the jumpin' up and down and I can't do that. . . . You always see some people leave when that comes on, and there's another core of people coming on to the dance floor.

The dance floor becomes a space that is claimed and reclaimed by the different regional identifications that have been transplanted to the United States and that still filter into the second generation. Some young men and women I spoke with, especially those who grew up amid strong regional networks, said they would like to marry someone from their own regional group, not just another Indian. I found that social cliques among Indian American youth, too, are sometimes bounded by regional identities, and even those who do not belong to them note the persistent salience of these identities, as in comments on "a trend of Malayali boys going with Gujarati girls." Intertwined with the contest for cultural authenticity, then, are conflicts among the pan-ethnic, national, and regional identities that are adopted by, and re-created in, the second generation.

The Paradoxes of Petrification

The ways in which Indian American youth make meaning of this youth culture reveal paradoxes of identity that challenge unified notions of what this popular culture signifies. Hebdige emphasizes that "the meaning of subculture is, then, always in dispute, and style is the area

"Balle balle!" (a Punjabi shout out). A Sikh man
performs bhangra moves on the dance floor.
(Courtesy of Srinivas Kuruganti)

in which the opposing definitions clash with most dramatic force"
(1979, p. 3). Some of the same youth who participate in the club scene
and hang out at desi parties also describe this hybrid popular culture as
"diluted" or somehow not authentically Indian. Vijay, a second-s-
generation man who grew up in Forest Hill, Queens, posed the dichotomy between "real" and "inauthentic" Indian cultural expressions
quite starkly:

> You have a dichotomy of, sort of, two cultures, you have an Indian culture
> which is sort of a real Indian culture, which, you have, Bharata Natyam
> [classical Indian dance] and other people who are really interested, and you
> have another sort of culture, which is the bhangra culture, you know, where
> you're looking at Bally Sagoo [a British Asian musician] remixes as a means
> to explore cultural identity, which is not exactly . . . I mean I enjoy listening

to those songs as well, but, er, there has to be a separation between what is real, and why you're really doing something.

Timothy Taylor cites a dismissive posting on the Internet that characterized "bangra" music as essentially "American" and therefore un-Indian: "Bangra is a music for [those who] . . . are willing to show shame towards their own culture. I really don't like Indian music either, but I have respect for it because it is a display of Indian culture. If y'all start listening to bangra, y'all are giving up on your own culture" (1997, p. 166). For many second-generation Indian Americans, authenticity is still tied to a vision of India that is based on classical arts, selected historical traditions, and religious orthodoxy.

This ethnic orthodoxy is based on a definition of culture filtered through the socialization of immigrant parents, whose desire to preserve an "authentic" culture overseas has led to the selective importing of elements and agents of Indian culture, with religious specialists, classical musicians, dancers, and film stars touring the United States and performing at community events. Thus, while a hybrid popular culture circulates in the diaspora, including music remixes and Indian films that are often a cultural pastiche, a parallel transnational circuit has helped reify images of Indian identity overseas (Prashad 1997). The cultural practices and productions selectively imported from the subcontinent travel the frozen furrows of memory and are driven by the politics of nostalgia, with immigrants harking back to the India they left a few decades ago or to a mythical land of spirituality, "good values," and unchanging tradition. The production of nostalgia is predicated on *absence*, a cultural anchor that is both missing and missed, and on the assumption of an earlier time of cultural wholeness that is now at risk of fragmentation, if not dissolution. Commenting on the rise of bhangra youth culture in Britain, Gayatri Gopinath (1995a, pp. 309–10) writes of the tension that is produced as a result of this awareness of trying to recover something that was never lost:

> [E]ven while bhangra was being used as a way of positing a shared, essential identity, the radical impossibility of that identity was always being referenced by its very form: bhangra songs that "add the Western touch," for instance, inevitably involve an alteration of the "culture" that they are supposedly only deploying strategically. In other words, these statements are enunciations of loss, of a yearning and longing to recover and recuperate that which is also simultaneously acknowledged to be irrecoverable and irrecuperable.

The definition of ethnic identity as a finite substance to be protected from diminution or dilution in the diaspora has a powerful impact on the second generation. While many of these college-age youth are away from home and from the surveillance of their parents for the first time, they practice an often intense monitoring of one another's behavior, with peers seeming to take on the functions of parents in policing ethnic boundaries. The college years may, at first, appear to be a liberating period when youth can potentially experiment with identities, but as the Birmingham theorists pointed out, subcultures often perpetuate characteristics of the larger culture; they do not always overturn the ideological constructions of the culture against which they are reacting but often repeat them in mimetic fashion (Cohen 1997).

The yardstick of ethnic authenticity in this tight-knit youth culture is finely calibrated. Those who do not socialize exclusively with other Indian Americans or South Asians, or who are part of an alternative subculture—whether based on a different style, progressive politics, non-Hindu religious groups, or alternative sexual orientations—said they often felt marginalized. Paul Gilroy finds a similar tension in his analysis of Black diasporic culture and attributes these rigid boundaries to "rhetorical strategies of cultural insiderism" that support an "absolute sense of ethnic difference" and "construct the nation [or national identification] as ethnically homogenous" (1993, pp. 83–84). The regulation of ethnic authenticity is always being negotiated in youth cultural productions that challenge monolithic understandings of ethnicity or nationalism, so that the beats of "cool" are mixed into tracks that flow into nostalgia, and vice versa. The dialectic between these cultural complexes is a response to the conjoining of market forces with multiculturalist projects in education and commodity culture that encourage the performance of identity through markers of style and leisure practices and that locate subjects in a racialized and ethnicized social structure. Indian American youth in New York City use the rituals of popular culture to negotiate their racialized, gendered, and classed positioning in the wider social context, and sometimes to reshuffle their parents' expectations of racial identification, but the discourse of purity runs deep.

As Dirks succinctly observes, "Rituals were generalizable sites for struggles of all kinds, including . . . the struggle between discourse and event, between what could be said and what could be done" (1994, p. 494). I argue that the gap, or space of contradiction, between the discourse of ethnic authenticity among second-generation youth on the one hand, and the performance of hybridity in remix youth culture and in everyday life on the other, suggests that what is at stake in this youth subculture is not just a struggle over definitions of Indian music and dance; rather, this disjuncture also reveals conflicts over attempts by Indian American youth to be "authentic" in both local and diasporic spaces, the belief of immigrant parents in the American Dream, and the complicity of Indian Americans with U.S. racial hierarchies. Race politics is deeply implicated in the question of what it means for a young woman or man to become an (Indian) American subject and, for second-generation youth, in the question of what it means to participate in performances of urban cool or of collective nostalgia.

Appropriating Hip-Hop: Masculinity, Racialization, and Subcultural Capital

Dharmesh, a young man whose family lives in New Jersey, remarked that Indian American youth who grew up with Blacks and Latinos, and even some who did not, on coming to college often acquire "the style, and the attitude, and the walk" associated with urban Black and Latino youth culture. Hip-hop is not just "the Black CNN" but has become the channel for youth culture information in general, as Peter Christenson and Donald Roberts point out: "Of all the current popular music styles, the rap/hip hop culture most defines the pop cultural cutting edge, thus providing adolescents concerned with 'coolness' and peer status much crucial information on subjects such as the latest slang and the most recent trends in dance and fashion" (1998, p. 111; see also Perkins 1996, p. 13). The music and media industries have helped make hip-hop a language increasingly adopted by middle-class and suburban youth (Giroux 1996; Kleinfeld 2000; Roediger 1998), with White consumers accounting for about 75 percent of rap album sales (Christenson and Roberts 1998, p. 111). Hip-hop culture is re-signified by Indian American "homeboys" when it crosses class boundaries, as Sujata, a woman who grew up in suburban Connecticut, pointed out: "A lot of them are like total prep school, but they put on a, like, it's this preppie boy–urban look, you know, it's like Upper East Side homeboy, you know. Huge pants, and then, like, a nice button-down shirt, you know."

As Rose observes, "Black style through hip hop has contributed to the continued blackening of mainstream popular culture" (1994a, p. 82). Cultural critics take various, often hotly contested, positions on the issue of consuming cultural commodities across racial, ethnic, and class lines. Perry Hall (1997) argues that White America has a historical ambivalence about Black American cultural forms, arising from racialized structures of power and difference, that is expressed in the simultaneous denial of and attraction to popular forms of Black musical culture. The appropriation and diffusion of ragtime, jazz, rhythm and blues, disco, and rap at different moments have been marked by cycles of innovation of Black musical forms, suppression and aesthetic rejection by the mainstream, followed by co-optation by White artists, absorption into the mainstream, and, in some cases, rejuvenation by contact with dominant cultural forms (Hall 1997). David Roediger, in his writing on "wiggers," or "white niggers," observes that "the proliferation of *wiggers* illuminates issues vital to the history of what Albert Murray has called the 'incontestably mulatto' culture of the United States. The dynamics of cultural hybridity have long featured much that is deeply problematic on the white side. From minstrelsy through *Black Like Me*, from the blackfaced antebellum mobs that victimized African Americans to the recent film *Soul Man*, the superficial notion that Blackness could be put on and taken off at will has hounded hybridity" (1998, pp. 361–62).

The question of hybridity is doubly complicated for desi youth in New York, for they are reworking hip-hop not only into their own youth culture but into a *remix* youth culture, one that expresses the cultural imaginaries of second-generation youth from an immigrant community of color. Fundamentally, desi youth turn to hip-hop because it is key to marking their belonging in the multiethnic urban landscape of New York City. Sharmila noted that for many second-generation men, hip-hop style connotes a certain image of racialized hypermasculinity that is the ultimate definition of cool: "South Asian guys give more respect to African Americans than to Whites because they think the style is cool. The guys look up to them because it's down [fashionable]. They think, 'I'm kinda scared of them but I want to look like them because they're cool.'" Ravi, who began going to Indian parties while in high school in California and who has continued to do so in New York, reflected, "The hip-hop culture has just really taken off. It's really appealed to the Indians, maybe just listening pleasure, the way it sounds, I guess. Maybe the toughness it exudes." Roediger points out that "in a society in which the imagination of Blackness so thoroughly frames what both attracts and repulses whites," American male youth often "identify with violence, scatology, and sexism in rap rather than with Black music and culture more broadly" (1998, pp. 359, 361). Black style is viewed as the embodiment of a particular machismo, the object of racialized desire and, simultaneously, of racialized fear. The desi youth subculture not only is engaged with essentialized definitions of what it means to be truly Indian but also invests this ideal with essentialized definitions of what it means to be cool and to be "young, urban, and black" (Banerjea and Banerjea 1996; Hall 1996b). As Gary Indiana writes: "In its most exacerbated form, this sentimental tic of the white hipster locates all 'authenticity' in the black experience. To be really, really cool becomes the spiritual equivalent of blackness, and even superior to it" (cited in Giroux 1996, p. 81).

Some may argue that Indian American men are drawn to symbols of "tough" masculinity to counter the popular construction of South Asian and Asian American men as somehow emasculated. Oliver Wang, in his work on East Asian American hip-hop artists, argues that "Asian Americans use hip hop as a space to reshape their own self-image, to lay claim to a long-denied masculine and sexual character, and to challenge racially gendered stereotypes. . . . from sexually perverse and predatory opium addicts at the turn of the century to present-day caricatures devoid of masculinity and sexuality" (1997, pp. 6–7). Yet very few young desi men I spoke to felt strongly about mainstream representations of Indian American masculinity as emasculated; while some did speak of being pegged as model students in school, they did not—at least consciously—connect this to the lure of hip-hop. Rather, Sunil, a member of an Indian American fraternity, was concerned about class-coded images of Indian American men as "convenience store owners" or innately nerdy students. He associated these images with the two major waves of post-1965 Indian immigration to the United States, that of the professional classes in the late 1960s and 1970s and that of small business owners in the 1980s and 1990s: "Like toward the lower middle class, they say, 'You're the shopkeeper,' the upper middle class, they'd say, 'Oh, you're this intellectual.'" A male body that exudes toughness might well counter both stereotypes of Indian Americans: the supposedly asexual whiz kid or the 7-Eleven owner. (Regarding the latter stereotype, one may pause to consider that the shopkeeper Apu in the animated television series *The Simpsons* is not particularly brawny.) That a critique of emasculation did not explicitly resonate with these Indian American men does not mean they were unconcerned with the particular overtones of masculinity available to them through hip-hop—a line of argument that brings to light the ways in which "the authentic black subject in hip hop" is rendered hypermasculine in the context of wider racist constructions of Black and Latino men as hypersexual or macho and Asian American men as historically emasculated (Wang 1997, pp. 14–15, 17).[10] Listening to what these young Indian American men have to say, however, it becomes obvious that the powerful appeal of hip-hop as youth style, not to mention sheer pleasure in its rhythms, is what chiefly draws them to this youth culture (Kelley 1997; Rose 1994a). The resonance is "rhythmic" and not just "symbolic" (Christenson and Roberts 1998, p. 111).

"Hipness" is of premium value in this remix subculture, and "being in the know" carries with it a certain status or subcultural capital associated with being cool (Thornton 1997a). This underlying social logic of subcultures, Sarah Thornton argues, is objectified in the display of the "right" width of jean legs, crop of hair, or use of dialect; knowing which party to go to or displaying the style of the moment is a mark of social distinction. Thornton's notion of subcultural capital draws on Pierre Bourdieu's analysis of cultural capital and its role in hierarchies of taste that are used to differentiate social strata. Subcultural capital, like cultural capital, has the quality of appearing to be an innate possession, acquired without effort or education and thus naturalizing social hierarchies; club cultures are, in fact, "taste cultures" (Thornton 1996, pp. 3, 10–12). The construction of subcultural cool is rooted in the nuances of style and dialect, in connections to a social network, and in knowledge of urban spaces which have their own contests of power and codes of belonging.

Young Indian American men who are deejays possess high subcultural capital in the remix party scene. Male deejays acquire capital in the traditional sense as well, since they make money from their gigs at parties. As in other dance cultures dominated by men at the turntables, this perhaps has something to do with the emergence in the 1980s of deejaying as a source of income for young men of color who "put culture to work for them" (Kelley 1997), as do other young men who find themselves marginalized by the post-Fordist economy, according to Angela McRobbie (1999, p. 145). But the preponderance of male deejays, despite the prominence of DJ Rekha and a few other, less well known women deejays in New York, also reflects the larger patterns in the music industry: The ways in which musical knowledge and technology are shared and developed reinforce the homosocial bonds of masculinist music subcultures (Straw 1997; Whitely 1997, p. xviii). The remix deejay crews tended to be created by male deejays who trained other male deejays; for example, DJ Magic Mike, one of the earliest desi deejays in New York, trained DJ Kucha, who now has his own "boyz" working under his stewardship. Although I found that Indian American deejays sometimes work with women promoters, subcultural capital tends to be perpetuated through these homosocial relationships. A male deejay is also presumed to confer status on his girlfriend, who would then be known as "DJ Karma's girl" or "Lil' Jay's girl," drawing subcultural capital from the achievements of her male partner in rock groupie style. The dynamics of gender and sexuality in this subculture highlight deeper conflicts over the role of women and negotiations of class mobility among second-generation youth.

Thornton's theory of subcultural capital helps address the ambiguous role of class distinctions in this Indian American youth subculture, at least up to a point. She argues that uniform expressions of style, language, or music may sometimes purposefully obscure class differences within a youth subculture, and in some instances, distinctions of taste may even emulate or romanticize working-class youth style. Both of these "fantasies of classlessness" are more complex, and potentially more problematic, than Thornton suggests. A young man from a working-class family in Queens might to all outward appearances dress, speak, and move in exactly the same way as the son of an engineer from an affluent Connecticut suburb, and the two might not be easily distinguishable in a crowd, based on broad strokes of style. This does not mean, however, that there are no material distinctions at work in this youth culture; on the contrary, the commodification of hip-hop, and of youth style in general, has meant that brand-name "gear," such as jackets, shoes, and backpacks, are carefully noted by youth who are in the know. As Bourdieu succinctly observed, taste classifies, and it classifies the classifier (cited in Thornton 1996, p. 101).

Designer labels are symbols of buying power, but in some contexts subcultural capital is the more important, regardless of the "authenticity" of its label. Thus, Hilfiger wear or the Prada logo does not need to be the "real" thing on the street, but the distinctive bands of red, blue, and white or the recognizable buckle do matter. Rose writes, "Hip hop artists use style as a form of identity formation that plays on class distinctions and hierarchies by using commodities to claim the cultural

DJ Sharaab spins at the Mutiny party in Manhattan. (Courtesy of
Srinivas Kuruganti)

terrain. Clothing and consumption rituals testify to the power of consumption as a means of cultural expression. Hip hop fashion is an especially rich example of this sort of appropriation and critique via
style" (1994a, p. 36). Rose argues that for urban, working-class or poor
youth, sporting mock gold jewelry or "fake" Gucci and other designer
emblems is a way of parodying, and perhaps challenging, the affluence
of those who can afford to flaunt the real thing. Hip-hop culture may
in some instances be implicitly subversive or critical of consumerism,
but cultural critics of hip-hop acknowledge that it is always engaged
with the realm of commerce, as are other forms of popular culture that
are marketed, distributed, and consumed (Rose 1994a; Kelley 1997;
George 1998). In the desi youth culture, which includes upper-middle-
class as well as less affluent Indian American youth, those who sport
"real" labels may well notice which others do and do not. Vijay, who is
from a wealthy business family, pointed out that it would be obvious to
others that the jacket he was wearing cost a hefty sum of money, and
he in turn would certainly know the price of someone else's brand-
name sneakers or backpack. A double layer of appropriation operates
in this Indian American youth subculture, drawing on hip-hop style
and also adopting the re-creation of designer wear that is part of hip-
hop's own stylistic bricolage and commentary on consumption. It

would be facile to say that class distinctions have disappeared into sub-cultural appropriation and mimesis. If anything, the materially shaped discourse and practice of authenticity at work in this subculture are determined by buying power and class status. These material concerns are significant for youth who are from immigrant families that represent a range of class backgrounds, and whose parents are often deeply concerned about the economic trajectories of the next generation. The social distinctions of hip-hop are recreated within an Indian American youth culture and become intertwined with its contradictory ideologies of gender and ethnic authenticity.

Consumption becomes an important terrain for the negotiation of these young people's ideological projects because the use of music and fashion to express social identities in adolescence is an option made available by particular industries that target youth as eager consumers. At the same time, the overemphasis on the leisure activities of adolescents in cultural studies obscures the fact that many youth are inevitably concerned with school and with work. For example, the desi party scene is a source of part-time or sometimes even full-time income by deejays and party promoters who are young entrepreneurs, savvy to the economics of popular culture; Indian American deejays in New York charge anywhere between $200 and $500, sometimes more, for spinning at a party for one night, and many are now organized in conglomerates headed by a single star deejay. Further, while hip-hop has always been a hybrid form, based on the sampling of sounds and words, and while popular culture, by definition, is not private property, many of the Indian remixes that sample rap lyrics are bootleg albums that do not respect copyright laws (Sengupta 1997). As bhangra and Indian film remixes move into the mainstream and Indian deejays begin to consider the possibility of signing on to major record labels, as British Asian artist Bally Sagoo did with Sony, there might be greater pressure to legalize this appropriation; but this does not necessarily translate into equitable acknowledgment or economic payback for hip-hop artists, given the White-dominated ownership of the record industry (Feld 1988; Hall 1997). Perry Hall notes, "Award (recognition) and reward (compensation) structures often evolve that grossly enrich white appropriators, while only a few Black innovators have comparable levels of compensation" (1997, p. 32). Or as performance artist Danny Hoch sums up in *Jails, Hospitals, and Hip Hop*, his brilliant analysis of hip-hop and the White-dominated culture industry, "We'll take your culture from you, soup it up, and then sell it back to you." One way of rethinking the debates about "cultural appropriation" that holds in tension these material and ideological forces is offered by Daniel Miller, who describes consumption as a "moral project," and understands that commodities offer possibilities to reimagine cultural ideologies, such as those of "self" and "other." He explains, "Consumption is simply a process of objectification—that is, a use of goods and services in which the object or activity becomes simultaneously a practice in the world and a form in which we construct our understandings in the world" (Miller 1995, p. 30). The dual discourses of authenticity operating in remix youth culture—that of subcultural cool and of collective nostalgia—are embedded in each other and sometimes reinforce but also contradict each other, as their moral projects lead youth to different understandings of how to be Indian at this particular moment in New York. The hierarchies of authenticity and belonging that are created involve judgments of worth or value based on ideological and moralized projects of cultural consumption and reinvention. There may be no "authentic" reading of the consumption of hip-hop by desi youth. There is, however, a politics of authenticity that has meaning in the lives of these youth at this particular moment in New York City, and that is constantly being negotiated with reference to their positionings in a larger Indian diaspora and to global flows of culture.

The globalization of mass media in the era of late capitalism has certainly resulted in the seeping of Black-identified American popular culture and fashion into remote corners of the world, at huge profits to American and multinational corporations (Skoggard 1998). Youth living in rural areas in India can now listen to American rap or Indian remixes from the United States, and children of the transnational Indian elite wear Nike shoes that are manufactured in sweatshops in East and Southeast Asia (LaFeber 1999). Miller rejects a populist reading of consumption as the "transgressive tactics of the weak" (de Certeau 1984, pp. xviii–xx), as do other cultural theorists, arguing that "it is far more common for the tactics of the weak to be concerned with gaining access to resources than in using consumption as some kind of 'resistance'" (Miller 1995, p. 29). His work avoids both the emphasis on "creative individualism" and a so-called "vulgar" Marxist critique of consumption as reflecting only "producer interests" (1995, pp. 28–29), suggesting instead that "material culture is often the concrete means by which the contradictions held within general concepts such as the domestic or the global are in practice resolved in everyday life. . . . [O]ne of the key struggles of modern life is to retain both a sense of authentic locality, often as narrow as the private sphere, and yet also lay claims to a cosmopolitanism that at some level may evoke rights to a global status" (Miller 1998, p. 19). Through the consumption of music and style and the performance of remixed dance movements, desi youth participate in a vision of "authentic locality" that positions them as Indian Americans but also New Yorkers, and they construct a sense of belonging to a diasporic community that is embedded in the material context of immigration.

The Racial Politics of "Cool"

The appropriation of Black style obviously has different meanings for youth depending on the particular racial and class locations they occupy; an understanding of the politics of cool is necessarily conjunctural. Codes of hip(-hop)ness at work in Asian American youth subcultures are always in relationship to the racialization of Asians and the Black/White racial paradigm of the United States. Dorinne Kondo (1995, p. 53), commenting on urban Asian Americans who identify with African Americans and borrow their dialect, observes, "If you are Asian American or Latino, especially on the East Coast, white and black are the poles, and if you don't identify with one, you identify with the other." Gary Okihiro (1994) probes more deeply into the positioning of Asian Americans within this racial binary by addressing the political implications of the question "Is yellow Black or White?"—or, if you will, is brown Black or White? Okihiro (1994, p. 34) notes that Asian Americans, Native Americans, and Latinos are classified as either "near-whites" or "just like blacks," depending on the operation of model minority myths or their subordination as minorities: "Asian Americans have served the master class, whether as 'near-blacks' in the past or as 'near-whites' in the present or as 'marginal men' in both the past and the present. Yellow [or brown] is emphatically neither white nor black; but insofar as Asians and Africans share a subordinate position to the master class, yellow is a shade of black, and black, a shade of yellow." Okihiro concludes that the question as posed is a false proposition because it reinscribes the bipolar racial framework of the United States, disciplining ethnic minorities and erasing histories of alliances (1994, p. 62). Yet, like the very notion of racial formation, racial polarity is a system of representation that still plays a role in shaping social structures and individual experiences (Omi and Winant, 1994, p. 55). The turn to hip-hop by desi youth in New York could be considered a "racial project" in Michael Omi and Howard Winant's sense of the term—an ideological link between structures and representations of race, connecting "what race means in a particular discursive practice and the ways in which both social structures and everyday experiences are racially organized, based upon that meaning" (1994, p. 56).

This racial project can be seen as a response to the Black/White racial binary and the attempts of second-generation Indian Americans to position themselves in relation to the monochromatic racial boundaries of the United States. In this sense, the work of hip-hop for Indian Americans is similar to the use of images of Blacks in Japanese mass culture, which John Russell explains as a "tendency to employ the black Other as a reflexive symbol through which Japanese attempt to deal with their own ambiguous racial status in a Eurocentric world, where such hierarchies have been largely (and literally) conceived in terms of polarizations between black and white and in which Japanese as Asians have traditionally occupied a liminal state" (1995, p. 299). Russell identifies two reflexive uses of the Black Other: One is to accept the "racial status quo" but to compensate for this inferior status of Japanese/Asians by asserting superiority over the supposedly "backward" group, internalizing racist models from "the West"; the other is to "reject the status quo" and assert solidarity with other nonwhites (1995, pp. 306–7). These strategies mirror the findings of Nitasha Sharma's 1998 pilot study of Indian American youth at the University of California, Santa Barbara, where she found two predominant kinds of hip-hop fans. One group accepted the notion that Indian Americans occupied a mediating position in the Black/White racial hierarchy and tended to be interested in rap primarily for its beats rather than for the content of its lyrics. The second group viewed hip-hop as a social movement critical of the racial status quo and identified with other youth of color, distancing themselves from or feeling marginalized within Indian American communities. The Indian American youth I spoke to in New York City demonstrated both kinds of strategic identification, but the differences between them were not as clearly defined as those Russell or Sharma outline; rather, their crossing of racial boundaries seemed partial and conjunctural. In some instances, the youth I spoke with seemed to accept, or perhaps passively *not to reject*, the racial status quo, but in other contexts they explicitly identified as nonwhite and resisted anti-Black racism. What makes these responses complex and contingent is that the particular youth culture I discuss is not simply hip-hop culture but an Indian remix youth culture that *samples* the sounds and styles of hip-hop and therefore is an overt expression of ethnicity. The emphasis on an ethnic identity in response to racial ambiguity is perhaps a third reflexive strategy, or more plausibly, one that contains some degree of distancing from or solidarity with Blacks, or both.[11]

The discourse of ethnic identity, according to some youth as well as some scholarly commentators, is a way to resolve or perhaps deflect the question of racial positioning for Indian Americans. Chandrika, who was actively involved with Asian American student activism on her campus, commented, "No matter what it is, if you haven't been accepted, you're not going to be Black, like all your friends, or White, like all your friends, it's not going to happen. You seek refuge." Most of the second-generation Indian American youth I spoke to had not been drawn to articulations of Indian Americanness until they arrived at college and found a sizable community of ethnic peers and a racially segregated campus social life, created in the context of the ethnic student organizations and identity politics prevalent in U.S. colleges and universities. Chandrika thought this explained why some of her peers had begun to flaunt Indian symbols of dress and jewelry and literally to perform their ethnic identity with "bhangra moves" on the dance floor.

These moves reflect broader patterns of emphasizing ethnicity that some critics view as attempts to position Indian Americans outside the racial stratification of the United States and to deflect identification with less privileged minority groups of color (George 1997; Mazumdar 1989; Visweswaran 1997). Visweswaran suggests that these tactical evasions have historical precedents in the early twentieth century, when Indian immigrants and other Asian Americans were contesting their ambiguous racial classifications in order to become naturalized as U.S. citizens, then defined as "free white people" or as persons of "African nativity or descent" (Jensen 1988, p. 247).[12] In a landmark case in 1923, the Supreme Court rejected the petition for naturalized citizenship of Bhagat Singh Thind, an Indian immigrant, claiming that although Indians were technically Caucasian, the definition of race had to be based on the "understanding of the common man." Visweswaran (1997, p. 21) argues that by not "challenging the racial basis of the exclusion laws," Thind and other South Asian immigrants "actively disavowed" racial identification with other Asian (and nonwhite) groups in order to be counted as "White," whereas, after 1965, Indian immigrant organizations lobbied to be classified as "Asians," a minority group, in order to receive affirmative action benefits. Though it is important to point out that Thind and others did not attempt to overturn the fundamentally racist premise of naturalization laws in the early twentieth century, the case is complicated by Thind's own history as an open, although not militant, critic of British imperialist rule in India who also served in the U.S. Army during World War I. The political implications of Thind's move are not completely straightforward, given the anti-Asian racism enshrined in immigration and naturalization law during this period; as a result of the Thind decision, Indians were legally barred from acquiring citizenship, and this case became the basis of Asian-directed antimiscegenation laws, exclusion from immigration quotas, and denial of land ownership in California (Daniels 1989; Takaki 1989a, 1989b).

At the turn of the millennium, notions of racial and cultural citizenship in U.S. public discourse and media may still reveal suspicions of Asians as aliens or potential traitors (Palumbo-Liu 1999, p. 5), but the category "Asian American" is a racial project now available to Indian Americans as a pan-ethnic identification, as are multiculturalist constructions of ethnicity, particularly on college campuses. Second-generation performances of ethnicity are motivated by needs seemingly more complex than a simple evasion of racial classification. As youth of color who, unlike their parents, grew up in the United States, these young people have been molded by the ethnic identity frameworks available to them and by their experiences of growing up as minorities. The question is whether these youth can build a racial politics that will allow them to participate in spheres based both on ethnicity *and* on alliances with youth of color, and whether they can resist the ethnic chauvinism of South Asian student organizations that view other group allegiances with suspicion. Chandrika observed that Indian Americans who participated in the remix subculture at Columbia University did not unite with African American and Latino students in the coalition of students of color that had been battling the university administration for adequate representation in the curriculum. In her opinion, students belonging to the South Asian student organization on campus were less politicized than other ethnic student groups and more interested in organizing events to promote "cultural awareness." While small groups of youth within most South Asian student organizations in New York are interested in building alliances with other minority student groups, I found that what most of these South Asian student organizations share is an emphasis on performing a strictly cultural Indian/South Asian American identity in an exclusively Indian/South Asian American social space. The larger backdrop for second-generation youth who are involved in this desi subculture is one in which identification as Indian American is generally not a political stance, let alone a position of solidarity with other youth of color.

The segregation of many New York desi youth from the racial group whose cultural productions they draw on in their remix subculture is not unprecedented in U.S. popular culture. As Perry Hall observes of the crossover of earlier forms of Black music, there is a "tendency of the forms to become disassociated, in the discourse and perceptual framework of the white-dominated mainstream, from the African-American experiential context that created them" (1997, p. 37). Commenting on discussions of "keeping it real" in hip-hop, Ross (1994, p. 287) notes the cruel irony that the "authentic" group—young Black males—is itself vanishing, under attack from and incarcerated by the state. Black style travels more freely across racial and class borders than young Black men do.

Remix youth culture's sampling of hip-hop allows desi youth to hold the two impulses of ethnicization and participation in the U.S. racial formation in a delicate balance. As a racial project, it defers the question of "Black or White" through the ambiguity of adopting Black style in an ethnically exclusive space. If the production of cool symbolically crosses racial boundaries, it is still, for some youth, only a transitional flirtation with Black popular culture, and one that has been, for many, almost an American rite of passage in adolescence (Roediger 1998). Jeffrey Melnick observes that the crossing of racial boundaries through music tends to wane as adolescents move into adulthood and is "temporally bounded by the fact that . . . teenagers have to grow up into a labor economy deeply invested in racial division" (1996, p. 227). Sunita, who grew up in Queens and in Stamford, Connecticut, believed many desi youth immersed in hip-hop culture "at the back of their minds are thinking, this is not long-term." She commented that the appropriation of what is perceived by the mainstream to be an oppositional style is mediated by the often unstated but always present location of class status, and she remarked, "I know for me there's this

cushion, my parents are supporting me, they're paying for my college
. . . you know [the identification] is only up to a certain point, there are
big, distinct differences." This was exemplified by a conversation I had
with an Indian American man in his mid-twenties at a conference organized by the New York chapter of the Network of Indian
Professionals (NETIP). He had been immersed in the desi party scene,
but as an adult in the workforce, he felt unmoored. What would re-
place the desi subculture that he had identified with when he was
younger? Clearly, his question was partly answered by the conference
itself, sponsored by an organization formed largely to support networking and heterosexual liaisons among young, upwardly mobile
Indian Americans.

In New York, many college students I spoke to seemed to envision
a future in which they would move into the professional, college-
educated class, in order to realize their immigrant parents' aspirations
for upward mobility. Unlike the creators of hip-hop, the youth who
participate in the Indian remix subculture are not necessarily using it
to recognize limited options for economic mobility. Most Indian
American youth I spoke to did not view this remix popular culture as
resistance to a system of economic and racial stratification; in fact, several seemed bent on succeeding within that system. Although as youth
of color they are often targets of racial discrimination, many did not
believe that would translate into economic discrimination in their own
lives. Second-generation youth who grew up in less affluent, racially
diverse neighborhoods, however, often know what it is like to live in
communities struggling for city and state resources, and regardless of
class location, many of these youth have experienced racial harassment,
sometimes because they are mistakenly identified as Black or Latino.
(For more on the politics of misidentification, see George 1997.)

The emulation of urban African American style has subtler implications if situated in differentials of privilege and generational divides
over racial politics. For some youth, the turn to hip-hop is clearly related to a rejection of the hierarchies in the dominant U.S. racial formations—and of their own families—and for a few, the interest in hip-
hop grew out of friendships and intimate relationships with other
youth of color. Sunita, who has been going to "Indian parties" since she
was in high school, thought that for her Indian American peers, "identifying with hip-hop is a little more rebellious" than adopting other
youth styles "because it's not the norm associated with White culture."

She pointed out that the adoption of hip-hop sometimes becomes a gesture of defiance against parents who, like her own, belong to the wave of Indian immigrants who came to the United States in the mid-1960s and 1970s and were highly educated professionals and graduate students. Manisha, who grew up in a middle-class neighborhood in Spring Valley (now New City), New Jersey, and who has been friends with and dated Black and Latino youth since she was in high school, said that although her parents do not object to her listening to rap, some Indian parents don't want their kids listening to "that music": "I think because it's definitely associated with Black . . . people. And I definitely know that there's *big* racist views in the community and they don't like . . . the fact that a lot of Indian kids are heading towards that, the hip-hop scene, which is mostly the Black and Latino scene, and we're getting real associated into that."

Manisha has an astute materialist analysis of how other people of color read the racial and political alignments of affluent Indian Americans. In response to an African American student in her class who had "heard that Indians are like the Hindu whites," and ignoring the distorted label for the moment, she observed, "I said the basic reason I think that we're associated like that is because most of them that come over here came with an education and we got wealthy pretty quick even though we were poor when we came over, we right away got wealthy, we moved into the White neighborhoods and that scattered us . . . we assimilated quicker in a sense." Manisha was very critical of the racism she had witnessed toward youth of color in her high school and of racial discrimination against people of color in general. Alluding to the Thind decision, she concluded that she could not understand how an Indian American might "feel like the Hindu White . . . because it [racial categorization] is like the definition of what the common man would see now, and that's not us, you know."

For several lower-middle-class as well as upper-middle-class youth, identification with African Americans sparked conflicts with immigrant parents on issues of race politics. Women who had dated African American men and struggled with parental disapproval expressed perhaps the most emotional critique of the anti-Black prejudices of immigrant parents. For instance, Purnima, who lived in New Jersey and then attended a high school with a large Black student population in North Carolina, had participated in several race relations workshops and spoke of the anger and frustration she felt on hearing her mother and her Indian relatives say, "You can't bring a kallu [darkie] home." She eventually ended the relationship with her Black boyfriend but said that she was unable to forgive her mother for her racial prejudices and the family was "torn apart." The anti-Black prejudices of South Asian immigrants are reinforced by the Black/White lines of American racial formations and the historical scapegoating of African Americans by new immigrants (Kondo 1995; Mazumdar 1989; Morrison 1994; Prashad 2000; Singh 1996). As Toni Morrison writes in her incisive essay "On the Backs of Blacks," "although U.S. history is awash in labor battles, political fights, and property wars among all religious and ethnic groups, their struggles are persistently framed as struggles between recent arrivals and blacks. In race talk the move into mainstream America always means buying into the notion of American blacks as the real aliens. Whatever the ethnicity or nationality of the immigrant, his [or her] nemesis is understood to be African American" (1994, p. 98).

Second-generation youth who participate in the desi youth culture are not unaware of the contradictions of consuming Black style and are often uneasy about the politics of this "cultural appropriation" in light of anti-Black racism. DJ Baby Face articulated this paradox clearly at an Indian party held in the cavernous tunnels of a Manhattan club, with the beat of Indian remix pounding against the walls: "Blacks are the scapegoat for Indians, but when it comes to fashion and style, we hold them high, they have power." His succinct observation reveals the underlying politics of being cool—the group emulated in style is also the one on whose back immigrants tread to preserve their sense of superior status.

The racialized entry of Indian immigrants into the United States and their relationship to African Americans is further complicated because they have left one color-conscious society, with a history of caste stratification, for another (Ogbu 1978; De Vos 1990; Mazumdar 1989). In *The Karma of Brown Folk* (2000), however, Vijay Prashad cautions against an easy acceptance of the "thesis that desis have a racist tradition that can be seen in the mysteries of the caste complex," pointing to radical South Asian traditions of solidarity with Black liberation that have been have been articulated by the likes of Mohandas Gandhi, Jawaharlal Nehru, and the poet Faiz Ahmed Faiz—and that have largely been erased in the diaspora. Prashad argues that many Indian and other South Asian immigrants accept anti-Black racism as part of the "conservative desi culture that is being created in the U.S." (2000, pp. 175–77), in their need to belong to a diasporic community that will bolster their sometimes fragile foothold in a new country. Prashad is right, I think, in pointing to a dynamic view of cultural tradition and of history that does not leave all Indian immigrants branded irrevocable racists but that simultaneously points to the willingness of some to accommodate to anti-Black racism.

Manisha, for example, points out that immigrant parents view the identification with hip-hop among desi youth through the framework of an assimilationist "moral project" that constructs White America as the preferred destination for their children, refusing to acknowledge that hip-hop is an integral part of White American youth culture as well: "Because on the one hand, they're like, 'Don't become Americanized . . .' and that's mostly faced towards the whiter side of it, but even though the hip-hop scene is Americanized too it's the other side of it, so they wouldn't like it either way, but I think they would rather it be on the other side, on the White side of it, than on the Black and Latino side because to them it's bringing in fights and all the bad stuff, that's all they see, that's all a lot of people [see] from the media and everything." Manisha's comments echo the views of those who argue that the Indian immigrant elite strives to ally itself with "White middle-class America" (Helweg and Helweg 1990; Hossain 1982). Amritjit Singh notes that some affluent Indian immigrants complain, as did an acquaintance of his, that "if middle-class people like us are paying unusually high taxes, it is only because of 'all those blacks on welfare'; that blacks do not want to work or work hard; that blacks have contributed 'brawn' but no 'brain' to the development of this country" (1996, p. 99). This rhetoric of anti-Black racism among Indian Americans reached its most publicized extreme in the writings of Dinesh D'Souza, infamous author of *The End of Racism*, who resurrected the specter of the model minority as a "weapon against African Americans" with his question: "Why can't an African American be more like an Asian?" (cited in Prashad 2000, p. 4).

Yet the hardening of racist beliefs in relation to the model minority myth among Indian immigrants in the United States is violently jolted by racial assaults on Indians, disrupting the denial of their presence as people of color in this country. Sucheta Mazumdar argues that incidents such as the attacks on Indian Americans in Jersey City in 1987 by the Dotbusters (see also Misir 1996) have evoked two kinds of strategic identification by Indian Americans: One has been an effort to assimilate into White American culture as much as possible and to play the "near-White" model minority; the other has been to form political alliances with other people of color to combat racial violence and discrimination (Mazumdar 1989). In the aftermath of the Dotbusters episode, it was a group of young South Asian American activists who mobilized to bring justice against the perpetrators of the attack and formed one of the first community-based progressive South Asian youth organizations in New York, Youth Against Racism (Misir 1996).

Some theorists argue that the turn to hip-hop among desi youth is explained in part by the alienation of second-generation youth from the model minority leanings of their parents, including the stereotype's manifestation as anti-Black racism. Singh is hopeful that second-generation youth have been socialized into a different kind of race politics, mediated through Black popular music: "Unlike their parents, they have African American friends and have developed a better understanding of how racism and poverty operate in American society. . . . [M]aybe the deep sense of 'alienation' expressed in contemporary black music resonates with their own sense of rebellion against their parents' double standards: an insistence on seeing African Americans harshly through the prism of caste even as they cloak themselves in the highest ideals of fairness and equal opportunity" (1996, p. 98). Some of the youth I spoke to expressed an awareness of race politics that had grown out of friendships and everyday social interactions with other youth of color, as in Manisha's case, and had developed into a critique of institutional and community racism, as articulated by Chandrika, Sunita, and others. Yet I distinguish between an "alienation" felt by youth who are politically or economically disenfranchised or critical of the status quo—a "structural alienation"—and a resistance arising out of a generational difference—a "social-psychological alienation" (Epstein 1998, pp. 5–6). Adolescent rebellion against parents and the generational ideologies they represent is a trope that has long been embedded in theories of adolescence and coming-of-age narratives in the United States, even while these have varied by gender, ethnic, and class location (Erikson 1968; Mead 1961). Rebellion through popular music, moreover, is a familiar rite of youth culture—often a particularly masculinized one (Whitely 1997)—that may offer Indian American youth a cultural form to express their distancing from parents. For some Indian American youth, however, a style that subverts their parents' expectations and racial prejudices may simultaneously be an expression of their own critique of the racialized caste stratification of U.S. society.

Desi youth's turn to hip-hop in the 1990s is rooted in a larger history of appropriation of Black music by non–African Americans as part of the reinvention of ethnic identity by various groups. The resonant connections between the work of cultural studies theorist George Lipsitz (1994) and anthropologist Michael Fischer (1986) on this issue provide interesting insights into the implications of Indian American hip-hop. Lipsitz, commenting on White American artists who were drawn to African American and Latino musical traditions, writes, "Black music provided them with a powerful critique of mainstream middle-class Anglo-Saxon America as well as with an elaborate vocabulary for airing feelings of marginality and contestation. They engaged in what film critics Douglas Kellner and Michael Ryan call 'discursive transcoding'—indirect expression of alienations too threatening to express directly" (1994, p. 55). For Indian American youth, this alienation may be partly a result of what Fischer calls "ethnic anxiety," a deep desire to maintain a sense of difference in the face of homogenization and to redefine the relationship between self and community (1986, p. 197). The ethnic anxiety of second-generation youth may be a response to ethnic identity politics in the United States, assimilationist pressures, and their own experiences as objects of racism. Lipsitz argues that for certain American musicians of Greek, German, or Jewish descent, this anxiety sometimes arises from a political understanding of relationships of racial dominance and subordination; engagement with Black music may signal the re-creation of a "moral vision" of the meanings of community and tradition (Fischer 1986, p. 197). For Indian American youth, the turn to hip-hop is not always based on clearly articulated political dissent or moral outrage, but it may at least provide a discourse for coding an alienation from parents that is bound up with struggles over what it means to be Indian in the United States. This alienation may not simply be a rejection of parents' racial ideologies but may also express an ambivalence toward the upwardly mobile path their parents have attempted to carve out for them, with its burden of suitable educational fields and careers.

This alienation is not always to be found in bald statements by youth about their class positioning. Nevertheless, the pressure of living up to the Asian American model minority image that the larger society has created and that their parents have reinforced is real for second-generation youth, as is occasionally acknowledged in the Indian American community when news surfaces of tragic suicides by youth unable to live the assimilationist dream (Pais 2000). Sharmila, who chose to pursue a career as an actress against her parents' wishes, commented that most of her peers seemed to sacrifice their own interests because of notions of "money and providing" that were deeply "ingrained" in them by their parents: "I think a lot of them will always have other interests in other things, they won't be as willing to . . . they won't have the guts, in a way, to [pursue those things], it's really difficult emotionally; is it worth it at the end? A lot of them will be like, I might as well just do this, make money and all because I want to make my parents happy, and therefore I'll be happy." The price of the model minority myth for these youth is often self-denial, guilt, and frustration. Using Lipsitz's argument, these and other "hidden injuries of class" are perhaps indirectly expressed through cultural alignments with a subculture that symbolically represents a different lifestyle. Sherry Ortner points out that there is often "a displacement of class strain and friction into other areas of life," at least for middle-class American families, and that the adolescent rebellion against middle-class parents through "representations of lower-class affiliation" is threatening precisely because youth are challenging not just their parents' class values but their investments in class reproduction (1991, pp. 171, 177).

This analysis echoes the Birmingham school's theory of youth subcultures, but it too does not presume that the appropriation of Black popular culture is an intervention with lasting social or material impact. Neither do I want to veer too close to a functionalist reading of class alienation from the "parent culture." Rather, as suggested by Peter Stallybrass and Allon White's analysis of carnival, I propose that hip-hop's insertion into Indian American youth culture is but "one instance of a general economy of transgression and of the recoding of high/low relations across the whole social structure" (1986, p. 19).

The politics of bhangra/remix youth culture in New York, and in the United States more generally, stands in contrast to that in Britain, where the late 1970s and early 1980s saw a "new symbolic unity primarily between African-Caribbean and Asian people" through identification with the category "Black" (S. Sharma, 1996, p. 39). This coalitional identification, Sanjay Sharma notes, was a political project involving "autonomous, anti-racist community struggles in Britain." Stuart Hall also points out, however, that the label "Black" "had a certain way of silencing the very specific experiences of Asian people" (cited in S. Sharma 1996, p. 39). Bhangra remix emerged as a "new Asian dance music" that offered an Asian identity as a possible racial location, but still one that, in Sharma's view, "continues to be intimately tied to rethinking the possibilities of the Black anti-racist project" (1996, p. 34). Keeping this contrast in mind is instructive, because it is a reminder that South Asian remix youth culture is not inherently subversive but is differentially politicized, depending on the historical, economic, and national contexts of particular immigrant communities.

Containing the Paradoxes of Ethnic Authenticity

Reflecting on the complex contradictions that emerge from an analysis of Indian American youth culture in New York, I find that this ethnic youth subculture not only tends to accommodate itself to the dominant racial and class framework, but it also uses a pervasive American means of expressing identity, that is, the marking of ethnic boundaries, as well as common commodities and social practices, such as fashion, music, and dance, associated with American youth culture. Georges Balandier points out, "The supreme ruse of power is to allow itself to be contested ritually in order to consolidate itself more effectively" (cited in Stallybrass and White, 1986, p. 14). This is not to dismiss the significance for many second-generation youth of a social and cultural space they can claim as their own, outside direct parental and community control, or the importance of cultural production by youth of color, but is rather to recognize how this subculture, instead of overturning established trajectories of socialization, recreates gendered sanctions or moralized judgments that reinforce a conservative discourse about ethnic purity. Instead of subverting the dominant tropes of cultural identity at work in the second generation, this subculture has provided a setting in which to *contain* the presumed paradoxes of second-generation experiences, by performing a hybrid identity that many of these youth nevertheless question. This popular culture contains social paradoxes of cool and nostalgia that are produced internally, within the youth subculture and immigrant community, as well as externally, in response to the racial and class structures of the wider society. Gopinath also concludes that "bhangra as performance must be understood, then, not as a manifestation of the free play of a hybrid identity but rather as a creative response to the demand for coherence and stability within specific racial and cultural contexts, a means by which to 'work the trap that one is inevitably in'" (1995a, p. 312). The management of hybridity serves an important purpose in the lives of social actors, particularly for immigrant and second-generation youth, but it has limited possibilities for broader change given that it is a strategy that serves both global capital and the multicultural, even imperial, state (Hall 1997; Hardt and Negri 2000).

A point that speaks to the internal paradox of hybridity in this subculture is that youth themselves often couch critiques of this second-generation popular culture in the rhetoric of authenticity. Images of the ancestral culture portray traditions as "pure" and "innocent" while mainstream American cultural tropes are "seductive" and "polluting" influences from which ethnic identity must be protected. The language that both first- and second-generation Indian Americans use in evaluating identities is that of chastity and corruption. The debates over gender and sexual roles in the second generation have a powerful moralizing dimension, one that has real consequences for the lives of young Indian Americans. James Brow argues that the "moral authority" that allows tradition to become "doxa," or the natural order of things, stems from a process of imbuing ethnic ties with a certain sanctity, so that "the primordiality of communal relations is preserved only by their incarceration in the doxic prison of innocence" (1990, 2–3).[13] While Brow makes an interesting link between ethnic absolutism and a process of sacralization, he does not make the connection to gender and sexuality, the other half of the tension in this instance of ethnic orthodoxy. Feminist and postcolonial theorists have pointed to a particular gendered view of culture in immigrant communities or nationalist movements where women are used to signify tradition and so must be controlled in order to maintain the boundaries of community or nation, as is discussed in Chapter 4.

A *sexualizing* of ethnic identities occurs that imbues them with a moral force, enabling the enforcement of notions of cultural purity in the second generation. A discourse centering on female sexuality is thus inserted into the rhetoric of ethnic authenticity to uphold a dichotomy of identity choices. The sexual undercurrents of this subculture—the preoccupation with dating and body image, the slipping out of the clothes of a "good" Indian girl into those of a popular clubber—express the generally shared concerns of adolescents but are also cast in a way that reflects on questions of second-generation identity and reveals the limitations of hybridity when expressed in the realm of style alone. The production of subcultural "cool" is intimately intertwined with the performance of nostalgia, for remix parties are always haunted by the specter of cultural authenticity. Desi youth construct a vision of second-generation coolness by working markers of urban youth style, such as hip-hop, into the nostalgia for an uncontaminated Indian culture. Clearly, these performances of desi cool and collective nostalgia are not in opposition to each other; one is embedded in the other, although this dialectic is often unevenly and viscerally felt, especially by young women.

Cultural theorists, however, have sometimes privileged notions of fluid, fragmented identities without paying sufficient attention to how actors may negotiate both shifting identities and reified ideals in their everyday lives; the contradictions on the ground are sometimes more complex than theorists acknowledge. Critiquing theories which insist that identity is a fluid "process" and never a static object, Taylor counters, in his study of South Asian British musicians, that identity is a "process both toward and away from a thing—a stable identity—that many musicians and fans hold onto" (1997, p. 164). Yet Indian American youth disrupt the very fictions of authenticity they construct, as in their use of hip-hop to mark a style that is distinctly diasporic. Dirks points out that the performative nature of ritual events demonstrates the contingent nature of authenticity: "Each ritual event is patterned activity, to be sure, but it is also invented anew as it happens. . . . [T]he authenticity of the event was inscribed in its performance, not in some time- and custom-sanctioned version of the ritual . . . inscribed in its uncertainty and contestability" (1994, p. 499). Authenticity, then, is not located in some authentic moment of expression. The practice and rhetoric of nostalgia for these second-generation desis is premised on the social fiction of authenticity, but at the same time it is a fiction that is continually retold in performance because it *does* have tangible cultural and political significance in the lives of youth who coproduce this expression of yearning for ethnic purity.

While authenticity may be seen as "inauthentic," a social construction rather than an essence, hybridity may also have its authenticating standards. As the juxtaposition of rap music and hip-hop style with Indian music counters the reification of nostalgia, it may reinscribe its own essentialist definition of "cool." Desi B-boys and B-girls, who are drawn to hip-hop's beats and "breaks," practice what Lipsitz (1994) dubs "strategic anti-essentialism," drawing on Gayatri Spivak's notion of strategic essentialism: "Strategic anti-essentialism gives the appearance of celebrating the fluidity of identities, but in reality seeks a particular disguise on the basis of its ability to highlight, underscore, and augment an aspect of one's identity that one can not express directly. Sometimes strategic anti-essentialism stems less from the fear about expressing oneself directly than from the parts of one's own identity that come into relief more sharply from temporary role-playing" (Lipsitz 1994, p. 62). Yet, unlike the Maori youth in New Zealand whom Lipsitz describes (1994, p. 63), who adopted hip-hop in the late 1980s as a symbolic expression of a "common struggle" shared with "Black America," Indian American youth are not clearly encoding a vision of solidarity with youth of color. Their antiessentialist practices are strategic insofar as they disturb the fantasy of essential Indianness, but they still return to the notion of an exclusive ethnic community and redraw the boundaries of insidership. The racialization of Indian American youth and the class schisms in the Indian community in New York leave a certain ambiguity in the meanings of desi hip-hop, but it is an ambiguity whose strategic value is still to be developed.

Lipsitz's use of strategic essentialism is an example of a shift away from analyses that valorize hybridity and dismiss performances of authenticity and toward an acknowledgment that the authenticity/hybridity dichotomy sometime overlooks the uses of essentialism in social practice. The next chapter looks more closely at the production of essentialist notions of Indianness and the nature of second-generation nostalgia, arguing that Indian American youth participate in and produce performances of culture that remix elements of "tradition" and "modernity," the "authentic" and the "hybrid."

Conclusion

When offering a critique of subcultural studies, it is necessary to pay attention to the implications of reflexivity in cultural studies analyses. The theories that one uses to understand youth can be applied to the theorists, who are consumers—even fans—of popular culture as well. Frith contends that "popular music is a solution, a ritualized resistance, not to the problems of being young and poor and proletarian but to the problems of being an intellectual" (1992, p. 182). He argues that

Ethnic yearnings and other desires: a boat cruise party at Pier 83. (Courtesy of Srinivas Kuruganti)

underlying much work in cultural studies is "the deep desire of intellectuals not to be intellectual." In my own work, the focus of my research did not necessarily develop to provide an escape from intellectualism, for I do not see a barrier at the university gate, where intellectual critique suddenly ends to give way to a purported "real(er) world." My research on second-generation Indian American youth popular culture, however, clearly allowed me to engage in particular ways with Indian American communities in New York. It has been a medium for reflecting on my own history of migration to the United States at the age of seventeen and on the significance of my liminal ("1.5 generation") positioning, and perhaps also a way to indulge my latent Punjabi identity through the rousing beats of bhangra. Yet the gendered dynamics of these parties meant that I never felt comfortable being in these spaces on my own; I shared the ambivalence many Indian American women felt about these spaces even as we took pleasure in the music and dance.

While presenting his cautionary observation about reflexivity, Frith extends the critique of popular culture studies by pointing out that "the paradox is that in making pop music a site for the play of their fantasies and anxieties, intellectuals . . . have enriched this site for everyone else too" (1992, p. 179); for example, Hebdige's work purportedly gave new attention to British punk, and a growing body of work focuses on South Asian diasporic popular cultures as objects of study (Baumann 1996; Gopinath 1995a, 1997; Hutnyk 2000; Sharma, Hutnyk, and Sharma 1996). A mutual influence always exists between "the researcher" and "the researched," no matter what the area of inquiry. Even more salient for the study of popular cultures created by immigrant or ethnic minorities is cultural studies' "voracious appetite for all that is labeled 'hybrid'" (Sharma, Hutnyk, and Sharma 1996, p. 1). The fetishization of ethnic popular cultures is indeed a danger to be mindful of, and so-called insider accounts are no less susceptible to exoticizing cultural marginalia than those by "outside" observers. This does not, however, mean an end to all analysis or interrogation in this area. Rather, it is important to integrate a critique of essentialization in studies of popular cultures with an approach that draws on lived experience and daily practice, to guard against the inclination to devise mythical interpretations in solitary engagement with cultural "texts." The romance of popular culture should not cloud our insights into the ways in which second-generation youth cultures still remix strains of nostalgia and beats of gendered myths.

3

Nostalgia

Ideology and Performance

"This Third Place Where We Are"

I met Veena and Kaushalya soon after I moved to New York City in 1996. Both women were undergraduates at New York University (NYU) and were sharing a suite in their East Village dormitory with two other Indian American women. Veena and Kaushalya grew up in New Jersey, the children of Indian immigrants who came to the United States after the Immigration Act of 1965. Their stories paralleled each other in some areas and diverged in others; their family histories of immigration reflected some of the major arcs of the Indian diaspora in the last half of the twentieth century and patterns of migration to the United States in particular.

Veena's family originally came from the state of Gujarat in western India and belonged to the Patidar caste, a Hindu landowning community with a long history of migration and entrepreneurship around the Indian Ocean. Her father had migrated from rural Gujarat to Uganda, then a British colony, and established a business there, as had numerous other Gujarati Patidar families for generations before him. When the family was expelled from Uganda in the mid-1970s with the creation of independent nation-states in East Africa, Veena's father migrated to New York City and the rest of the family moved to London. Transnationalism was writ large in Veena's story, but she had learned about these multiple migrations only in bits and pieces. Ironically—or perhaps not so ironically, considering the parental propensity for protectiveness despite family histories of adventurousness—Veena's parents had been nervous about her move across the river to an urban campus; only after she began living in Manhattan did she learn that her father had worked in a business in New York City when he first arrived in the United States.

Kaushalya's parents hailed from the Telugu-speaking community in Andhra Pradesh in South India but had lived in Madras, a major city in Tamil Nadu, and so had already experienced geographic and cultural displacement within the borders of the nation. Her father came to the United States in 1965 to study engineering, sponsored by his sister, who had migrated earlier and was working as a doctor. He returned to India in 1975 and was introduced to Kaushalya's mother, who came to the United States with him after their marriage. Kaushalya was born in the Bronx in New York City, and like other immigrants who initially arrive in urban areas, her parents moved to suburban New Jersey after a few years. Her parents socialized mainly with other Telugu families in the area and were active members of the Telugu association for North America. Her father had been president of the association for a year, and Kaushalya had regularly attended their conferences, one of which drew ten thousand Telugu families to Long Island. Similarly, Veena's family belonged to a transplanted network of Gujarati Patidar families known as Panch Gam (literally, "five villages"), bounded by their geographic locality in India and by codes of endogamy, or in-marriage, in the diaspora. Her parents hoped that she would marry into one of the families who belonged to the Panch Gam community, just as Kaushalya's parents hoped she would marry a "nice Telugu Naidu boy" who belonged to the same caste and linguistic-regional group. Yet Kaushalya had violated her parents' ultimate taboo by dating an African American in high school, a relationship she hid from her parents for over two years.

Both young women were concerned about parental pressures to marry within the group and about sanctions against dating, especially for daughters. Kaushalya reflected, "It's funny 'cause I think, I know my parents and the parents in our circle are stuck in how it was when they were in India and they come here and they're stuck with the ways they had when they were back there, . . . whereas you go there, and the girls of our age, their Indian parents have kind of gone with the flow

because they've seen the changes and they've seen what's goin' on."
Cultural fossilization creates the paradox of a community that is socially and ideologically more conservative than the community of origin, clinging to mores and beliefs that have remained static, albeit contested by their children. The implications of this cultural petrification
for the second generation is one of the key themes explored in this
chapter.

Despite her parents' monitoring of her social behavior, Veena managed to go to quite a few parties in New Jersey while she was in high
school, but these were mainly events organized by various Indian and
regional associations or by other young Indian Americans. At NYU,
she was initially wary of the cliques that were notorious for dominat-
ing South Asian student organizations and was hesitant to join Shruti,
the NYU student club for South Asian Americans. Veena recalled her
early impression of Shruti—"It's a cult"—and Kaushalya rejoined,
laughing, "Once you're in, you don't get out!" Kaushalya, too, had not
expected to become a part of the South Asian student social network
on campus but was drawn into it after meeting her Indian American
roommates.

John and Upkar were both active members of Indian American associations that were attempting to create different kinds of communities for second-generation youth. Both young men studied at Pace
University, a private, commuter college in Manhattan. Upkar was president of the Indo-American Association at Pace, an organization that,
despite its appellation, included Pakistani and Sri Lankan American
students. John was a member of Iota Nu Delta, a recently formed fraternity for Indian American college students in New York State, whose
long-term goal, he explained, was to form "a network . . . of Indian
professionals." John's father was a federal government employee and
his mother, like many other immigrant women from the state of Kerala
in southern India, was a nurse. His mother emigrated first, which is not
typical of most Indian immigrant families, and later returned to India
to get married. John's father had been working in the family rubber
business and, after moving to the United States, took some university
classes and did "odd jobs" for a while. John was born in Staten Island,
and his family later moved to Queens and eventually to Long Island,
which has a growing Indian immigrant population. Like many other
Keralites, John's family were Catholic; his father was president of the

Indian Catholic Association in Long Island. They were also members of FOKANA, a national organization of Keralite associations in North America.

Upkar grew up—not too far away from John's home—in Flushing, Queens, an area that also has a large Indian immigrant population. He told me his family lived in an "upper-middle-class" neighborhood with very few other Indians. His father's story also traced the wide arcs of the Indian diaspora, for he had migrated to Vietnam to work as a salesman in Saigon and later came to the United States after getting married. Upkar had gone to a predominantly White school in Queens but had become involved in organizing the fragmented South Asian student community at Pace. In addition to taking the helm of the Indo-American Association, he was actively involved with a youth forum that he had established with other members of the Swaminarayan temple in New Jersey, a Gujarati Hindu institution with chapters throughout the far-flung Gujarati diaspora. Upkar continued to work with this youth forum after going to college because he was troubled by the lack of communication between young Indian Americans and their parents and felt there was a need for mentorship and initiation into the temple.

Upkar and John acknowledged that their parents did not monitor their social behavior as rigidly as they did that of their sisters, and they were critical of the gendered double standard in their families and for Indian American women in general. John elaborated, "From what you see in old-world India and what you see in Indian movies, like, older Indian movies . . . how your parents kind of mold your sister to be . . . a certain way, for Indian women to be a supporter, take care of the family, . . . that pressure is still placed on them." Yet both men also thought that Indian American women should embody a certain domesticity, modesty, and virtue. John commented, "I always do think that the women are the center of the family and that sort of helps us . . . she gives you the morality, it's like the center." Upkar thought that the temple was important for young Indian American women because it would "make sure that they stay on the right track" and not be corrupted by what he saw as the sexualized youth culture of high school.

In another echo of each other's stories, Upkar and John both said they had been headstrong when younger and had often gone against their parents' wishes. Interestingly, they admitted that they had done things they hoped their own children would never do, or that at least they hoped their children would be able to talk about such things more freely with them: "'Cause now I think about it and I know I'm wrong, and that's why I tend to revert more to the traditional thing," reflected John. Upkar, too, felt strongly about the need for adherence to moral and social codes, particularly those derived from religion, but was concerned about the dichotomization of identities in relation to the much-maligned "American society" feared by the immigrant generation: "It's almost as if, if we disagree with our parents, we're part of the rest of society, because either you're good or bad. . . . Because we definitely don't agree with everything our parents do, and by doing that, we're already wrong. But we definitely don't agree with everything society says, like there's this third place where we are, you know."

This chapter critically examines the construction of this third place and the ways it is shaped by gendered and classed experiences. This third place is not a fixed location but an emerging set of disparate, sometimes contradictory, experiences and narratives of hybridity and nostalgia in the second generation. As Homi Bhabha writes, emphasizing that the third space is a shift away from originary notions of culture as pure, discrete starting points: "The importance of hybridity is not to be able to trace two original moments from which the third emerges, rather hybridity to me is the 'third space' which enables other positions to emerge. This third space displaces the histories that constitute it, and sets up new structures of authority, new political initiatives, which are inadequately understood through received wisdom" (1990, p. 211). The practices and rhetoric of cultural reinvention in the second generation suggest, however, that the positions emerging from this third space are not utopian or liberatory and do, in fact, create "new structures of authority." The abstraction of theories of "third space," as outlined by Bhabha among others, is challenged by the complexity of cultural practices and relations of power in daily experience. A deep desire remains among many Indian American youth to find a clearly defined point of origin and to circumscribe the locus of tradition, even as these yearnings are challenged by the everyday paradoxes of second-generation lives. For many of the youth I spoke to, the notion of being "truly" or "really" Indian involved possession of certain knowledge or participation in certain activities, and these criteria differentiated those who were more essentially ethnic from those who were not.

The nostalgia that is produced in Indian American youth subculture rests on underlying ideologies of authenticity that create status systems and moral hierarchies, ranking individuals in a social order. Ethnic authenticity is an ideology in John and Jean Comaroff's sense of "an articulated system of meanings, values, and beliefs of a kind that can be abstracted as [the] 'worldview' of any social grouping. . . . [T]his worldview may be more or less systematic, more or less internally coherent in its outward forms. But, as long as it exists, it provides an organizing scheme for collective symbolic production" (cited in Hall 1995, p. 262). This ideology of nostalgia is not simply the ethnicized flip side to a notion of subcultural "cool" based on American youth culture, reproducing and reifying the tired binary of assimilation/authenticity, but a layered complex of ideas and practices that has its own internal contradictions. Embedded in the yearning for ethnic authenticity is a particularly second-generation self-consciousness about culture as produced, performed, and commodified, a reflexive understanding that flows into popular cultural productions of youth in music and dance. Yet this artisanal or even consumerist notion of culture as needing to be made or acquired coexists with a naturalization of tradition that is paradoxical but not surprising, given the imperatives of multiculturalism and the prevalence of ethnic student organizations on college campuses.

The longing for ethnic authenticity in the college years has to be placed in the historical context of the unfolding lives of second-generation youth, in the kinds of responses to spatial and cultural displacement suggested by the thumbnail biographical sketches of the four youth that opened this chapter. The ways in which cultural nostalgia or coolness is produced by youth in late adolescence or young adulthood are shaped by childhood experiences of managing what Kathleen Hall calls "cultural fields": "Cultural fields exist as 'relatively autonomous social microcosms,' each composed of constellations of power and authority, cultural competencies and influences that are 'specific and irreducible to those that regulate other fields'. . . . The regularities of routine practices in a cultural field both reproduce and create cultural expectations for bodily gestures and dress . . . as well as cultural knowledge people use to interpret social interactions" (1995, p. 253). Hall's study of the cultural fields inhabited by British Sikh teenagers in England, such as the school, the gurudwara or Sikh place of worship, and "English nightlife," is informed by the practice theory developed by French sociologist Pierre Bourdieu.

Bourdieu's analysis of different forms of capital—cultural, social, and economic—and unquestioned systems of classification, or "doxa," brings a Marxist critique of social structures and class reproduction to an ethnographic understanding of cultural symbols and daily action. Bourdieu argues that adolescence is a socially constructed rite of passage that is part of a larger social taxonomy that serves a political function by "symbolically manipulating . . . the boundaries which define age-groups" and often "disadvantage . . . the young." These generational categories are marked by "the symbolism of cosmetics and clothing, decorations, ornaments, and emblems . . . which express and underline the representations of the uses of the body that are legitimately associated with each socially defined age" (Bourdieu 1977/1994, p. 160). These uses of the body are part of the "habitus" of adolescence, to use Bourdieu's "taken-for-granted term for dispositions of daily life" that perpetuate social structures and divisions of labor (Knauft 1996, p. 116). Bourdieu's work has been criticized for not sufficiently emphasizing individual agency and for focusing on class structures at the expense of gender, ethnic, and racial ideologies. (See Knauft 1996 for a review of critiques.) As refined in the work of American anthropologists such as Sherry Ortner and in Sarah Thornton's research on British youth culture, however, the attention to cultural practice in Bourdieu's work has offered a way to think about the connections between ideology and daily experience and the bodily expression of cultural distinctions.

In this chapter, I explore five discourses and cultural practices that feed into the ideology of cultural nostalgia and also are informed by it: (1) the mapping of discrete cultural identities onto distinct cultural fields; (2) rituals of "going back" to India and "coming out" as ethnic; (3) the performance of nostalgia at culture shows and the creation of ethnic student organizations; (4) participation in religious nationalist and secular organizations; and (5) expressions of desire and ethnic purity. Before I delve into this analysis, I briefly sketch some of the ways in which theorists across different disciplines have attempted to define ethnic identity in the United States.

Mapping Ethnic Identities

Different models of ethnic identity have emerged at particular historical moments in debates over immigration, citizenship, and cultural difference in the United States, for ethnicity is an ideological construct, a
cultural system that makes claims about the condition and direction of
society (Aronson 1976). This is clear in the shift from "straight-line"
theories of assimilation to more nuanced, contingent views of ethnicity as dynamic, multiple, and even deterritorialized. During the influx
of European immigrants to the United States in the early twentieth
century, Robert Park and the Chicago sociologists predicted a "race relations cycle" of "contact, accommodation, assimilation," and ultimate
"amalgamation" of ethnic groups through interracial marriage and social interaction across generations (Kivisto 1990, p. 462). This "melting pot" model was challenged during the Civil Rights struggles of the
1960s and 1970s by pluralistic theories which argued that ethnic
groups would continue to maintain their identities in later generations
(Alba and Nee 1997, p. 827; Glazer and Moynihan 1963; Greeley
1974; Novak 1971). While these "salad bowl" approaches were an im-
provement over the ethnocentrism of the melting pot, they did not
fully acknowledge the historical inequalities between ethnic groups
that were embedded in the racial structures of U.S. society (Kitano
1980; Patterson 1977; Steinberg 1981). Later work in the 1980s and
1990s attempted to analyze social and historical determinants as well as
subjective, situation-specific ethnic identifications (DeVos 1982; Gans
1992; Kim and Hurh 1993; Kivisto 1990; Ramirez 1984; Roosens
1989; Waters 1990).

Sociological research on the children of post-1965 immigrants has
suggested a model of "segmented assimilation," proposing that different groups of second-generation youth enter different economic sectors and subcultures in American society (Gans 1992; Portes and Zhou
1992; Rumbaut 1994; Waters 1994; Zhou and Bankston 1998). Some
of this research, however, tends implicitly to create a racialized hierarchy of assimilation trajectories and to suggest that second-generation
youth who identify with urban youth of color are throwing in their lot
with a maladaptive or delinquent group, sometimes coded as "under-
privileged and linguistically distinctive" or "adversarial" youth subcultures (Zhou and Bankston, 1998, p. 7). This stigmatizing portrayal of
urban Black and Latino youth is a consequence, perhaps unintended,

of instrumentalist approaches to ethnic identification that focus primarily on its implications for opportunities for upward mobility and academic achievement; the refutation of homogeneous portraits of second-generation youth sometimes comes at the expense of understanding the psychological nuances and ideological implications of young people's daily experiences and cultural productions.

Disciplinary approaches and schools of thought also vary in their emphases on the subjective or structural aspects of ethnic identity, reflecting the range of theories of identity implicitly or explicitly used in debates about cultural essentialism, invented selves, and political and material constraints. Ethnicity often overlaps with other social constructs, such as race and culture, and while the distinctions between these are not always kept clear, there has been a move away from "primordialist" or biologically deterministic definitions of ethnic identity in the research literature for quite a while (Isajiw 1974, cited in Royce 1982). An emphasis on common "origins" and "culture," however, is still an element in traditional sociological theories of ethnicity (Glazer and Moynihan 1963; Yinger 1994). Other theorists clarify that cultural beliefs and practices are not necessarily inherent in an ethnic group but are the cultural "content" marked off by the boundaries of the ethnic group, constructed as part of the process of "ethnogenesis" (Barth 1969; Roosens 1989).

A discussion of ethnic group origins, similarly, often suggests a spilling over of ethnicity into nationalism, since both ethnic group and nation are "constructed symbolically and presuppose the existence of boundaries" demarcating membership (Guiberneau and Rex 1997, p. 5). Ethnicity, however, is not always correlated with citizenship (the basis for "civic nationalism," among other things), and it is these disjunctures that lead to struggles, if not violent conflicts, between ethnic group and nation-state (Greenfield 1992, cited in Guiberneau and Rex 1997, p. 5). Contemporary studies of immigration suggest that often what is at stake in the conflict between ethnic and national identities is the claim to cultural citizenship, as new categories of citizens or social movements organized by disenfranchised citizens demand both state "recognition" and "redistribution of resources" (Rosaldo 1997, p. 30; Lowe 1996; Tuan 1999). Notions of cultural citizenship are made more complex by work on transnational immigrants or diasporic communities whose social and economic ties cross national boundaries, and who may use these transnational links to provide ideological or material resources not available to them within a single nation-state (Basch, Glick Schiller, and Szanton Blanc 1994; Ong 1999), or in some cases to practice a form of "flexible citizenship" (Ong 1999). It is against the backdrop of this "ethnoscape," or movement of people in the era of global capital (Appadurai 1996), that the stories of second-generation youth such as Veena and Kaushalya, Upkar and John, must be understood—as attempts to make meaning of and manage their ethnic, gendered, and class locations.

The Discourse of Situational Ethnicity

Indian American youth experience early in their lives the ways in which the different social spaces, or cultural fields, they occupy are associated with particular notions of generationally appropriate behavior and ideologies of citizenship and ethnicity. Second-generation youth learn in childhood that they have to negotiate different ideals of youthful behavior in specific contexts and select certain images or identifications within particular social and structural constraints. This manipulation of contexts is not unique to second-generation Indian Americans, even though the cultural "content" of the strategies may vary among ethnic communities and social classes. (For other studies of Asian American youth and situational ethnic identifications, see Thai 1999; Yang 1999; Park 1999.) I was interested initially in learning how Indian American youth strategically managed these different models of adolescence while moving from one cultural field to another; for in a sense they sometimes had to switch not just linguistic codes but their general habitus, their embodied worldview—or so the academic and popular discussions about "biculturalism" and second-generation "identity conflict" would suggest.

All the youth I spoke to grew up managing situational, or context-dependent, ethnic identifications that generally took their most compartmentalized form in childhood. (For studies of situational ethnicity among first-generation Indian Americans, see Helweg and Helweg 1990; Saran 1985.) Many of them spoke of having an "American" social circle during the week, when they socialized with White American children at school, and an "Indian" set of activities and friends on weekends. Sujata, who went to an all-White Catholic school in Windsor, Connecticut, until sixth grade and then to a public school that had a predominantly White student population, said, "That's when I was taking Indian dance, so my culture was a lot more forced on me, and then, I basically, it was basically I had two different lives, I had like my American life and I had my Indian life, and by the time I went to public school I didn't mind that, you know, I was okay with being Indian." Sujata defined her American life with non-Indian friends as consisting of activities such as "going to the mall, being with my friends, just like hangin' out, going to parties, you know, driving around, doing whatever . . . that didn't really constitute to my Indian life, which was more religious. I also have an Indian group of friends, you know, like, from my dance class, there's like a group of us, and we used to all, like, get together on the weekends and have sleepovers and parties and stuff but it was, like, different, you know." Sunita, who also spent most of her childhood in suburban Connecticut and socialized with her Indian cousins on the weekends, said, "It was definitely like my weekend life versus my weekday life; Fridays, there was definitely a difference." The difference between these cultural fields is sometimes articulated in terms of differences in social practices, but at other times the distinctions were not as tangible. Yet it became clear from the ways in which almost every second-generation youth I spoke with described this experience of "situational identities" that these different spaces and times were always associated with different structures of feeling—or "meanings and values as they are actively lived and felt" as "inalienable elements of a social material process" (Williams 1977, pp. 132–33)—that were coded as "American" or "Indian." Not only was there a mapping of discrete cultural lifestyles, defined in terms of nationality and ethnicity, onto different cultural fields such as home and school, but these ethnic and national categories were also temporally organized, with a "weekday" life distinguished from "weekends."

I found that Indian American youth developed varying ways of conceptualizing this compartmentalization of their daily lives in space and time and of dealing with this shifting habitus. Madhu, who was one of a handful of Indian American students throughout her school years in Hazlitt, New Jersey, experienced it as unproblematic because it was simply her daily reality. Recalling the distinct social activities with her "American" friends and with members of the Halari (Oswal) and Kutchi Jain caste associations to which her parents belonged, she commented, "It was just the way it was, when I'd go to the Halari parties, it was all my Halari friends, and when I went to the Kutchi parties, it was all my Kutchi friends, and when I went to the association parties, it was all my association friends. I just got used to that kind of thing."

The partitioning of social worlds is not binary, as the popular rhetoric of "being torn between two worlds" suggests, but multiple; for Madhu, even the "Indian" cultural field was subdivided into the different groups to which her mother and father belonged. While her family networks may have been particularly complex, other youth also concluded that their movement among different cultural fields was, at least for a few years, not something they questioned but simply the way they lived their daily lives. So, did this rhythm of daily or weekly switching among modes of being and socializing entail a clash of different habitus for these youth, or did it, in its complex and layered entirety, represent their own habitus, their life unquestioned until they encountered the nativist doxa of monoculturalism?

Some second-generation youth felt a sense of guilt or unease about what seemed like acts of dissimilitude, a tension that apparently had less to do with the juggling of different performances than the production of these different "selves" for agents of authority, particularly parents. Pulling wool over one's parents' eyes is an age-old ruse, by no means particular to Indian American or even second-generation youth, but it is clear that for these youth, the "selves" performed were not just "good" (parent-approved) or "cool" (peer-approved) but were ethnically and nationally marked, "American" and "Indian." Some of this switching of cultural codes involved using style and language that evoked varying images of youthfulness in different situations. Ravi, a young man who grew up with a large Indian American social network in southern California, spoke of being respectful, conservatively dressed, religiously observant, and more "Indianized" in speech at home and of adopting one of a range of youth styles when on "the outside." For Ravi, the "outside" performance of identity was experienced as less inhibiting than that associated with family and was viewed as an expression of choice rather than of a dutifully prompted image; "on the outside," he could choose the style he wished. Kathleen Hall, too, suggests that the school is the cultural field where British Sikh youth not only feel "the most English" but, as one student put it, free to be "what they want to be" (1995, p. 256), implying that it is the "English" habitus that is freely chosen by youth. Yet any style of self-presentation is selected, and then perhaps recreated, from a particular repertoire of available options, and these selections, far from being arbitrary or willfully chosen, connote particular kinds of economic or "cultural capital" in society, in Bourdieu's sense of the term. Looking or acting like the dominant group or participating in the "structure of feeling" associated with a particular mode of being an American youth is an ideologically informed practice that cannot be understood outside the context of schooling as a site of cultural reproduction, where youth are socialized into the national culture and workforce (Eckert 1989; Suzuki 1995; Willis 1977). These inflections of style or language also carry with them different kinds of "subcultural capital," allowing youth entry into various social groups or images of being "cool"; adolescents imagine, adopt, or reinvent different style codes from these subcultural repertoires. Ravi's "slicked-back look" outside the home was deliberately chosen to evoke a certain image—of "wildness," perhaps—which is as culturally coded as the "traditional" appearance favored at home.

Furthermore, as Ravi pointed out, the stress inherent in these performances is sometimes heightened for young women, creating a gendered tension in the management of different images. The literal switching of feminine styles, from demure to sexy, on the way to a party emblematizes the different habitus represented by the cultural fields of family and youth culture. For women in particular, the division of social spaces by cultural proscriptions of gendered behavior is linked to ideologies of "true Indian womanhood" that are used to control the sexuality of young Indian American women, as is explored in the next chapter.

Other youth interpreted the opportunity to belong to a social network parallel to the one at school as a social advantage. Bina, who grew up in Spotswood, New Jersey, and went to a predominantly White school, reflected that a dual social life offered an alternative context for winning acceptance not available to her non-Indian friends, who had "to go out of their way to be Number One with" the other students at school, whereas she could always "hang out" with the "Indian crowd": "You had that escape when you're, like, you have the school and then you have the escape. Whereas these people in the high school, they couldn't do anything, they had to be friends with these people, there was nothing else." Echoing the enjoyment in access to dual social worlds that other Indian American youth express, Bina considered having a peer group apart from her school friends a social resource and perhaps even a source of additional subcultural capital (Thornton 1996).

On the Border: Partitioning Cultural Fields

For second-generation Indian Americans, the tension in performing situational identities derives not just from the actual switching of codes or clothes but also from the responses of the other social actors. Many of their non-Indian friends, their teachers, and their parents do not know about or do not understand the reasons for the different social roles that second-generation youth enact on a daily basis. John, who went to a predominantly White Catholic private school, commented: "Actually it was very weird . . . because all my [White] friends in high school didn't know my friends outside of high school and vice versa." The management of different social identities was often driven by immigrant parents' ignorance, presumed or actual, of their children's adoption of forbidden behaviors or styles. The discrepancy between varying cultural (and subcultural) ideals of success made the experience of situational identity, of changing the presentations of the self across social contexts, a highly performative one for many youth. Sujata's reflections are especially illuminating on this issue. Since her parents prohibited dating, she had to lie about her boyfriend, but she thought her parents believed that what they saw was *all* of her: "I liked to do wild things, which constitutes a lot of lying, you know [we both laugh] a lot of sneaking around, so no matter what social situation they saw me in they thought it was just me, you know. . . . I don't think they really noticed the difference in that degree but that's just because they didn't *know* what was going on in my life on a more social level, [they just thought of me as their] Indian child." What is interesting, however, is the self-consciousness with which Sujata and other second-generation youth understood this ideal as a cultural performance to be elicited in particular settings for specific audiences, and the degree to which they were able to articulate the situational, if not relativistic, nature of the moral codes or ideologies of goodness embedded in these performances.

The complex ways in which youth internalize this compartmentalization of their lives became apparent in my conversations with these young Indian Americans. The seemingly impermeable division between sets of experiences was often not the result of a conscious partitioning but rather a manifestation of the degree to which these differences were felt to be incommensurable. The discrepancies were clearly embedded in broader political structures of race and class. Swapna, for example, spoke of her experience growing up in a predominantly White community in Florida: "In my prep school, it was a very distinct [population], it was like, old South Tampa White families; everyone had streaked blond hair, everyone had the tan from being on the ski slopes, and I never felt comfortable, even with my closest friends, who totally knew me well, saying like, this is my religion, this is how I practice [it]. The mandir [temple] doors would always get closed when they came over."

For Swapna, the hesitation to talk with school friends about Indian cultural practices stemmed in part from a sense of inequality based on at least three perceptions of social difference. One was the awareness of racial, that is, phenotypic, difference: She is not "White" or "blonde." The second axis of difference she implicitly invokes is that of class, a privileged rootedness in the landscape—"old," well-established Florida families whose most recent migration was perhaps only to the "ski slopes," as contrasted with her own peripatetic, thrice-migrated mother and immigrant father. While her parents, both doctors, probably enjoyed an upper-middle-class status, Swapna described their concerns about consolidating their economic position in the United States and leaving behind the financial insecurity of newcomers who brought little with them except their educational and social capital. The third sense of difference was that of religious practice: Swapna recalled the closing of the doors of the family shrine when "outsiders" came to visit. Later discussions in this book explore the different ways in which religion becomes a source of internal boundary marking for second-generation youth, but for now it is enough to note that this shutting of doors is symbolic, perhaps too obviously but nonetheless evocatively, of the many levels of "cultural privacy" in spaces where immigrants and their children interact with others. Swapna's sense of difference demonstrates the many layers, particularly those of race, class, and religion, that have shaped many second-generation youth's early awareness of their lack of "cultural capital" in local status systems.

Cultural Normativity

Why did Indian American youth use the strategy of shielding the Indian realm of their lives from others or experience a hesitation in sharing aspects of this culturally "private" arena? As is clear from the biographical reflections of the youth I interviewed, facets of self become marked "identities" that are highlighted as "different" because of, first, the presumed normativity associated with certain experiences and, second, a questioning by youth of what they previously accepted as simply their way of life. The awareness of difference from a wider cultural norm was particularly acute for some youth when they were younger, especially in kindergarten or elementary school, when they were uneasy about standing out as different from their peers. A common anecdote among the youth I spoke to was that other children made fun of Indian Americans in the schoolyard or playground by yelling "Wha-wha-wha," in a mockery of a Native American war cry, not only drawing attention to the supposed primitivism of their Indian playmates but confusing their origins as well. Discomfort at being singled out as different or mistakenly represented is often due to the homogenizing impulses present in certain age groups and the socialization function performed by schools. Upkar, who grew up in the multiethnic neighborhood of Flushing in Queens, recalled being the brunt of "basic minority jokes" and being labeled "Hindoo." He commented that he moved from an early desire for reassuring conformity to a rejection of assimilationist pressures. The uneasiness that lingers for adolescents who are reluctant to open up their "Indian lives" to their non-Indian, particularly White American, friends may stem from a similar early understanding that these social categories are embedded in cultural ideas about normativity and relations of power.

Some of this awareness of the political meanings of cultural "difference" in the United States comes from not just the peer group but also the media. John, who grew up in what was initially a predominantly White community in Long Island, before the arrival of other Indian immigrant families, reflected, "When I was really younger, growing up where I did, I always denounced my Indianness. . . . When you're younger you feel always like, you see the things on TV, how they make fun of people and stereotype and so subconsciously you [accept these stereotypes] and as you get older, and it's more open and more accepted—being Indian—it's easier for you to come out [and be comfortable being Indian]." This observation illustrates the role of both structural and subjective evaluations, which is key to Frederik Barth's (1969) interactionist perspective on ethnic identity: ethnic identification is the result of both self-ascription and identification by others. The marking of difference and of ethnic boundaries for these second-generation youth occurs in symbolic interactions that are embedded in wider social, economic, and political contexts. Second-generation Asian Americans seem to share the experience of a swing from an early desire to "fit in" a mainstream peer culture to an often intense identification (akin to a "coming out") as an ethnic subject in the college years (Hong and Min 1999; Leonard 1999; Thai 1999). This shift is propelled, perhaps, by the development of cognitive capacities to reflect on social identities and to question power relationships (Keating 1990; Torney-Purta 1990), as well as by changes in peer group dynamics and the new ethnic identity politics of college campuses.

In addition to the social and psychological shifts of adolescence, which offer opportunities to rethink ideas of power and belonging, second-generation youth have access to *transnational* norms of family and child-rearing through travel to India or family visits that provide an alternative frame of reference. For example, Madhu commented, "I always knew our family was close-knit, and we always just did things together. . . . But I mean, like, big differences like, I didn't even realize 'til high school, a lot of things . . . and that's when I was like, 'Whoa! My family's like, is this normal or abnormal, you know?' Here it's abnormal but in India, it's like, maybe normal, you know." National representations of the "normal" American family—a myth challenged by the diversity of family arrangements even as it is reified—were complicated for Madhu because she had traveled to India and developed an awareness that another set of cultural norms existed elsewhere. For second-generation youth, cultural relativism becomes not an abstract idea but a lived experience that prompts a cross-cultural or transnational analysis of one's own daily realities. This is also true for African American, Latino, and Native American youth, and for anyone whose lived experience cannot be bounded by the mythologized white picket fence of middle-class White American family life.

Madhu's comments, and those of other Indian American youth, suggest that second-generation Indian Americans often learn to consciously reflect on and to articulate the various cultural norms to which they are exposed. This reflexive, self-conscious ethnic identity is characteristic of the experiences of second-generation children across national boundaries, as indicated in the work of anthropologist Eugene Roosens (1989) on second-generation Moroccan and Italian children in Belgium. Roosens observes that second-generation children who are forced to question the normativity of their experiences may objectify their family culture, viewing it analytically or "from the outside," even as they maintain an emotional attachment to family or community. This increasingly reflexive vision can lead to an awareness of cultural margins and multiple identities, which some of the youth I spoke with thought of as a unifying factor underlying the varied experiences of Indian American youth. The awareness of difference is thus construed as a commonality among second-generation Indian Americans.

Second-generation youth lent meaning to the partitioning of their everyday life; it was "weird" but at the same time "just the way you live," "the best of both worlds" but also an experience understood as particular to second-generation youth and as inevitable. These contradictions were not at all lost on these youth; rather in hindsight they were understood as *integral* to the young people's self-fashioning. Contrary to the psychological models discussed earlier, dissonance can be woven into a narrative of identity, rather than understood as loosening or rupturing its fabric. Self-reflexive or autobiographical narratives of second-generation identity, as Fischer points out, attempt to "find a voice or style that does not violate one's several components of identity. . . . [S]uch a process of assuming an ethnic identity is an insistence on a pluralist, multidimensional, or multi-faceted concept of self: one can be many different things" (1986, p. 196). Integrity for these Indian American youth was very much about the plurality of identities, for it was inextricably bound up with their experience of day-to-day life. This shifting of self-presentations was, in a sense, their habitus— their routine, embodied disposition of daily life—only not understood or accepted as such by others who did not share the same experience. It is possible that this notion of a habitus that actually involves managing more than one habitus pushes Bourdieu's original concept further, allowing it to encompass the complexity of diasporic lives. Yet, at some moments in their adolescence, the Indian American youth I interviewed realized the specificity and uniqueness of their daily or weekly switching, forcing the taken-for-grantedness of the habitus to slip. They consciously acknowledged that at certain moments they lived a life of parts, although one to which they were deeply accustomed.

The negotiation of multiple, situational identities extends beyond the case of second-generation adolescents to the conceptualization of identity more generally by individuals who manage a range of social roles (Strauss 1995; Strauss and Quinn 1994; Waters 1990). A person may identify as a mother in one situation, an employee in another, a member of an ethnic group in a third, an American when outside U.S.

borders, and so on. Acknowledging that *all* social actors routinely manage multiple cultural frameworks normalizes cultural complexity, instead of attributing it only to those who presumably deviate from a monocultural norm (Amit-Talai 1995). What makes this conceptualization of identity particularly important to theorizing second-generation ethnicity is that studies have traditionally portrayed second-generation Americans, or Europeans or Australians for that matter, as being preoccupied primarily with only *two* identities: that of their family's ethnic ancestry and that of the nation-state in which they live. Analyses of second-generation experiences that frame questions of ethnicity in this way not only let gender, class, race, and other dimensions drop out of the picture but also lead to a particular politics of "culture" in which immigrant families are positioned as outsiders to the nation. Social anthropologist Gerd Baumann critiques the simplification of the "between-two-worlds" trope of identity commonly used when discussing second-generation South Asian youth in Southall, London:

> I could not work out why they should be suspended between, rather than be seen to reach across two cultures. More importantly, which two cultures were involved? Was there a homogeneous British culture on the one hand, perhaps regardless of class or region, and on the other hand some other culture, perhaps one which was shared with their parents? If so, how were these parental cultures defined: was it on the basis of regional origin or religion, caste or language, migratory path or nationality? Each of these could define a community, culture, and an ethnic identity in the same breath, it seemed. So between which two cultures was any young Southallian suspended? (1996, p. 2)

Kathleen Hall notes that the second-generation British Asian youth in her study used this rhetoric of "two worlds" themselves, even while their daily lives suggested a more complex picture of multiple cultural influences. She argues, "These contradictions—and the sets of oppositions such as Indian/English, traditional/modern, black/white to which they conceptually correspond—each exist at the level of ideology as objectified forms of culture abstracted from the more fluid, ambiguous, and plural processes of cultural production that occur in daily life" (1995, p. 248). Shifting from an emphasis on duality and so-called biculturalism to a picture of multilayered identifications and social locations leads to a more complex understanding of the ideologies of ethnicity that are available to and reshaped by second-generation youth, and of the strategies they use to manage these cultural and political fields.

Hall's insight, not quite fully developed in this summary of her study, is that the discourse of "two worlds," while contradicted by the multiple cultural influences of daily life, is a strategy used by British Sikh youth to make sense of the contradictions they witness as they move from one cultural field to another. The processes that underlie the construction of these contradictions themselves help shed light on the ideological work of these "cultural contradictions" and their implications for youth and for narratives about nation. These felt contradictions of ethnic identity are ultimately about questions of power and the relationships of immigrant communities to the nation-state; it is these definitions of cultural citizenship and racialized nationalism that help keep this rhetoric of "between two worlds" alive, in the face of individual creativity in managing multiplicity in an era of massive global migration. In the case of the Indian American youth in New York to whom I spoke, this discourse of keeping worlds separate seemed partly internalized, because it was a framework offered by ethnic institutions and the family as well as by higher education institutions and the mainstream media—a result of both American nativism, fueled by Orientalist notions of Asian "traditions," and immigrant nostalgia. The rhetoric and strategy of compartmentalization become, for many second-generation youth, a necessary response to a situation created by very real historical processes and ideologies of difference that guard the borders of nation and citizenship in the face of growing immigration from the "Third World."

The dichotomization of cultural fields and identifications—for instance, "American" versus "Indian"—occurred, first, because when these Indian American youth were going to school in the 1980s, most lived in towns without many Indian or South Asian families or, when they could afford it, their parents sent them to private or Catholic schools where there were even fewer South Asians. Second, for many youth, ethnic activities were associated with specially organized events, such as religious festivals, dance performances, and language classes, and with weekend gatherings of Indian immigrant families and social activities with other Indian American children that rarely spilled over into daily, schoolgoing life. The "public" world of school thus rarely overlapped with the "private" spaces that represented things Indian for second-generation youth, and their weekday or public life was experienced as non-Indian, coded as "American." This division of cultural fields was partly the creation of their parents, who attempted, successfully, to produce a parallel social world for their children and whose economic resources generally allowed them to live outside urban ethnic enclaves, where less affluent Indian Americans tended to cluster, or to send their children to private schools. The ethnic infrastructure that Indian immigrants have created in the form of national, regional, or religious organizations provides an institutionalized social context largely intended to reproduce, and sometimes to reimagine, the social maps that the first generation carried with them to the United States— maps of regional subcultures, religious communities, or nationhood.

Immigrant Organizations and Networks

With the increase in the number of Indian immigrants to the United States in the 1980s and 1990s, the number of ethnic organizations and organizations for specific regional subcultures has mushroomed (Fisher 1980; Lessinger 1995; Maira and Levitt 1997; Shukla 1997). The pages of Indian community periodicals, such as *India Abroad*, *India Monitor*, *News India Times*, and *India Today*'s North American special edition, and ethnographic studies of Indian Americans feature regular reports of regional association conferences. Nearly all the youth I spoke to said their parents were connected to a local network of Indian immigrant families and were, to varying degrees, involved in pan-Indian or regional organizations in their local communities. In general, Indian immigrants in the New York City area tend to create organizations along national, if not regional, boundaries rather than as part of broader, pan-ethnic alliances. Nationalist celebrations draw huge crowds of Indian Americans in Manhattan, most notably the Federation of Indian Associations' (FIA) India Day Parade on Madison Avenue, an annual display of national pride on Indian Independence Day. In New York City, however, there are tensions between groups that are strictly national in focus and those with emergent pan–South Asian identifications. These divergences stem partly from political contestation of membership in these national categories, tensions that are sharpened in public stagings of national identities. In the case of the India Day Parade in New York City, the FIA actually barred South Asian organizations from participating in their annual national celebration for several years on the grounds that organizations must be exclusively Indian in membership (Lessinger 1995, p. 153).[1] Not coincidentally, however, the banned organizations, such as the South Asian Lesbian and Gay Association, were politically progressive in orientation and undermined the construction of the nation as family, based on heterosexual reproduction (Mukhi 2000; Sengupta 1997). In these ethnicized spaces, ideologies of nationalism, gender and sexuality, and class are produced and also challenged, offering to Indian American youth multiple understandings of "community," its orthodoxies, and its subversions.

Local ethnic newspapers and magazines that target Indian immigrants also tend to sustain national identifications, appealing to home-country allegiances with names such as *India Abroad*, *News India Times*, *India Monitor*, and *Little India*, with some recently created newspapers targeting specific local communities, such as *India in New York*. At the time of my research, only a couple of periodicals, such as *Asia Observer* and *Asia Online*, had an explicitly South Asian focus and agenda. To build on Anderson's (1983) argument about "imagined communities" based on national identity, one can see that these publications recreate collective imaginings outside national borders, within which print capitalism may have first helped to support nationalism in newly independent nation-states.[2]

Second-generation youth who did not have access to an ethnic organization sometimes had other links with Indian Americans through practices of consumption generated by businesses targeting ethnic communities. Sunita, who grew up partly in Queens and mostly in Stamford, Connecticut, made trips with her family to Jackson Heights, where restaurants and stores selling South Asian food products, music, clothes, and publications are concentrated (Khandelwal 1995). This "Little India" enclave was the source of "all Indian things" for Sunita and her family, for there were very few other Indian Americans and no such ethnic resources in her hometown.

Sunita also came into the city with her family to attend religious meetings of the Jain Society while other youth sometimes accompanied their parents to the nearest temple or church in their area. Biju, whose family belongs to the Syrian Christian community from Kerala in South India, attended the Marthoma church in Long Island, which serves the large Malayali community in the New York City area, and also participated in the national convention of the Federation of Keraltes in North America (FOKANA). A couple of youth went to summer

"Whose h(om)e-land?" A store with a Hindu-inflected title around the corner from a restaurant welcoming South Asian Muslim customers, Lexington Avenue, Manhattan.

camps sponsored by branches of Hindu nationalist organizations, such as the Vishwa Hindu Parishad (VHP), a worldwide Hindu organization linked to the Hindu fundamentalist organization Rashtriya Svayam-sevak Sangh (RSS) and the right-wing Hindu nationalist Bharatiya Janata Party (BJP) in India (Mathew and Prashad 1996; van der Veer, 1994). These organizations have attempted to portray a convergence between Indian and Hindu identity and have targeted diasporic Indian Hindus in the United States for fundraising campaigns as well as for drawing in young members from the second generation, as is discussed later in this chapter.

Indian American communities are organized not only around trans-planted religious identities but also along the lines of regional/linguistic and geographic groupings, which seem to be reproduced by second-generation youth who are socialized into various subcultures that come with their own versions of ethnic pride. These regional identifications have assumed growing institutional significance in rapidly expanding

Indian American communities such as that in New York, where Indian immigrants can now cluster according to more specific levels of difference. For example, Sujata attended a weekend program for Indian American children where she learned Gujarati, but while her father is (broadly speaking) North Indian, Sujata's mother is from South India and encouraged her to learn South Indian classical dance. For Sujata, these organizations transmitted different regional languages and traditions that did not always coexist easily. Other youth pointed to a certain degree of regionalism, if not parochialism, among first-generation social networks that undermined a pan-Indian identity. Nikhil, who grew up in New Brunswick, New Jersey, said, "I would have to say, there was a level of . . . disassociation . . . [among] my parents' friends, first of all, there's so many to choose from, so many Indians, North, South, whatever, that it wasn't an issue of like, actually, exclusivity, it was just that my parents chose to associate, in a group, in a large circle, where there were mostly North Indians." It is also striking that second-generation youth sometimes express regional biases and cultural stereotypes about, for example, "North Indian" versus "South Indian" social behaviors. What is troubling to some is that stereotypes associated with the cultural geography of India are being transplanted from the "old world" to a new spatial context and reproduced in the second generation. As Nikhil and others observed, pan-Indian cohesiveness among social networks is less evident in areas where Indian American communities have become large enough to break down by region. Thus, there are tensions between regional identifications and pan-Indian associations in the second generation, although these are not as impassioned as they might be for first-generation Indian Americans.

While many of these students grew up with connections to Indian American communities, a few complained about the hostilities and internal divisions that they and their parents encountered within these communities. These contestatory regional and religious affiliations sometimes become enmeshed with the production of second-generation nostalgia in the Indian American youth subculture in New York. Indian American associations and social networks socialize second-generation youth into a model of multilayered but still tenuous pan-Indianness that they must grapple with when they create their own organizations in college.

Rites of "Going Back" and "Coming Out"

The college context offers many second-generation Indian Americans the opportunity to become part of an Indian American peer group on campus and, for those studying in urban areas with large concentrations of Indian American youth, exposure to a specifically Indian American youth popular culture. Nearly all the interviewees thought that the transition to college had strengthened their ethnic identification, as is the case for many other Asian American youth (Leonard 1999; Park 1999; Yang 1999) who experience a surge of interest in ethnic identity as they move into contexts where "difference" is acknowledged, even celebrated, within the limits of multiculturalism. Reena, who is now at Hunter College, noted, "I think college really changes you so you become proud of who you are. In high school it's like, you want to be mainstream, and be like, I want the Gap clothes." The sense of ethnic or national pride that Reena described as emerging when she came to college was mentioned by others as well. Madhu commented on the Indian American students who belong to the South Asian association: "The members of, the Shruti people, they're like, very Indian pride–type people."

For Sujata, who like Madhu was at NYU but who did not completely identify with "Shruti people," this nationalistic fervor in the college years was akin to the display of gay pride, an overt display of an integral part of identity that had been suppressed for many years: "So I think they've come to this point, where it's almost like they're coming out of the closet, you know [we both laugh] they're like flaming all over the place with this Indian heritage stuff. All their life they've just been kind of like, 'I'm Indian' [in resigned tone], you know, and now they're just, like, ahhh, jumping out, going crazy." Interestingly, the metaphor of "coming out" to describe this ethnic revival crops up in narratives of other second-generation Asian American youth who experienced the shame attached to this "closeted" and racially stigmatized ethnic identity in childhood, demonstrating the power of social context to produce ritualized affective responses that reflect the political predicament of a collectivity. Sujata was cynical about this ethnic "coming out" because she felt the enthusiastic celebration of Indian heritage among her peers was somewhat superficial; their ethnic pride was not based on the kind of ongoing process of education in specific

Indian traditions that she had received and that she considered the basis of a "true" Indian identity.

For youth who had not grown up with an Indian American social network, the most salient aspect of the transition in college was the connection to other second-generation Indian Americans. Purnima, who had an ethnically diverse group of friends in New Jersey and North Carolina and who was at Columbia University when we spoke, said, "Now my best friends are all Indian, because I think when you come to college, I never thought I'd do this, but you just kind of bond with people that you have the most in common with. It just ended up to be Indian people because you don't have to go that extra step, you know. You already share this common background, common values, common rules, almost."

After years of being one of the few Indian Americans in her hometown in North Carolina and of feeling caught in the middle of the Black/White racial polarization in the South, Purnima gravitated toward the Indian American students she met on campus. Yet Purnima herself was surprised at the degree to which her social circle became exclusively Indian American, and she was ambivalent about the ethnic segregation she thinks is endemic to college socialization. Part of her immersion in the Indian American community on campus was voluntary, but her social choices were also shaped by the ethnic self-segregation that students observe across campuses in New York City. Ethnic student organizations and the social relationships they encourage are supported by a multiculturalist vision of ethnic identity and difference, which is used by the academy "in its claim to be an institution to which all racial and ethnic minority groups have equal access and in which all are represented, while masking the degree to which the larger institution still fails to address the needs of populations of color" (Lowe 1996, p. 41).

Yet the discovery of an Indian American peer culture was not equally salient in the lives of all the youth to whom I spoke. Sunita, who was also at Columbia but grew up close to her cousins in Connecticut and made visits to Jackson Heights and the Jain temple in Queens, did not think entering college marked as significant a change for her as for some of her peers. The entry into an Indian American youth subculture in college thus depends on several factors: access to an Indian American social network or ethnic resources at other stages in life, the desire to be part of an ethnic peer group in college, the extent of identification or involvement with the campus South Asian/Indian American student organizations, and the degree of inclusiveness or ethnic self-segregation on campus.

A couple of men pointed out that the transition to college is deeply gendered and can be far more significant for Indian American women who had led "sheltered lives through pre-college years," according to Ravi, and then "lost it" on moving away from home for the first time. Another young man, Vijay, who was at NYU, thought that college provided Indian American women with a new freedom from their parents' rules and sanctions, and he observed that students who had not grown up in the New York metropolitan area or who came from suburban towns generally threw themselves into social life with greater vigor than he did. While these men's observations of Indian American women out on the town demonstrate an undertone of paternalistic protectiveness, and perhaps some disapproval, most young men were also sympathetic to the frustrations of female friends who encountered harsher restrictions than the males had at home. Some British Asian men in Hall's 1995 study echoed these views, pointing out that women suffered doubly because of parental control; they were constrained while living with their families and then overly distracted by the catharsis of unfettered social lives, sometimes at the expense of academic performance. Among the Indian American youth in New York, however, the price women pay for newfound social autonomy in college is not academic achievement but evaluation within a sexualized framework of "good" and "bad" girls, as I discuss later.

"Coming out" as Indian American is thus not a uniform rite of passage in college but is contingent on gendered experiences of parental control, on previous exposure to the social opportunities of an urban context, and on material realities such as notions of economic mobility and career expectations. These factors that shape the transition to college influence all students, not just Indian Americans, but family norms for children's behavior and gendered sanctions tend to be culturally coded.

In addition to the entry into an ethnic peer culture and multicultural educational context in college, transnational ties and travel often spur a rethinking or new interest in ethnic ancestry for second-generation Indian Americans in late adolescence. Just before or after they enter college, when they are old enough to travel to India on their own and make decisions about their course of study, second-generation Indian

Americans often use visits to India to engage in a specific cultural (and political) project of "authenticating" their ethnic identity. Travel to India requires material resources that not all immigrant families have available for their children, but it was remarkable how many of the second-generation youth I interviewed spoke of the trip to India, particularly the first visit, as a critical turning point in their understanding of ethnicity and nationalism. Vijay recalled his visit to his mother's hometown in Rajasthan in western India: "I discovered, sort of, my heritage. I went back to Jaipur and I was, like, when you're younger you don't realize any of these things, but when you come back now, you know, my grandmother was doing all these big ceremonies because I've been past the age of eighteen, so now I'm a man, whatever." Vijay's statement reveals two interesting aspects of journeying to India to "discover" one's Indian identity: (1) the sense that this experience is a rite of passage for many second-generation youth and (2) the notion of return, or "going back" to a presumed point of origin. Both tropes are writ large in second-generation travel narratives that are part of the everyday discourse of Indian American youth, as well as in the media (for example, Kalita 1999).

The ritualized nature of this journey was highlighted for Vijay by the coming-of-age ceremonies his grandmother performed for him, which created a sense of passage into a new phase of life.[3] While none of the other youth I interviewed mentioned participating in a formal ritual on the visit to India, many who experienced a turning point in their self-identification on the trip pointed out that for the first time they had traveled to their family's place of origin on their own, unaccompanied by family, which heightened the aura of "discovery" that surrounds narratives of such journeys. A couple of youth I spoke to described their visits to India as involving a "mission" to acquire knowledge of Indian languages, religion, or aspects of Indian cultural tradition. Madhu said, "I went back to India and at least, I don't know if my parents saw it as a mission, but my uncle saw it as a mission to make me very aware of my Indian culture and my Indianness and got me involved in everything that was Indian. So . . . one aunt made me take religious classes, that was one year, and another year, my uncle made me learn to read and write the language, going to a tutor."

The "culture mission" that Sujata and Madhu describe has a ritual dimension, a search for specific knowledge and traditions, that is associated not just with the catalyzing visit-to-India narrative but also with the larger question of what constitutes second-generation ethnic identity. The word *mission* evokes the purposefulness of the quest and the importance of the task to be achieved, echoing the goals of someone setting out "with authority to perform a special service," such as the work of religious missionaries "to preach, teach, and convert" or that of a delegation sent to a "foreign country" to accomplish a task across national borders (*Webster's New World Dictionary*, 3rd college ed.). While none of these formal aspects of a mission was directly engaged on the visits to India, it is not far-fetched to say that Madhu's uncle, for example, wanted to inculcate in her or convert her to an awareness of a particular perspective on Indian culture and religion. The metaphor of a mission and emphasis on discovery of cultural "roots" conceals the imaginative nature of this project, as Stuart Hall points out, for there is no premade, packaged cultural identity waiting to be revealed. Rather, "the act of imaginative rediscovery which this conception of a rediscovered, essential identity entails" for diasporic subjects is an "act of imaginary reunification . . . imposing an imaginary coherence on the experience of dispersal and fragmentation" (Hall 1990, p. 224). Cultural identity, Hall emphasizes, is an act of production, not an artifact waiting to be unearthed, in which second-generation youth are engaged through the telling of travel stories. The trope of cultural mission, however, suggests a fervor associated with this journey to India; indeed, *nostalgia as faith* is at work here—a belief in the authenticity of "Indian culture" as unifying hitherto fragmented lives.

The Indian tourism industry has eagerly exploited this quest for "authentic" cultural knowledge associated with travel to the country of origin. Travel agencies that target affluent diasporic Indians and their children package and commodify the cultural authenticity recovered through the rite of "going back." Johanna Lessinger notes, "Tourist agencies in India now use the Indian immigrant press to promote the educational value of family travel to the country's historic sites, nature preserves and great temples" (1995, p. 56). An article in the Indian American press underscores that the desire to visit India is tied not just to the acculturation issues of the second generation but also to business ventures spurred by the liberalization of the economy: "Suddenly everybody is headed for India—from businessmen in search of a piece of the post-liberalization cake to NRIs [non-resident Indians] taking their children on a discover-your-roots trip. Or so the mushrooming agencies that cater to India would have one believe. . . . This [Indian travel] is a sector that has grown by 14 percent over the last year."[4] The same article goes on to report that Air India, the government-owned Indian airline, "plans to target second-generation Indian Americans by giving them incentives to plan a mini-vacation while in India to visit relatives." Travel packages now include "off-beat" destinations of special interest to returning immigrants; the socially and politically aware can arrange tours to study the exploitation of women in carpet factories, while Guyanese and Trinidadian Indians are offered visits to Hindu pilgrimage sites.

As Vijay Prashad (1996) points out, these tourism packages play on immigrant nostalgia and construct a romanticized glimpse of India, with an unabashed "roots" sentimentality that is evident in the advertisement for a lavish train tour: "'Embrace the land your ancestors ploughed,' says the Royal Orient, a company which arranges short train tours of 'India's most culturally fascinating states.' In search of 'memories of a lost world,' the NRI will travel in a train 'modeled on the grand coaches of the Maharajas.' . . . The romance of the advertisement is almost overwhelming" (Prashad 1996, p. 225). Second-generation Indian Americans also view travel to India as facilitating a particular intellectual project of acquiring cultural knowledge, which for a small minority of students I spoke to involved learning about contemporary social issues. An Indian American student I knew at Harvard helped found a program for other second-generation youth to do AIDS education in India while also learning about "the culture," and an Indian American tour operator who designs travel packages for Indian American youth who are visiting with their families arranges for them to see Indian villages and, ostensibly, to participate in public service projects.[5] This rural tourism, however, is often framed as encouraging "charity" work (Melwani 1995, p. 23) without fostering an understanding of the underlying issues of development and globalization that link First and Third Worlds, not to mention Indian economic migration and the country's "brain drain" to the United States (a problem more generally apparent in many "global community service" programs for U.S. college students).

What is illuminating in second-generation narratives of visits to India is the second theme in Vijay's story about Rajasthan: the recurrent use of the phrase "going back" or "returning." For Vijay, this statement is factual; he was born in Jaipur, Rajasthan, and came to the United States at age eight. Yet I interviewed Indian Americans who were born in the United States or elsewhere and who nevertheless spoke of "going back" to places they had never, technically, left. Roosens points out that the second generation can simulate but never actually "return to a 'former culture' that they never had" (Roosens 1989, p. 138; see also Gans 1979). Even in the case of actual relocation, cultural beliefs and practices, being dynamic, will be different from those their parents left behind. For the second generation, the language of return expresses a sense of displacement that is, in most cases, based on emotional and political rather than geographic dislocation; it is their parents who were spatially displaced, and the legacy of nostalgia for the country of origin lives on in the second generation. As Arjun Appadurai observes, "one of the central ironies of global cultural flows, especially in the arena of entertainment and leisure," is that they are often marked, in the diaspora, by a "nostalgia without memory" (1996, p. 30). There is indeed a collective memory, but it is a *re*created popular memory based on a myth of pure origins—a yearning to recover a presumed missing link—that is historical, cultural, and personal. What this language of return indicates is that cultural recovery is most charged at moments when the naturalized basis of ethnicity or tradition is in perceived doubt, when the trope of return expresses a sort of collective mourning for a seemingly lost culture (Dirks 1994; Suárez-Orozco 1995), as is evident in the discussion of bhangra remix youth culture in New York. As Marilyn Ivy notes in her analysis of the work of cultural nostalgia, national culture industries that uphold "a past that is sometimes troped as 'traditional'" provide "a recognition of continuity that is coterminous with its negation," for "such reassurance would not be necessary if loss, indeed, were not at stake" (1998, p. 97).

The desire to "return" stems from layers of second-generation experience, many of them imbued with emotional significance, that give rise to wishes to learn more about family history and background, to feel a sense of "belonging," or to resolve conflicting identity issues. At the same time, many Indian American youth clearly romanticize the "ancestral homeland." Kathleen Stewart (1992, p. 252) suggests that nostalgia is an interpretive strategy individuals use in response to "an increasingly fluid and unnamed social life" in late capitalist culture. While her postmodernist emphasis on identity fragmentation is rather abstract and overdrawn—and one also cannot veer into indulgence of an intellectual or historical nostalgia for a time of greater social certainty, a nostalgia that is itself culturally produced—she points to the longing for wholeness or completion that seems to underlie the work of cultural nostalgia for second-generation youth. In Ameena Meer's novel *Bombay Talkie,* a second-generation Indian American adolescent fantasizes: "Maybe in India she'd be able to straighten it all out, she'd thought. Maybe she'd be able to find a happy medium between what her parents wanted her to do (the good Indian girl) and what she wanted to do (the bad American girl). Maybe she'd figure out what it was she really wanted to be" (1994, p. 35). India and America represent moral choices, standing in for the conflict between duty/responsibility and freedom/wantonness, yet the ancestral homeland remains the hoped-for site of self-discovery, thus individualizing this cultural dilemma.

In the second generation, it can be said that there is a "second migration" (Leman 1982, cited in Roosens 1989) that may take the form of a "psychosocial return to the ethnic group" or a geographic relocation, a "radical remigration." On a psychological level, the second migration may express a need for a sense of closure in second-generation individuals who turn to ethnic origins to "complete" their identity or family history (Suárez-Orozco, personal communication, 1996). It also echoes the refrains of the American ethnic identity trope of "the search for roots"—the idea that ethnic identity origins need to be recovered and authenticated. Identity politics in the United States encourages this view of ethnic identity as a search for validating origins, as a claim that must have geographic roots elsewhere (Prashad 1997; Waters 1990), contributing to the production of nostalgia. Ethnic yearnings are based on imaginings of the place of origin that are reinforced by these larger cultural narratives and structural factors.

The "second migration" may be a passage in psychosocial development as well, for traditional American conceptualizations of adolescence figure the transition to adulthood as involving a literal journey away from the family and into a new social context as well as a symbolic "journey into the self" that involves shifts in ethnic and other social identities. Developmental psychologists conceive of late adolescence in particular as a period when individuals reflect on their identities and their relationships to their community and society (Erikson 1968). As other theorists have suggested, ethnic identity is closely intertwined with rites of passage and crises in the life cycle; coming of age is a rite of passage that may be a "highly emotional symbolic reinforcement of ethnic patterns" (DeVos 1982). Arnold van Gennep's (1960) pioneer-

ing use of the concept of "rites of passage" is built on a sequence of separation, transition, and incorporation that can also describe the experiences of late adolescents who move away from home—which was true
of some, though not all, of the youth I interviewed—and who enter a
new social arena or academic context. This sequence provides a
metaphor for the psychological development that may accompany this
displacement, for the emergence of a capacity for greater differentiation followed by integration is a fundamental principle of developmental stage theory.[6] Rites of passage, however, are always created in
the juncture between psychological development and social and material contexts; for instance, travel to India involves economic resources
that may or may not be available to Indian American youth. Moving
out of the home to live on a college campus also involves a substantial
expense that some youth are unable to afford; approximately one-third
of the students I spoke to lived with their families and commuted to
college in Manhattan. The transitions that geographic mobility creates
are perhaps largely shared by those middle-class Indian Americans who
have the financial capital to make the ritualized passages possible.

While the visit to India may have crystallized an interest in ethnic
identity for some youth, for others it evoked a realization of the rela-
tivity of their ethnic identification across geographic contexts, for in
India they were often categorized as "American." Nikhil described this
shifting scale on which authenticity is assessed: "When you're there,
you realize to a much higher degree how very non-Hindustani you are,
how very Americanized you are . . . by the way you act . . . how you
carry yourself, all these things are different. The more you realize this
the more you realize that that's not a part of who you are." Being labeled "American" by those whose authentic Indianness second-generation youth find themselves working hard to emulate can produce a
sense of disappointment. Sunita thought that her relatives in India
viewed her and other second-generation Indian American women as
inherently less traditional and hence less acceptable as brides for the
young men in their family. While Sunita was not interested in being
the perfect bride and fiercely valued the freedom to work and pursue a
career, the implication that second-generation women were somehow
culturally less adequate for having grown up in the United States upset
her: "I know there's certain parts of my family . . . 'Oh, she's like an
Indian girl raised in America so she's different,' I mean, people in my
family will say it like right in front of me, and I'll get very angry."

Recollecting her relatives' comments, Sunita felt she needed to defend the authenticity of her ethnic identity, for this was what was at stake in the cross-national comparison. Visits to India and transnational family relationships, while catalytic, can both support and challenge second-generation Indian Americans' sense of ethnic identification; they can bolster the ideology of ethnic authenticity and simultaneously lead to an awareness that "true" Indianness is contingent on the place where it is enacted. While the ritualized visit to India is a nostalgic project that binds together second-generation youth who share a certain diasporic experience, it is ultimately part of a larger politics of authenticity in their lives, for some are seen as "more truly Indian" and thus culturally and morally superior to others. As Nicholas Dirks observes, "While rituals provide critical moments for the definition of collectivities and the articulation of rank and power, they often occasion more conflict than consensus" (1994, p. 488).

Furthermore, while some second-generation youth idealized India as a mythical place of origin, for others the nostalgia projected onto India as the embodiment of authentic culture was disrupted by the realities of cultural change apparent on their visits there. Indian immigrant parents often uphold a dated, if not idealized, vision of the India they left anywhere from ten to thirty years ago, clinging to a fossilized definition of social mores that they then hold up as a yardstick for their children's behavior (Agarwal 1991). Second-generation Indian Americans are sometimes surprised to find that the dynamism and globalization of culture have changed many of the social norms their parents described to them as epitomizing Indian "tradition." For Ravi, this encounter with "Westernized" Indian youth in urban areas was read in terms of a temporal trajectory of modernity and contemporaneity in popular culture: "If anything, kids there have really progressed as well. They're not too far behind, if anything they could be ahead. But they're not far behind in things, or in dance . . . they're very Westernized, and I think the parents have moved on as well. . . . Whereas I think over here, Indian parents are still back where they left India, you know what I mean?" While Ravi depicted the liberalization of social norms and the Westernization (i.e., Americanization) of style as "progress," he also associated this modernity with the "vices" that Indians commonly cite in lamenting the "immorality" and crime that presumably tarnish U.S. society: drugs, prostitution, and, inevitably, AIDS.

India can thus no longer be held up as a model of social virtue and unchanging tradition, for cultural beliefs and practices, being dynamic, have evolved. This leads to a paradoxical situation in which second-generation Indian Americans, especially those visiting middle-class relatives in urban areas, find they are more familiar with formalized cultural rituals and more likely to use traditional symbols of regional or ethnic identity than are their peers in India. Their relatives on the subcontinent do not need to assert a symbolic ethnicity, as Madhu observed of her Indian cousins:

> In terms of culture . . . I felt, sometimes I felt I was more involved in everything being here, they took everything for granted. To me, dancing and going out for Navratri [Gujarati festival] and things like that was always, like, things I wanted to do; I have like, at home, I have like, five or six chania choris [ethnic dress], whereas my cousins and my friends have like one or two, you know. And they're like, "Oh, we don't go!" And they don't even know how to play dandiya raas [Gujarati folk dance] or things like that, and I'm like, "Oh my gosh! Those are big things for me, you know!" . . . And in some sense, yeah, I just felt like I was more of aware of being Indian than they were.

Many second-generation Indian Americans have adopted ethnic clothing, performances of traditional dance, and celebrations of Indian festivals as emblems of ethnic identity. For Madhu's cousins in India, however, these symbols, while more easily accessible, were probably not imbued with the same emotional significance that they held in the diasporic community. These emblematic features of second-generation identity are the focus of rites of "coming out" or "going back"; they are the commodities or events discovered, or recovered, by these "journeys," but they are also in a sense *created* by this search. Ethnic authenticity becomes commodified through the use of various objects that come to stand in for tradition, such as clothing, and through cultural practices of consumption involving food or music that are part of a cultural economy of nostalgia.

Both the self-consciousness of these ethnic identity constructions and the ritualized participation in activities that uphold ethnic identification are addressed in theories of the "symbolic ethnicity" of the second generation. Herbert Gans's (1979) notion of symbolic ethnicity was based on a study of middle-class third- and fourth-generation White Americans; according to Gans, ethnic needs are "neither intense nor frequent" in the third and fourth generations, so individuals look for "easy, intermittent" expressions of "voluntary" ethnicity that do not conflict with their largely assimilated lifestyles (1979, p. 8).[7] Symbolic ethnicity involves the use of popular culture (traditional food, music, or dance), material culture (cultural artifacts), and political culture (a discourse of ethnic interest issues), which become emblematic for the group (Steinberg 1981). Second-generation Indian American youth, particularly in the college context, often display these symbolic aspects as they organize "culture shows" and begin wearing Indian clothing in public. The paradox of symbolic ethnicity among these youth is that an essentialized ethnic identity is not considered contradictory to the notion that this objectified "commodity" can be acquired and refined. The experiences of Indian American youth, however, differ from Gans's view of symbolic ethnicity in at least two important ways. First, for visible minorities, ethnic identification is not always voluntary, in contrast to the White Americans in Gans's study or in Mary Waters's *Ethnic Options: Choosing Identities in America* (1990). Second, for the children of immigrants, as opposed to the later generations studied by Gans, the first generation is still a living presence and the family is still a crucible for ethnic identity development.

The subtler aspects of symbolic ethnicity have been drawn out by cultural anthropologists in ways that shed light on the issue for second-generation Indian Americans. In contrast to Gans's primarily instrumentalist approach, Roosens (1989) emphasizes the expressive dimensions of symbolic ethnicity for second-generation Moroccan and Italian children in Belgium and the notion that ethnic attachment is not based on "objective" continuity with cultural tradition. Roosens points out that "to see and use one's culture as a right" (or consciously to reflect on one's cultural identity), one must first gain distance from that culture by questioning it or being questioned by "forced acculturation" (1989, p. 150). This self-consciousness about ethnic identity takes particular form in the diaspora, where the children of immigrants are often reminded of their ethnicity by others' questions or taunts and do not live in an environment where family language and culture are seamless with those of the larger society. Second-generation adolescents' intellectual, consciously articulated engagement with their ethnic identity, coupled with their immigrant parents' desire to transmit their own national, regional, and religious allegiances, leads to the formalization of a certain diasporic identity politics.

Bhabha's notion of cultural translation addresses this objectification of culture by second-generation youth, who constantly move among different systems of meaning. He writes, "By translation I first mean a process by which, in order to objectify cultural meaning, there always has to be a process of alienation and of secondariness in relation to itself" (1990, p. 210). For example, Sharmila decided when she visited India during her junior year in high school that she wanted formal instruction in her family religion, Jainism, because she had gone to a Catholic school and because at the Indian Sunday school she had attended, the other students were Hindu. In seeking a formal, intellectual approach to religion, Sharmila took her parents and her relatives in India by surprise, for to them religion was to be accepted uncritically as a part of life. Few young Indians made this kind of deliberate effort to seek out philosophical training from a priest, as Sharmila pointed out:

> Even all my [Indian] relatives were like, "So tell me about Jainism?" Like, just as a joke, because they didn't really understand, like they know, but they never questioned anything, and I wanted to know why, you know, all the reasons, and I was just asking all the time, and he [the priest] was like, "God! These girls from America!" You know, how they say these things, like, "Why do you have to know everything?" And I'm like, I need a reason, you know, because I'm not going to believe in something that I can't, you know, whatever, and he was giving me these reasons and giving me these books, "Fine, you look it up!"

This analytical, reflexive approach to ethnic identity emerges from the ability of diasporic or postcolonial subjects to see their culture "from the outside" (Roosens 1989, p. 151). The sense of desiring something ("Indian culture") to which you feel close and yet from which you feel removed is also, according to Stewart, the fundamental condition of nostalgia, which "sets in motion a dialectic of closeness and distantiation" (1992, p. 253). This dialectic of nostalgia is visibly apparent at the "Indian culture shows" produced by Indian American college students, where the performance of "tradition" both brings it closer to "home" and calls attention to itself as a theatrical moment removed from daily life. The next section considers the meaning of these performances for second-generation youth in light of their experience of movement among cultural fields in childhood and the cultural translation that it necessitates, as well as their ritualized "coming out" as ethnic subjects in college.

Performing Tradition

The South Asian student organization at NYU, Shruti, held its annual culture show at a high school in Chelsea in April 1997, and for weeks beforehand there was intense planning and preparation, a gradual buildup of excitement, nervousness, and the occasional organizational glitch. The last-minute cancellation of the on-campus venue seemed almost overshadowed by the controversy over which party promoters were officially hosting the much-anticipated "after party." But now, in the large auditorium, with friends and families in attendance, all attention focused on the show, titled "Harmony, Pride, and Heritage." As the president of Shruti explained in the program, "We try to bring our members together in *harmony*, we take great *pride* in our culture and our *heritage* is something most of us hold close to our hearts." The goals of the culture show were explicitly tied to ethnic pride and the project of cultural authentication: "Through each act, you will observe the magnificent beauty of our culture; your eyes will witness the richness of our diversity. . . . These acts portray who we are and manifest the fact that all of our acts come from some sort of ancient tradition." In keeping with this manifesto to define "our culture," the opening performance was a Bharat Natyam dance performance; in fact, almost every South Asian or Indian American student culture show I have attended has opened with a classical Indian dance, performed by a woman, as an exemplar of "real culture." In the same month, Club Zamana, the South Asian student organization at Columbia, staged its own culture show, "Tamasha," which the students defined as "exciting spectacle." The program announced that Tamasha's purpose was "bringing the splendor and richness of the South Asian culture to life for students here," suggesting that this spectacular enactment would revitalize a cultural tradition lying dormant in the diaspora.

Culture shows fulfill two important functions: They showcase definitions of what constitutes "Indian culture" (or pan-South Asian culture, as both student organizations emphasized) for second-generation college students, providing theatrical displays of idealized as well as contradictory versions of culture; and they provide a medium for the performative aspects of symbolic ethnicity in the second generation, creating a formally organized occasion for enacting ethnic identity at the event and during rehearsals. These shows are a site for packaging

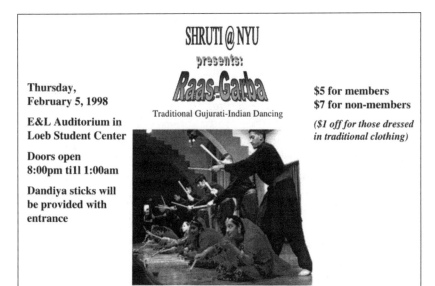

SHRUTI @ NYU

presents:

Raas-Garba

Traditional Gujurati-Indian Dancing

Thursday,
February 5, 1998

E&L Auditorium in
Loeb Student Center

Doors open
8:00pm till 1:00am

Dandiya sticks will
be provided with
entrance

$5 for members
$7 for non-members

($1 off for those dressed
in traditional clothing)

A Gujarati dance performance encourages students to attend wearing
Indian clothes.

and performing cultural nostalgia, but in performing the dialectic of
closeness and distantiation, they also highlight some of the contradictions of the ideology of ethnic authenticity, especially when situated in
the context of ethnic student organizations and the Indian American
youth subculture at large. At the Shruti culture show, several of the acts
that followed the classical dance performance reenacted dance sequences from Hindi films, and interspersed with these were the
mandatory fashion shows and a couple of bhangra remix dance numbers. The dance sequences were highly polished and perfectly coordinated, the participants having viewed and re-viewed the film performances to reproduce them on stage.

This mimetic performance had a surreal quality for me as I sat in the
Manhattan auditorium, far from Bollywood—as the Indian film capital
of Mumbai is called—and it brought home the irony of transnational
popular culture. Though I spent the first seventeen years of my life in
India, I am still incapable of singing a single Hindi film song (perhaps
a few lines, if my life depended on it); nor can I easily slip into "filmi"
dance gestures that bear any close resemblance to on-screen perform-

ances. (Perhaps some Indians would describe me as an inauthentic desi.) It is apparent that, in the United States, the circulation of videos through Indian grocery stores and screenings at selected theaters has made the viewing of Hindi films a marker of second-generation Indian American identity. Hindi films offer a contemporary resource from popular culture for fashioning a symbolic ethnic identity, but they also can be used as boundary markers in the politics of authenticity. Nikhil, who had little interest in watching Hindi films but was passionate about theater, recounted that he was labeled "Indian trash" by his friends who thought him less Indian because of this "aberration": "Some of my friends would object, on different occasions, they'd call me Indian trash. . . . Indian trash is a phrase used for somebody who's really very White, is Indian, and because I never took an interest in Hindi films . . . my friends always used to get together and watch Hindi films, maybe it [his presumed inauthencity] was because of me taking an interest in acting."

Hindi films are not only considered a canonical element in an authentic Indian identity but also provide a template for second-generation performances of ethnic identity at culture shows. The emphasis in the reenactments of film sequences was on verisimilitude and mimetic precision, and indeed, the students seemed to have rehearsed every flirtatious shrug of the shoulder and coy glance; and though I had never seen the "original" performances, the expressions and movements struck me as faithful reproductions. The "culture show" evokes for the spectator the experience of being a tourist, in a sense, watching staged fragments of what are clearly not everyday cultural practices. Edward Bruner (1996) argues that in cultural spectacles performed for tourists who are well aware that this is theater, the concern of the audience is not with issues of authenticity but with verisimilitude. In these student culture shows, however, the question of authenticity cannot be so easily separated from the emphasis on credibility and aesthetic quality. These performances stage a particularly diasporic version of the project of authentication, which is understood as having a purpose very different from that of the "original" performances in India; their authenticity feeds into a politics of nostalgia that may or may not be relevant to Bruner's tourists in Indonesia. Sunita Sunder Mukhi, commenting on a Hindi-film dance performance by a young girl at the Indian Independence Day culture show in New York City, suggests that the mimesis involved in this act produces a vernacular nationalism capable of being reproduced and embodied in the diaspora: "Using Michael Taussig's definition of the mimetic faculty as the 'nature that culture uses to create second nature,' I can say that the child's self-taught mimicry of the dance naturalizes her talent and her Indianness ... persuades us, comforts us, that Indianness is indeed, second nature ... that it is alive and well in the body of our children and will continue, even on Madison Avenue, New York City, United States of America" (1998, p. 193).[8]

In contrast to the "tainted" culture of remix club music and dance, performances of Hindi film dances are seen as representing "traditional" Indian culture and evoke a "distant India" for the immigrant community, according to a study of second-generation Indian American women and dance performances (Ghei, cited in Leonard 1997, pp. 136–37). This is somewhat ironic since Hindi film dances are themselves hybrid performances and often exhibit influences of American and European dance and fashion trends, but they are read as being virtuously Indian and imported directly from the homeland, hence lending authenticity to the women who perform them. Few acts on Shruti's program were hybrid performances; only three or four out of a total of twenty were choreographed to remix music and used club dance steps rather than classical or "filmi" movements. The costumes, likewise, were for the most part traditional; for the fashion show, the women wore saris while the men wore blazers, and all the "models" bowed their heads with a traditional Indian "namaste," hands folded, at the end. The fact that the female models wore traditional clothing while the men wore American- or European-style jackets is indicative of the gendering of this cultural reproduction. At remix parties, too, flyers often state that while men should wear "proper or elegant attire," even specifying jackets at some events targeting upwardly mobile youth, the recommended dress code for women is "ethnic attire," and a club sometimes will bestow a discount on the cover charge for women who sport "Indian dress."

The expectation that Indian American women should embody a community's ethnic identity is powerfully enacted in *Miss India, Georgia* (Grimberg and Friedman 1996), a documentary film that follows four second-generation women who compete in a beauty pageant for Indian Americans. Not only are the women in the film literally paraded on stage as the "prizes" of the community, but the pageant clearly favors "traditional" dress and classical dance over any kind of syncretic style or performance. Women are expected to embody unsullied tradition, chaste Indian womanhood, which underlines the double standard that applies to sexual behavior for young South Asian American women and men. Sayantani Das Dasgupta (in Das Dasgupta and Dasgupta 1996, p. 386), a second-generation Indian American woman, writes:

> Throughout my life, I have been involved in Indian community dances, poetry recitals, musical festivals, and pujas. While and I countless other little Indian girls were sari-swathed, paper-flower-garlanded, primped, and prodded for most our youth, our male counterparts got off, for the most part, scot-free. The young women I met at a recent Indian American 'Youth' Conference perhaps said it best. "We girls are expected to deck out in Indian clothes at every bhangra," they complained. "But the guys can just wear their baggy jeans and backwards baseball caps. They dress like homeboys and no one says anything."

Das Dasgupta and Dasgupta conclude, "The daughters of the community [are] disproportionately burdened with the preservation of culture in the form of religion, language, dress, food, and childrearing" (1996, p. 386). The gendering of tradition in the diaspora is a critical issue to which I return in the next chapter.

The performances at the Tamasha show, in contrast to the Shruti event, drew to a somewhat greater degree on hybrid enactments of Indian dance and music. The opening act was performed to a remix by DJ Karma, a local Indian American, and except for a couple of classical and film dance performances, most sequences fused Indian and American dance, clothing, and music. A hybrid aesthetic was at the forefront of this show, in contrast to the largely mimetic performances staged by Shruti; yet individual youth on both campuses spoke of performances of Indian classical or folk dance and classical music as stagings of "real" Indian culture.

These performances reveal several levels on which ideas of cultural authenticity are played out: One is the level of discourse or rhetoric about ethnic authenticity; another is the level of theatrical performance; and a third is daily action or situated cultural practice. Contradictions emerge among expressions of ethnic authenticity in these different spheres, so that youth may say they think one thing and then enact another view on stage or in an everyday situation. There is a gap between everyday cultural practices and staged events, between discourse and performance. Individuals who were critical of one criterion to evaluate cultural authenticity still defended another's ability to measure "true" and thus superior ethnic identity. Sujata, for example, was critical of her peers' dismissal of non-Hindu Indian Americans as less authentically Indian, but she also thought that Shruti's (few) hybrid performances of ethnicity were not truly representative of "culture":

> I mean they try Indian things . . . but I think the biggest problem, the reason why they have it so forced and the reason why they're trying so hard, is because overall it's not a cultural organization. As Indian as they say they are, like, at the fashion show, for example, we go on stage to this Indian song, and then, the next segment, the fashion show, people are going on stage and the Fugees [a Haitian American R&B group] are playing in the background, you know, and they're wearing saris, and I'm just like, what are you doing, you know? Or they have this, like, rap music playing in the background.

The production of hybrid "cool," as discussed in the previous chapter, mixes uneasily with the performance of nostalgia evident at culture shows. The dichotomy second-generation youth create between "pure" Indian traditions and an "inauthentic" mixed aesthetic overlooks the reality that hybridity has shaped even so-called authentic cultural traditions on the subcontinent, which has had a long history of multiple cultural influences and cross-fertilization with other cultural traditions. This point is emphasized by the British social anthropologist Pnina Werbner (1997, p. 4), who, drawing on Mikhail Bakhtin's theory of linguistic hybridization, argues that a more useful distinction is that between "conscious, intentional hybridity" and "unconscious, 'organic' hybridity." Intentional "aesthetic hybrids" use "deliberate, intended fusions of unlike social languages and images," but they build on the foundations laid by organic hybridity, which is a feature of all cultures. Werbner points out, "Despite the illusion of boundedness, cultures evolve historically through unreflective borrowings, mimetic appropriations, exchanges and inventions. . . . At the same time, . . . organic hybridization does not disrupt the sense of order and continuity: new images, words, objects, are integrated into language or culture unconsciously . . . 'organic hybrids remain mute and opaque'" (1997, p. 5, citing Bakhtin). Hence organic hybridity creates the historical foundations on which aesthetic hybrids build to shock, challenge, revitalize, or disrupt. Second-generation Indian Americans may choose to enshrine classical dance and music and Hindi films as repositories of ethnic authenticity because they represent "illusions" of pure, discrete cultural traditions. These presumably organic hybrids are aspects of culture that apparently do not represent a challenge that would compromise the authenticity of ethnic identity. Yet these cultural forms also help materialize an ideology of nostalgia that infuses a larger youth subculture that has its own conflicts of power and social hierarchies. The tension between notions of nostalgia and coolness is played out in a system of status distinctions in the social spaces created by ethnic student organizations.

Student Organizations and Campus Subcultures

Student organizations are the vehicles that second-generation college students most often use symbolically to affirm and perform ethnicity, and as such, these groups participated in the multiculturalist politics of difference in U.S. higher education in the 1990s. A fact that few students I interviewed chose to mention is that university adminisrations generally are the funders of ethnic student organizations, and the availability of material resources often funnels youth into these ethnically demarcated spaces of campus social life. College also offers the first opportunity many youth have to participate in ethnic or pan-ethnic organizations that are created and led solely by their peers, not by adults from their parents' generation. New York University's Shruti had approximately 270 members in 1996–97. At Columbia University/Barnard College, the South Asian student organization was Club Zamana.[9] (There was also a recently formed Organization of Pakistani Students at Columbia at the time.) Pace University's student group, although called the Indo-American Society, included Pakistani, Nepali, and Bhutanese students among its 150 members in 1996–97, some of whom were students taking evening classes. According to the society's president, many of the members were first-generation students from India, unlike Club Zamana and Shruti, where the majority of members were second-generation Indian Americans. At Hunter College, students spoke of an Indian Club, but with little enthusiasm, and reported that there was also a Bengali Club for both Bangladeshi and Indian Bengali youth. Although the organization sponsored one or two cultural events and parties every year, no students were in their meeting space during the times I stopped by, unlike the other ethnic clubs on the same hallway, where students chatted and music blared. Among the youth I spoke to, involvement in student organizations ranged from active leadership roles to almost complete disengagement. (Membership at some campuses was assumed to be de facto for all students identified as ethnically South Asian, but only a fraction of these were generally actively involved.) Some students belonged to other kinds of Indian organizations, for example, the Hindu Students' Council at Hunter College, sponsored by the VHP.

Pan–South Asian organizations are a more recent phenomenon on college campuses in the United States. They emerged as student groups realized the value in creating stronger coalitions and as the label "South Asian" gained greater currency as an umbrella category, uniting those whose families originated in India, Pakistan, Bangladesh, and Sri Lanka (and, in much smaller numbers, in Nepal; even fewer trace family origins to Bhutan or the Maldives). This pan-ethnic identification, however, is somewhat different from the forging of Asian American coalitions in the 1960s, which were responses to shared experiences of political discrimination based on race (Espiritu 1992; Wei 1993). Today's creation of South Asian organizations is also a politicized strategy but more often is a response to the partitioning of ethnic identity politics in academic institutions, where ethnicity and geography are the accepted boundaries of student organizations, academic study, and institutional funding. South Asian or Indian American organizations also constitute a site for students' socialization into the fabric of U.S. society as ethnic subjects.

The creation of ethnic-based collectivities, however, has also given rise to tensions and fissures, for second-generation youth sometimes resist pan-ethnic alliances. Some students argued that this category erased important differences among immigrant groups from Asia, while others protested that the label "Asian American" is often used synonymously with "East Asian American" and so does not include South Asians. (See Gupta 1998 for a discussion of this issue at other colleges in the Northeast.) Yet some students I spoke with who were actively involved with Asian American organizations on their campuses, such as those at NYU and Columbia, believed that Asian Americans shared cultural and historical commonalities and that the need to build coalitions outweighed any differences. For them, as for other youth who identify with the coalitional label, identifying as Asian American is an expression of a particular vision of pan-ethnic solidarity (Lee 1996).

Indian American students on different campuses unanimously described the motivation for joining ethnic organizations as stemming from two major interests, social and cultural. The structure of student organizations at the time, not coincidentally I think, tended to mirror this dual focus, with "social committees" and "cultural chairs" taking care of fulfilling these needs for both immigrant and second-generation youth. For most youth, the most widely shared expectation was that ethnic student organizations should engage in some sort of cultural education or in the promotion of certain aspects of "Indian culture." The youth subculture that these organizations created seemed to bolster a politics of authenticity, tinged by cultural nationalism and a desire to reproduce the ethnic community created by middle-class and elite immigrant families. Yet the subculture that Indian American college students create is also shaped by the particular needs of second-generation youth and infused with specific cultural and political agendas.

Many students viewed ethnic organizations as providing a way to learn about or maintain a cultural identity as Indian or South Asian. The underlying belief seemed to be that culture could be practiced through programs that involved symbolic displays of ethnicity, such as celebration of Indian—generally Hindu—festivals, performances of classical or folk dances, and opportunities to wear traditional clothing. At Pace, for example, the president of the Indo-American Society said that the organization's first public event, "Colors of Holi," named after a North Indian spring festival, included three dances and a fashion show—"good stuff that shows Indian traditional wear and Indian traditional dances, and demonstrates an Indian wedding." This kind of orchestrated performance reinforces symbolic ethnicity (Gans 1979) and also expresses collective nostalgia for tradition and an "authentic" past. Public, celebratory enactments of ethnicity are what some Indian American youth learned to associate with ethnic identity because these rituals were staged at the "Indian" community events they attended with their parents. Some of the young people I interviewed said these organizations provided a youth subculture where they felt at "home" and a sense of continuity with the social networks to which many had belonged before college. Nikhil emphasized that ethnic student organizations attempt to reproduce the symbolic functions of ethnic community organizations and the immigrant family's "preservation" of ethnicity: "I'm in Zamana, I'm active in it, . . . not necessarily because I'm afraid I'm going to lose anything but I feel I haven't had the chance to actually get really heavily involved, just because of the fact that there was never a need to, it was always there in front of me, like there was never a need to throw a Diwali party because there was one at my parents' house, whatever."

Yet there were murmurs of dissent from the agendas of ethnic organizations among many students I spoke to, who felt frustrated with the vision of community and culture recreated by their generation; others attempted to negotiate a position within the Indian American subculture while resisting its essentializing codes of membership. A common complaint about Indian/South Asian student organizations at nearly all the campuses was that they were mainly "social" or "party" organizations that held dances and dinners but did not organize enough, or adequately focused, "cultural" activities. For example, Madhu's initial motivation for joining Shruti was the possibility of socializing with other Indian Americans, in which she was partly prompted by her parents' encouragement to "at least try to meet some Indian people," perhaps in the hope that she would continue their own involvement with local Indian social networks and organizations. But Madhu became increasingly frustrated with Shruti's emphasis on socialization, saying, "Especially recently I've felt more and more, that their organization, the only thing that it's become part of, is parties, parties, parties, parties." A small minority of students on each campus seemed concerned that the organizations did not focus on "political" issues or did not take a progressive stance on social concerns, and those who expressed this criticism generally felt marginalized and frustrated by the Indian American student community. Jay, who was a junior at NYU and had been teaching at a public school on the Lower East Side attended by Bangladeshi immigrant students, said, "A lot of people do stuff on their own, instead of having to find Shruti as a medium to go through to do certain things, like community service, or helping out the Indian community." Some student activists tried to change the organization from within, while others left altogether and joined other, more politicized student groups, such as Asian American coalitions. (The criticism of political apathy was sometimes mentioned with regard to the larger Asian American student organizations as well.)

In addition to staking their claim in a multiethnic institutional context, ethnic student organizations create a youth subculture that has its own social hierarchies and codes of authenticity. Some students felt alienated from the student organizations because, in addition to emphasizing particular activities as appropriate expressions of ethnic identity, their implicit criteria for belonging rested on definitions of subcultural authenticity. Sujata reflected on Shruti's activities: "I mean that's cool, that's fun, I go to those Shruti parties, but at the same time I'm not considered a Shruti person. Most of the Indians, like a lot of people from Shruti, they look at me, like, 'Ohh, she's not—,' because it's very like, if you're in Shruti, you need to be hard-core Shruti, you have to hang out with all the Indian kids and you have to be into, like, rap music, have to have your Tommy Hilfiger, pants down to [your knees]. That's just my opinion on Shruti." For Sujata, who was more interested in "alternative music" and who actually played in her own band, popular music allegiances were one aspect that set her apart as someone who was not "a Shruti person," pointing to the ways in which many youth subcultures are built on local distinctions of taste (Bourdieu 1984; Thornton 1996). Hip-hop music and style constitute a visible badge of membership in an emerging Indian American youth subculture in New York City, particularly at NYU. Sujata also observed that this essentialized definition of membership—to be "hard-core Shruti"—involved socializing exclusively with other Indian Americans.

These criteria for membership in student organization subcultures create boundaries between those who possess subcultural capital and those who do not. Swapna, who was at Columbia, complained of that university's South Asian student organization: "Zamana's very cliquey . . . because these people have known each other for two more years and they're all friends and it's been established. But at the same time, there's no effort to like open it up to other people without giving them a once over, and you know, how do you move? How do you dress? Can you dance? Can you be all coy and cute and whatever?" Style, participation in popular culture, and a certain kind of femininity or sexuality emerge as criteria for popularity in the exclusively Indian American cliques on campus. For some students, the cliques that form the core of the student subcultures are an extension of the social networks they had before college, especially at an institution such as NYU which attracts many local youth from the tristate area. Thus, while ethnic student organizations aim to help students find a sense of belonging and experience some kind of ethnic camaraderie, they marginalize those who do not conform to the subculture's norms.

Cliques or social groups with rigid codes of acceptance are not unique to Indian American youth subcultures; they are part of the larger context of ethnic self-segregation visible on these campuses in

Manhattan and, indeed, in colleges across the country (Kibria 1999). At NYU, Indian American students who belonged to this subculture congregated in a particular area in the cafeteria in the Loeb Student Center. Biju, who was on the Executive Board of Shruti, observed that this clustering by ethnic tables was true of African American, Korean American, and Chinese American students as well and saw it as simply an expression of ethnic solidarity, saying, "I don't think there's anything really wrong with it, as long as like, it's not like, you have a problem with the other group or whatever, I mean, you want to stay with your culture and these are your people." Yet some students thought this clustering created social divides outside the cafeteria, erecting boundaries between Indian American students and other students of color as well as within the subculture. Manisha commented, "I've heard other Black and Latino friends say to me, 'Wow! Those Indians hang really tight in Loeb, it seems like that you can't even hang out with them.' I was like, 'Trust me, I know! I can't.'"

Critics of this youth subculture have pointed to the ways in which the subcultural capital associated with status in these cliques is tied to both economic capital, or material resources, and social capital, or whom you know, to use Bourdieu's framework of cultural distinctions at work in social stratification (as developed in Thornton 1996). Swapna recalled an insight of a non-Indian friend at a program celebrating Diwali, the Indian festival of lights: "At the end of the program, when everyone's coming and mingling around, she's like, 'I get the distinct impression that status is a big thing here.' . . . I think she meant a combination of money, image, um, kind of networking, who knows who, who's in the scene, who's in the clique." Social status in this middle- and upper-middle-class milieu rests, according to Swapna, on economic affluence, social connectedness, popularity, "image," and acceptance in the dominant cliques. The "social logic" underlying this subculture (Thornton 1996) is not just of style but also of social connections and class status. There is, in addition, a *cultural logic of authenticity* that creates distinctions and hierarchies among youth in this subculture and that underlies the politics of nostalgia. As Thornton observes of club culture in London, "Rather than subverting dominant cultural patterns in the manner attributed to classic subcultures, these clubber and raver ideologies offer 'alternatives' in the strict sense of the word, namely other social and cultural hierarchies to put in their stead.

They may magically resolve certain socio-economic contradictions, but they also maintain them, even use them to their advantage" (1996, p. 114).

Ethnic Purity, Desire, and Dating

Culture shows and codes of subcultural membership perform the work of constructing and distinguishing between the often blurred but always charged categories of "Indian" and "American." In the Indian American youth subculture on New York college campuses, being "more Indian" is desirable and intrinsically superior to somehow being "less Indian." These standards of ethnic essentialism are potent because they carry a moral force. Sociologist Jean Bacon (1996, p. 60), in her study of first- and second-generation Indian Americans in Chicago, observes that discussions in Indian American public forums and the immigrant press reveal "a deep ambivalence within the Indian community concerning the status of Indians in America. Are Indians 'better' or 'worse' than the mainstream? . . . [T]he debate about two worlds that pits Indian against American values and practices often places Indian values and practices on top, as clearly superior to the American alternatives." Furthermore, Bacon writes that "anxiety" about "superior/inferior status" is associated with the development of clearly defined criteria for distinguishing one's position in this hierarchy "in some absolute and definitive way" (1996, p. 65).

Ravi explicitly described a hierarchy of knowledge of cultural traditions, with the parental generation being "superior in knowledge" that was waning in the second generation, reproducing the trope of the second generation as culturally confused—as in the pejorative label "ABCD" (American Born Confused Desis). In Ravi's view, ethnic authenticity is quantifiable, something that will diminish across generations: "I mean after parents have said so much . . . the second generation has come out with whatever they've produced, but they in turn are going to produce something to a lesser degree for their own, third generation, and that's what I fear that slowly and slowly it's going to become less and less India-based. . . . People are going to have [a] more Western mentality, so to speak." The underlying idea is that two cultural poles are available to the second generation, "Indian" and "Western," and that the former is clearly tied to a superior, truer ethnic identity. This cultural dichotomization of India and the West illus-

trates a "totemic attitude of selective perception" that promotes differentiation by seizing on incipient differences for their emblematic value
and by emphasizing contrasting traits rather than similarities
(Schwartz 1982). This symbolic contrast is often learned from immigrant parents as they attempt to reproduce ethnic identity in the second generation, as Baumann points out: "The very process of encul-
turating children entails the necessity of isolating elements, traits, and
norms that stick out as distinctive and which are thought, in the widest
sense, proper to a cultural 'us'" (1996, p. 13). The binary classification
of Indian (culturally superior) versus Western/American (culturally
lacking) is perhaps an attempt to reverse the racial hierarchy imposed
on immigrant communities of color by asserting a cultural nationalism
in response, a defensive move to compensate for the degradations of
racism. However, this subcultural orthodoxy is one that ultimately not
only marginalizes and excludes some people but also perpetuates the
Orientalist framework of a spiritually rich India or Asia holding on to
its cultural riches and legacy of ancient civilizations despite the domination of the West, which, though materially wealthy, ultimately lacks
spiritual enlightenment (Prashad 2000).

The reification, and perhaps self-Orientalization, of Indian culture
in opposition to the invasions of "America" is very visible at the student
culture shows and is also apparent in the use of the imagery of cultural
dilution and ethnic contamination in this subculture. For example,
Nikhil thought that second-generation identity—his own as well as
that of other desi youth—was inherently "weak" or culturally "diluted," a concern that was particularly acute for him because he was in
a "serious" relationship with a White American woman at the time. He
worried that marrying a non-Indian would result in a sullying of his
children's ethnic purity:

> Just because I'm not living in India, I don't know Hindi as fluently, I don't
> know my culture, I'm not completely surrounded by, you know, the culture,
> twenty-four hours, and so I'm a bit watered down, and so, for me to even
> marry a second-generation Indian, my kids would be even more watered
> down, even if they're still pure, even if they're still one hundred percent, just
> because I've lived in America my whole life, they'll already be more watered
> down, and if I just marry a White person, it would be even more drastic and
> not like it's a bad thing, but they become more assimilated.

India is thus the site of cultural authenticity, and in order to remain
potent, ethnic identity requires immersion in an authentic cultural

environment. Growing up in America or marrying an American inherently contaminates the purity of ethnic identity. This rhetorical resistance to Americanization among second-generation youth inverts nativist critiques of immigrant culture, reversing fears of immigrants sullying the essential national culture of the United States. Yet, ultimately, both ideologies of authenticity are based on a conception of culture as a chemical-like substance that is ideally uniform and contained, rather than porous and complex.

Perhaps this underlying view of culture expressed by Indian American youth is shaped by assimilationist sentiments in the United States, but it also, more immediately, seems influenced by the subcultural pressures and cultural orthodoxies of immigrant parents and ethnic peers. Crossing group boundaries to date a non–Indian American, according to Sujata, is construed as a betrayal of the ethnic community: "And then, at NYU, it's very much, Indians want to date other Indians. [S: Really?] Like, they have huge Indian parties every weekend, you know, and it's basically just a meat market [laughs] and you know, which is another reason why Shruti considers me a sellout, because I have a White boyfriend and all the Indians here know that. And I walk into the cafeteria and I have a White guy next to me. Whereas everyone else is sitting at tables, four or five Indian people."

Straying from the fold can be construed as not just a betrayal but a moral flaw. Nikhil's dilemma about his interracial relationship was exacerbated, or perhaps even precipitated, by his Indian American friends' disapproval and suspicion of his "character." Nikhil was critical of his friends' judgments but also vulnerable to their moral evaluations because they played into his own fears that an interethnic relationship would be at odds with a "pure" ethnic identity. He was not the only one to succumb to the orthodoxy of pure culture and to use the imagery of cultural dilution; Purnima, who had dated an African American in high school only to break up with him under parental pressure, seemed to have internalized the ideology of ethnic authenticity with crusader-like fervor.

Resistance to the ideology of ethnic authenticity was not an easy matter for the Indian American youth I spoke with, and even dissenters rejected some tenets of the subcultural orthodoxy only to espouse others. After vehemently critiquing her Indian American peers' policing of interracial relationships, Sujata invoked another marker of ethnic authenticity, her knowledge of Hindu prayers as a result of attending a

VHP summer camp, in order to defend herself against accusations of ethnic betrayal: "They don't consider me, like, Indian, because I have a White boyfriend, but you go ask any of these people for like, to re- peat any Indian prayer or what type of cultural upbringing they've had, and they're clueless, they're really clueless." The desire to prove one's cultural worth according to the terms of the subculture is a social and emotional need that cannot be easily dismissed.

Biracial Indian Americans or youth of Indian descent who grew up in other parts of the diaspora encounter the orthodoxy of ethnic purity in particularly embodied ways. Madhu, for example, had a roommate at NYU who was half Indian and half Irish American and who felt that Indian American students "were turning away from her . . . just be- cause she wasn't fully Indian." Madhu added that she herself had found it hard to gain entrance into Shruti's tightly knit social networks, so being biracial may have only heightened the gatekeeping in this sub- culture. Indo-Caribbean Americans often seem to have an uneasy rela- tionship with those who are "Indian from India" (as I am sometimes described by Indo-Trinidadians); Indian immigrants are not always ac- cepting of those whose ancestors crossed the "kala pani" (black water) several generations ago to work as indentured laborers on colonial plantations in the Caribbean. Manisha's comment about an Indo- Guyanese student in her high school illustrates how moral judgments are made of those whose genealogies are presumably diluted by murky waters: "I hung out with the *badder* Indian kids [we both laugh], . . . but actually, . . . they weren't even that bad, they were just thought of bad, because actually one of the kids was Guyanese, he wasn't really, well, *pure* Indian I guess, how they would say; none of the parents liked him, there was all that stuff, so that's why they were considered the bad kids." The politics of authenticity dividing Indo-Caribbean and Indian American communities in New York has sometimes been forced into public debate at moments of crisis.[10] In 1998, after a brutal racist at- tack on an Indo-Trinidadian man in Queens by three young men who resented the "Indian" presence in their neighborhood, Somini Sen- gupta wrote, "East Indians from the Caribbean and the subcontinent have remained strangers at best in New York . . . rarely if ever, joining the same cultural or social networks. Many Indo-Caribbeans . . . have complained about being looked down upon as inauthentic Indians" (1998, p. B1). While the public admission of this internal hierarchy of authenticity provoked some unease among even progressive Indian

Americans, the incident provoked a strategic alliance of Indo-Caribbean and South Asian activists, who united to protest the assault and to demand legal justice.

Authenticity is an ideology shaped by complex historical and political processes within any subculture or community and is a difficult creature with which to do battle, as the sometimes contradictory discourses and performances of ethnic purity among second-generation youth suggest. The only Indian American youth I spoke to who explicitly rejected the fundamental idea of cultural authenticity, and also the hierarchy it creates, was Chandrika, a Columbia student, who said of another Indian American: "Like there's this one guy I know . . . who I heard talking to many of his friends once, and he was like, 'Yeah, 'cause she's not really Indian, some of my White friends are more Indian than she is,' and I was like, 'What does that mean? And how are you defining that? And why are you imposing that definition of her? And who gives the right to deem her Indian or non-Indian?' you know what I mean?" Chandrika pointed out that definitions of authentic Indianness are shaped by others' perceptions of India and Indians. The image of India in the American public imagination, in the popular media and in literature, has been often been tinged with exoticism and colored by the mysticism associated with Orientalized visions of Asia, even as Indian immigrants in the United States were depicted as dirty "Hindoos." Second-generation Indian Americans may not consciously be aware of these perceptions as they enact notions of ethnic authenticity, but there is clearly a performative dimension to symbolic ethnicity that has a ready audience among Americans fascinated by "exotic" cultures. Chandrika described a young Indian American at Columbia who was a fan of Indian remix music and would greet "random people" with his hands folded in a traditional Indian greeting of namaste, wearing "prayer beads," to "project this image to non–South Asians that this is what it means to be Indian." Chandrika firmly rejected the notion that authentic Indianness can be embodied and regulated: "I have to say that they have no clue of what it means to be an Indian, because . . . that's not something that one person can define."

Though individual second-generation Indian Americans may challenge the imposition of ethnic essentialisms, it still appears that there is a convergence of views of what constitutes authentic "Indianness," an orthodoxy of cultural knowledge to be performed, if not flaunted, by youth in this second-generation subculture. These definitions were not created by second-generation Indian Americans alone; they were shaped by immigrant parents' own nostalgia, anxieties, and selective memory of India. In the 1990s, notions of ethnic authenticity in diasporic communities also have to be situated in the context of right-wing political movements in India, as religious fundamentalists waged a campaign to define the nation as Hindu and to capture the wallets of affluent NRIs and the hearts and minds of their children (Mathew and Prashad 1996; van der Veer, 1994).

Religion, Language, and Nation

Religion is an arena in which diasporic Indians' quest for ethnic authenticity has met with highly organized institutional responses. Depending on the relationship they posit between religion and national identification, institutional programs often intensify the politics of authenticity by positing particular congruencies or slippages between "Hindu" and "Indian" identities. Transnational Hindu right-wing organizations have attempted to draw on local articulations of ethnic ideologies in immigrant communities in the United States and to fulfill the desires of second-generation youth to be "truly" Indian. This is accomplished by producing a packaged version of Indian diasporic nationalism that has no room for non-Hindus and keeps its political truths hidden from most second-generation youth. Religion is thus inevitably, though sometimes covertly, politicized when it enters the space of ethnic ideology. Religious nationalism also both co-opts and is undermined by the politics of multiculturalism in the U.S. academy. Campus ethnic organizations provide an institutional structure for performing cultural nostalgia, but the case of Hindi nationalist organizations in the United States provides an example of how the ideology of nostalgia has been harnessed to a political platform.

Indian immigrants of all political persuasions and of various faiths have established religious organizations to educate youth in response to the particular diasporic circumstances of the second generation, who do not automatically learn about Hinduism, Sikhism, or Islam as part of their daily lives (Lessinger 1995; Miller 1995). The youth programs that religious institutions have established seem to draw second-generation Indian Americans not solely because of interest in religion but also because they offer spaces to focus on the more general social and cultural concerns of that generation. This is evident from the experiences of other second-generation Asian Americans as well, notably Chinese Americans and Korean Americans, some of whom who have turned to evangelical or fundamentalist Christian congregations in large numbers (Park 1999; Yang 1999). Upkar, a young man at Pace University, illustrated this mix of religious and secular concerns when he spoke of helping organize a youth group at the Swaminarayan temple in New Jersey, both to teach younger Indian Americans about this branch of Hinduism and to formalize mentorship of youth: "[N]ot much attention's paid to the younger kids, they get lost, especially at the temple, a lot of focus is put on doing things the right way, but it's hard to do that, you know, I mean it's difficult, especially with Indian parents, and these kids, they're not going to their parents if they have their problems . . . so we want to make sure that they know they have us." Upkar's youth group had eighty members and a Web-based newsletter that he edited, which underscores that these religious groups are highly organized spaces with the resources, technology, and programming to appeal to young people. Religious youth programs are also differentiated by the class base of different segments of the Indian American community. Camp Robin Hood, for example, a summer camp for Sikhs in Pennsylvania, is situated on sixty acres of land purchased by six Sikh doctors; the youth who attend these camps are the children of affluent Sikh Americans who were part of the early wave of post-1965 Indian immigration. The mission of the camp, as stated on the Web, is to wage a "battle . . . against the armies of ignorance and hatred, and the lure of assimilation" (Goodstein 1998, p. A7). Ignorance and hatred are forces many brown-skinned immigrants in the United States have to contend with, especially Sikhs who choose to keep their turbans, only to be called "ragheads," have their turbans torn off, or, in one infamous case, be denied entry to a New York restaurant.

Religion becomes a medium through which nonwhite immigrants mediate the vicissitudes of class and race, as is clear from other studies of Asian American youth (Park 1999; Yang 1999). Diana Eck, director of a study of world religions in the United States, notes that Hindu or Sikh summer camps mirror the programs created by Jewish immigrants for "consolidation of identity" (cited in Goodstein 1998 p. A7). But what is different for Indian immigrants is that not only are many of them non-Christian but most cannot pass for White. As Arvind Rajagopal writes of Indian immigrants drawn to Hindu nationalism,

"As relatively well-educated but dark-skinned immigrants confronting their ambivalent class status, they choose a safe and familiar means of defining themselves. In the U.S., religious identity becomes a way of evading racial marginality.... To be 'Hindu' is to bask in Orientalist visions of an ancient civilization and so compensate for its bygone glories today, while muting the stigma of racism" (1998, p. 15). The "ambivalence of class status" is elaborated on by Biju Mathew and Vijay Prashad, who observe that Hindu nationalist groups such as the Vishwa Hindu Parishad of America (VHPA), or "world Hindu council," offer a "'safe' space for expressions of nationalism and identity that have no place in corporate America" and that are "continuously mediated by the NRI's link to the American Dream" (1996, p. 40).

To attract second-generation Indian Americans, who have a different relationship to Indian nationalism and the American workforce than do their parents, the VHPA created the campus-based Hindu Student Council (HSC) in 1987, of which there were forty-five chapters across the United States and Canada in 1995.[11] HSC chapters, which are increasingly led by second-generation Indian Americans, generally organize study groups in Hinduism, Hindu festival celebrations, conferences, and summer camps. In addition, the VHPA and the Rashtriya Svayamsevak Sangh (RSS), or "national volunteer corps," organize summer camps and classes in the United States for Hindu youth of all ages, offering religious education along with games and outdoor activities. The programs thus superficially resemble American summer camps for youth, a format familiar and inviting to many second-generation Indian Americans, who can go away to camp just like their friends and be introduced to religious nationalist ideology in the process. Sujata, who was sent to Hindu summer camps while she was in high school, including a VHPA camp in New Jersey, said, "The VHP camp was not very religious, it was more a bunch of Indian people together at a camp doing American things. We did, like, woodshop.... [Both of us laugh.] But then we also had to, like, pray and ... we had to wake up at five o'clock in the morning and go to temple.... [M]y sister can probably open a book and speak any single Sanskrit prayer.... [I]t seemed a lot more cultural, you know, a lot like *Indian* people and we sat around and listened to stories about India." Sujata recalled that the emphasis was on a Sanskritized approach to Hinduism and socialization with Indian American youth from North Indian Hindu families. She seemed unaware of the political context of the VHP or VHPA, probably because this was strategically not alluded to during the camp, as part of the organizers' attempt to attract moderately religious middle-class Indian Americans eager to have someone teach their children about Hinduism and India.

This ignorance about the organizational link between youth programs such as summer camps and the HSC and VHPA seemed to be shared by nearly all the Indian American youth I spoke to, not just those interviewed for this study but other youth I have met who participated in the programs, including some whose parents were involved with VHPA activities. All of them were unaware that the VHP's ideology posits an essential Hindu identity for the Indian nation, asserts Hindu superiority over other religious groups, and supports caste privileges and patriarchal definitions of womanhood.[12] Two young Indian American women I spoke to belonged to the then newly formed Hindu Students' Council (HSC) at Hunter, which cosponsored events such as visits to temples, with HSC chapters at NYU and Queens College. Malika, from Astoria, Queens, and Priya, who lives in Brooklyn, said the organization had twenty-five members in 1996-97; both women joined because they were "friends to begin with anyway" and the HSC allowed them to "do things together." This largely social motivation stands in contrast to the reported ideology of the HSC, which defines itself as an "international forum for education and promotion of Hindu culture and heritage" (Internet posting by MIT chapter, April 26, 1996). Malika, in fact, disclaimed the very idea of a "Hindu identity," proposing instead a nonsectarian, nonnationalist identity: "I mean, if you read the Geeta [Hindu scripture] and [in] the Geeta it does not say, like, you know, it does not even have the word *Hindu* in it, it does not have the word *India* in it, so if we think about ourselves, we're just human beings, you know, that's it."

Malika and Priya, who were the first members of their respective families to join a VHPA-sponsored organization, thought that Hinduism was the most important component of their Indian identity yet were hesitant to define Hinduism in national or cultural terms. Being Hindu was a very important part of being Indian for both women, but they were not ready to frame the equation in the reverse, that is, to posit that all Indians are necessarily Hindu. The separation of religious identity from national or ethnic identity was still an open, if ambiguous, question for them. Yet both commented, at various moments, on how religion remained a divide in their relationships with non-Hindu youth. Priya, who initially said that Hinduism was "not a specific thing," went on to speak of the importance of her Hindu friends in college, "[w]hereas junior high school, like, I was, I had a lot of good friends, but they don't see things my way, because of my religion. And over here, we can relate to one another." In contrast, Malika repeatedly emphasized that she did not claim a "Hindu" identity, and when asked if there was any important issue that she would want to put on the record, she stated, "I'd say that everyone has their different experience and that we each have different beliefs." Malika remarked, "I have friends, Bangladeshi friends, and they were in my high school too, they came here. The only thing, it would happen, is religion, 'cause they always bring it up. See, they don't understand, it's spiritual, we don't just look at any group and say, 'That's bad.'" It is possible that some Bangladeshi students were strident about Islam—Malika did not elaborate on the conflict—but it is important to place this remark in the context of South Asian organizational politics at Hunter. While the Indian Club seemed to be dormant, the HSC was technically open to Jains, Sikhs, and Buddhists as well, which is consistent with the VHP's attempts to include these religions "as part of an all-embracing Hindu civilization"—excluding, of course, the "foreign" faiths of Muslim and Christian "intruders" (Van der Veer 1994, p. 658). At Hunter, according to Malika and Priya, the Muslim Club drew many Bangladeshi students (some of whom also joined the Bengali Club) and was larger than the relatively new HSC. In effect, then, Hunter had no active, secular, pan-Indian, let alone pan–South Asian, student organization to compete with these religious or regional-linguistic organizations.

The ambivalence and occasional self-contradiction the two women expressed about Hinduism's meaning—oscillating between a completely amorphous philosophy and a specific social identity—reveal the contradictory politics that second-generation youth must deal with in coming to grips with religious nationalism. Malika's ecumenical statement provides a window into the source of some of this contradiction, for, as Rajagopal points out, "new minorities craft religious identities within a sanctioned pluralism" (1998 p. 16). For second-generation youth in particular, the politics of multiculturalism in the United States sits in an uneasy relationship with the doctrine of religious nationalism. While groups such as the HSC offer a space in which to affirm ethnic pride, the exclusion of other religious groups from this Hindu nationalist project, even for those unaware of the VHP's platform of

"Hindutva," runs counter to the multiculturalist discourse of pluralism and inclusiveness that allows these groups to be formed on campuses in the first place. Rajagopal argues that "contemporary Hindu nationalism articulates a genteel multiculturalist presence in the U.S. with militant supremacism in India" (1998, p. 20). Yet in the second generation, this articulation is somewhat tenuous. It is true that the "VHP trumpets Hindu culture as . . . a contribution to America's multiculturalist experiments," as was evident in the programming for Women's History Month at NYU the year after I completed my research. The organization sponsoring the largest number of programs was the Hindu Students Council, with their discussions on Hindu women ironically sharing the bill with programs on feminism and queer politics. Yet, for some Indian American youth, it becomes difficult to reconcile the projects of U.S. multiculturalism and Hindu religious nationalism, particularly as these young people attempt to negotiate their own relationship to the U.S. nation-state through idioms of secularism and cultural citizenship.

These dilemmas surface in the "politics of recognition" and representation played out in South Asian student organizations (Taylor 1992). The negotiation of multiculturalism and religious nationalism is complicated by the ways in which religion becomes a medium for Indian American youth to assert their cultural authenticity within their youth subculture, thus making religious assertion a banner in the crusade for ethnic purity. Second-generation youth are thus both drawn to religious nationalist organizations and hesitant about how to use their ideologies in the joint production of nostalgia and coolness. Commenting on the Hindu Students' Organization at Columbia, Swapna says in a near lament, "HSO has a really small membership, like I feel like . . . people aren't interested in doing their religion in this big thing, they much prefer the Indian scene versus the Indian culture. Maybe individually it's different for everybody, like they are very religious and spiritual but collectively . . . people are just not interested." Religion thus becomes conflated with culture and drawn into the contest of ethnic authenticity.

Most South Asian student organizations on Manhattan campuses are predominantly made up of Hindu Indian Americans, even though they attempt to offer pan–South Asian, religiously inclusive or secular programs and events. At NYU, however, Shruti sponsored celebrations only of Hindu and Jain festivals. Swapna observed that, at Columbia, many Muslim Indians and, most likely, Pakistani and Bangladeshi students join the Muslim Students' Association. While Club Zamana does host a celebration of Eid-ul-Fitr, and notes this pointedly on the program for their cultural show, Swapna worried that this was only a "token effort" to appear inclusive to Muslim students. The students at Columbia I spoke to generally seemed more concerned with, or at least influenced by the rhetoric of, pluralism and secularism than those belonging to South Asian organizations at other colleges, yet some thought these emphases led to difficult choices in how authentically to represent Indianness in an institutional context. Nikhil recalled that he had created a flyer for Club Zamana's Diwali celebration that was rejected by the club's president because it had an image of the Hindu deity, Shiva. Nikhil acknowledged the validity of Zamana's "concerted effort" to be inclusive of all South Asian religious groups, but he seemed ambivalent about having to use the image of a classical dancer to represent the event:

> The president of Zamana would not allow me to use this flyer because she said that, even though it's a religious celebration, the celebration itself, the party itself is going to be very nonreligious and we cannot have a flyer that has any religious thing on it. . . . [W]hat she said, is that they've gotten into trouble with trying to promote a religious kind of thing. . . . So even though there's this tendency to embrace, you know, and open up to all, Muslims, Hindus, trying to keep things one, at the same time . . . because they're in a delicate environment, there's the idea to compromise.

Being able to display his religious allegiance in a space marked as ethnic, in this case pan-ethnic, was for Nikhil legitimate, even desirable; frustration and disappointment characterized his account of the flyer's rejection. For him, the "compromise" forced him to sacrifice on the altar of inclusive multiculturalism what he saw as an expression of his authenticity. But he did not reflect on how Muslim students might feel about their right to partake of this cultural authenticity. Evading the inherently politicized nature of this negotiation or the implicit concern over sponsoring secular events for fear of "trouble" (especially real in the case of a university-funded organization) only heightens the dilemma for second-generation youth who tend to frame their choices in the language of cultural authenticity. Yet secularism, too, can be imbued with its own authenticity—if one has to be persuasive within the terms set by the debate here—perhaps by pointing to long traditions of pluralism that can be claimed as Indian. The issues raised here are by no means simple, but youth could perhaps look to other models of re-worked cultural representation in the diaspora, such as the "Diwali against Communalism" celebrations created in England to address this very need (Grover 1996).

It is not always Hinduism per se that is considered an essential component of an authentic ethnic identity for second-generation Indian Americans; however, someone whose family is Christian or Muslim is more likely to be interrogated about their ethnic origins, and perhaps even authenticity, by other Indian Americans because his or her last name might be Hussain or Thomas. This approach obliterates the long histories that Islam and Christianity have had in India, histories that are often not included in college courses on South Asia or acknowledged by college student organizations. John, whose family is from the Malayalam-speaking Christian community in Kerala, where people commonly have last names such as Mathew or Alexander, was at NYU before he transferred to Pace University and recollected, "Before NYU, [the] majority of my friends were Malayalis, so you never knew the difference. . . . When I came to college, then you branch out and most of your friends are mostly diversified, either Gujarati, Punjabi, whatever, and then everyone's like, 'How's your last name Mathew?' I'm like, 'Why not?' And then they're like, they'll speak Hindi, and I'm like, . . . 'I don't speak Hindi, I don't know it.'" Sujata was more obviously angry about the exclusionary attitudes toward Indian religious minorities held by some of her Indian American peers at NYU:

> It's very close[d]-minded, another example is like, last year, I met this Indian boy, we were talking, he was just like, totally, very like pompous, arrogant, he was talking, "Oh, I know, can you believe it? There's people here with names like John and," 'cause [there are] Indians who are Christian, and he was just like, dissing them and saying all these things and I was just, like, "That's, what's wrong with that?" He's just, like, "Well, they're not Indian." And I was, like, "Yes, they are Indian, they just have a different—India is not a Hindu country." And that's how close[d]-minded people are.

For Sujata, national or ethnic identity was clearly distinct from religious identity; but this was not always acknowledged by other students, even as they were confronted with religious pluralism in India. The year that I was doing my fieldwork, the president of Shruti was herself a Keralite Christian, and Sujata commented, "A lot of people are weirded out at the fact that there's a president of Shruti's name is Mary. They're like, 'What?'" There is thus a rupture between religious identification and authentic ethnic identity for those whose families are not Hindu or, perhaps, Jain.

As John points out, non-Hindi speakers are also sometimes suspect in this construction of authentic Indianness as embodied by those who have origins in the Hindi-speaking regions of India (perhaps not entirely coincidentally, the Hindu fundamentalist base known as the "saffron belt" of North India). Ravi, whose family is Hindu, conjoined religious practice to language fluency as the necessary foundation for ethnic identity: "I think they really kept a really big Indian base on me from the beginning. My mom used to sit there with me from age two, three, upwards, and try to teach me Hindi. And I'm so lucky I can read, write Hindi. And she kept me into puja [worship], everything, prayer, mantras, everything. . . . I mean, we're not fundamental[ist] religious, you know, but we've kept that base, we've kept that base strong." The link between ethnic authenticity and the ancestral language in the second generation is a much-researched topic that merits a book of its own. Many second-generation Indian Americans, including several I spoke to, enroll in Indian language classes, both at college and on visits to India or semesters abroad at Indian universities. Courses in Indian languages are often a demand of students who lobby for South Asian studies, particularly within the area-studies approach of the U.S. academy. (See Visweswaran and Mir 1999/2000 for an analysis of the politics of South Asian studies programs, including Vedic Studies at Columbia.)

Language clearly symbolizes connections to nation and community in powerful ways, and, in addition to Indian music and dance and expressions of religious identification, becomes a way to perform ethnic authenticity (Heller 1987; also see Lee 1995 and Nunez 1995 for evocative fictional treatments of this issue). The role of English as a postcolonial Indian language was not always addressed by these children of largely English-educated, middle-class Indian immigrants. Interestingly, some youth observed that they were more anxious to learn their ancestral language than their parents were to teach it to them, a reversal of the common immigrant tale of parents speaking the native language at home to meet with replies from children in English. For Biju, speaking Malayalam is still very important even though his parents have reverted to using English at home. Although he cannot read or write Malayalam, he said he would like to marry a Keralite so that he could converse in Malayalam and retain his language fluency: "I don't know how I picked it up, I just talked Malayalam and I can speak it very well, now. I mean, sometimes I'll lose it, but, I try to speak it if I can. I like that . . . when I was young-young, they did teach it to me, but I just, it just stayed in my head, like I never lost it, I never lost it. . . . My parents speak English at home all the time now. Unless I speak something to them in Malayalam then they'll answer me back but otherwise they speak English." Echoing the preoccupation with "losing" this link to the place of origin, Manisha would urge her mother to speak Gujarati with her when at home: "I speak at home all the time, and even recently, I'll go home and I'll tell my mom, 'Mom, I'm losing my Gujarati, I'm not speaking it as well anymore because I'm not home, so make sure you speak to me in Gujarati, you know.' So, I want to make sure I know it, and I want to make sure I'm fluent in it." The fervor of Manisha's plea poignantly underscores how second-generation youth, in reviving their families' language of origin, sometimes come to feel that they are holding on to fragile identities in a "losing" battle to feel at "home."

An often unremarked but significant example of how ethnic authenticity is indexed by language fluency in the second generation is the pronunciation of names of Indian cities. For example, several Indian American youth used the technically correct Hindi pronunciation of "Dhil-hi" instead of the Anglicized "Delhi," which is still commonly used in India when speaking in English, or the Bengali "Kol-kotha" instead of "Calcutta." Yet, in another instance of diasporic irony, most middle-class, English-speaking Indians would probably not use the vernacular pronunciations. This effort to "get it right" highlights the ways in which second-generation Indian Americans cling to symbolic demonstrations of national authenticity more tenaciously than do their peers in India.

Conclusion

The nostalgia produced in this Indian American youth subculture is a multilayered structure of feeling—sometimes ambivalent, contradictory, and yet, ultimately, extremely potent. The notion of ethnic authenticity that it drives emerges in different sites and social practices in the second generation: the movement between cultural fields such as "home" and "school" or between temporal frames such as weekend and weekday; the ritualized travel "back" to the "homeland" and the "coming out" of ethnic pride; the performances of "culture" and evaluations of subcultural capital in campus organizations; desires for ethnic "purity" and concerns about heterosexual relationships and marriage; and participation in religious organizations and language classes. Second-generation Indian Americans are not, however, passive conduits for their parents' nostalgia or for images of India circulated by the U.S. media; they adopt and manipulate these cultural symbols in ways specific to their own experiences. Perhaps in doing so they illustrate aspects of Smadar Lavie and Ted Swedenburg's notion of "third time-space"—"an imaginary homeland" and "a process not of becoming a something but one that remains active and intransitive" (1996, p. 16). This view of identity builds on Stuart Hall's notion of identity as a process of "'becoming' as well as of 'being,'" "a production, which is never complete, always in process, and always constituted within, not outside, representation" (1990, pp. 222, 225).

The trouble with this processual, postmodernist view of identity is that, when observed in cultural practice, the identities postulated by these subjects on the hyphen often reveal yearnings to simply "be" something or someone, fixed, rooted, and clearly recognized. Bhabha's celebratory vision of a hypercreative third space has been critiqued for romanticizing the "new subject-formation in 'in-between' sites, inhabited by migrants as pioneer settlers," and for offering a largely theoretical and ungrounded view of these sites where "the 'past-present' becomes part of the necessity, not the nostalgia, of living" (cited in van der Veer 1997, p. 94). Presenting their notion of "third time-space" with some caution, Lavie and Swedenburg (1996, p. 17) attempt to "resist the new dualisms of a certain brand of postmodernism, a neo-orthodoxy that would privilege identity as constructed, hybrid, fragmented, conjunctural, and would reject any notion of identity as essence, fixed, rooted." While their conceptualization is more open to contradiction than many analyses, nevertheless this third time-space remains diffuse and abstract; Lavie and Swedenburg acknowledge that this concept is "evanescent" because of its "shifting, emergent character" and can offer only a few concrete examples, such as that of "inter-racial dancers at a rave" or "multi-ethnic youth gangs of the Paris banlieues" (1996, p. 17).

The notion of third time-space is conjunctural and cannot be abstracted from the specific, historical and local circumstances of its production. In the case of Indian American youth subculture in New York

City, the delicate and often conflictual relationship between structures of feeling such as coolness and nostalgia must be understood in the context of the particular social and material dilemmas of second-generation youth. I argue that the nostalgia felt and performed by Indian American youth in late adolescence is, in part, a response to the childhood framing of cultural fields as discrete and incommensurable. The degradations and exclusions of the school playground, where Indian American children learn that their cultural citizenship is in question, cannot be divorced from the intense need for an ethnic community in later adolescence, for a subculture to which they feel they finally belong. The cultural crusade for ethnic purity and the youth subculture that supports it can be understood as expressions of a desire for wholeness and belonging. These practices and structures of nostalgia, however, have created their own politics of belonging and exclude those who do not possess the requisite subcultural capital of ethnic authenticity. Yet second-generation youth are not dupes of nostalgic false consciousness; this is their attempt to make sense of, or at least to accommodate to, discourses of multiculturalism and racialization, and to respond to family narratives of class mobility and cultural displacement. Indian American youth fashion their symbolic ethnic identities deliberately and self-consciously and perform a nostalgia that is seemingly reflexive, their ability to orchestrate its production evident in stagings of culture shows on college campuses. Yet this reflexivity stops short, for many, of what could be a "critical nostalgia" (Clifford 1986a, p. 114, citing Raymond Williams).

While some second-generation youth were critical of the yardstick of ethnic authenticity, a dominant set of views about what constituted true Indianness seemed to hold sway within the subculture, with a surprising degree of consensus. While these opinions may not have congealed as yet into a naturalized doxa that is self-evident and unquestioned (Bourdieu 1977/1994, p. 160), the moral force attached to the idea of ethnic superiority makes the notion of authenticity a powerful orthodoxy that demands adherence to a set of standards monitored or assessed by other youth in the subculture. The yearning for ethnic authenticity is definitely greater than the sum of these several elements, and its contradictions are often literally embodied in ways that mesh with other, more corporeal desires.

4

Chaste Identities
The Eroticization of Nostalgia

n the introduction to *Nationalisms and Sexualities*, the coeditors of the collection observe, "Whenever the power of nation is invoked . . . we are more likely than not to find it couched as a love of country: an eroticized nationalism" (Parker et al. 1992, p. 1). The ideology of ethnic authenticity that is recreated in the New York Indian American youth subculture, I found, is articulated through an eroticization of nostalgia for India, the nation and site of "true" culture that has been "lost" to diasporic communities. A study of the "Maya Queen" beauty pageant in Guatemala by Carlota McAllister demonstrates that this love of nation is often linked to displays of the body, especially female bodies: "Nationalism . . . is a structure of feeling . . . which, internalized by the subjects of political entities, fills them with ineffable love. The premises that produce and reproduce the sentiment of nationalism are economies of pleasure. . . . Pageants, which project an idealized national femininity, directly engage these economies" (1996, p. 106). Ethnic culture shows, orchestrated to present "national culture," highlight these "economies of pleasure" in their rendering of flirtatious film dance sequences that stage heterosexual seductions. The classical dance performances by young women that are given pride of place at the opening of culture shows underscore the role women play in representing "authentic" tradition. Even at remix music parties, or perhaps especially in this hybridized youth culture, there is an intense focus on defining appropriate and desirable femininities as well as masculinities. Indian American youth do not simply become ethnic subjects, they are gendered and sexualized ethnic subjects, and they negotiate ideologies of gender and sexuality that articulate particular cultural and material concerns that they project onto men and women. The youth I spoke to were particularly concerned with gender and sexual norms in the cultural fields they inhabited, and issues of dating, desirability, and marriage were often uppermost in their minds, generally framed in a heterosexual context. This preoccupation, of course, is typical of most American youth in late adolescence, a time when individuals have crossed the threshold of puberty and, according to traditional developmental theory and dominant American ideas about the life cycle, are exploring their gendered and sexual identities (Brooks-Gunn and Reiter 1990; Katchadourian 1990).

Critical feminist and queer theory has challenged traditional definitions of sex as the "pre-social, pre-biological body" and gender as the "cultural script that socializes the body" (Puri 1999, p. 4; see also Caplan 1987; Lancaster and di Leonardo 1997; Zavella 1997). Judith Butler argues that "gender must also designate the very apparatus of production whereby the sexes themselves are established. As a result, gender is not to culture as sex is to nature; . . . one way the internal stability and binary frame of sex is effectively secured is by casting the duality of sex in a prediscursive domain" (1990, p. 7). Butler points out the "power relations that produce the effect of a prediscursive sex . . . conceal that very operation of discursive production," thus securing the notion of sex as binary (male/female), "natural," and culturally determined by gender. That is, sex is as implicated in relationships of power as is gender. This is not to deny or downplay the significance of bodily experiences and physical differences associated with sex or to view gender only in semiotic terms, as simply "a subject-position in discourse" or "performance," but to highlight how these experiences are not outside the domains of culture and politics (Connell 1995, p. 51). As feminist sociologist Jyoti Puri observes, "Sex enables the mechanisms of power upon the body that make it impossible to view a body outside the limitations of sex and to engender the compliance and consent of the individual to expectations of normal sexual and gender development" (1999, p. 7). "Sexual feelings and activities," as well as

gendered norms and ideals, "express all the contradictions of power relations—of gender, class, and race" (Ross and Rapp 1997, p. 154).

For second-generation Indian Americans, ideas about gender roles
and sexuality are constructed in both local and global contexts, shaped
not just by the expectations of youth cultures and mainstream media
but also by the norms held by immigrant parents and the ethnic community. Ellen Ross and Rayna Rapp point out that "community practices surrounding sexuality represent more than local traditions, for
communities are also termini of worldwide economic, social, political,
and cultural systems. . . . Many of the aspects of community sociabil-
ity—peer groups, the transmission of sexual knowledge, ritual boundaries to permissible or impermissible sexual relations . . . reflect both
the autonomy of community groups and the presence of a larger social
world" (1997, p. 157). Institutions such as the state, religion, medicine,
and the law, as well as phenomena such as migration and labor markets,
influence and delimit gendered and sexual experience, as do the mi-
crocosmic contexts of peer groups, family, and community. For example, immigration restrictions prevented Indian men who migrated to
California in the early twentieth century from bringing wives from
India, and antimiscegenation laws prohibited them from marrying
White women, so some of these men married Mexican and Puerto
Rican women whom they met while working in the fields as agricultural laborers (Hess 1976; Leonard 1992).[1] Marriage networks grew
between Punjabi partners and sets of Mexican sisters, and a Punjabi-
Mexican community flourished for a brief time due to this unusual
confluence of labor, migration, and legal forces. This history is often
not known to second-generation youth, many of whom trace the history of Indian Americans only to more recent migrations. Most immigrant parents who wield rules about marrying within the ethnic group
are (perhaps gladly) unaware that their predecessors in this country
were intimately involved in interracial relationships. Today, antimiscegenation laws are no longer in effect and immigration restrictions have
eased somewhat, yet class location and educational experience still influence the ethnic and racial composition of the communities in which
Indian Americans live and work, and thus the likelihood that second-
generation youth will find partners within or outside their ethnic
group.

My analysis of gender and sexual ideologies in this youth subculture
draws on observations at cultural events and social gatherings and on

individuals' own views on issues of gender and sexuality. I note Patricia Zavella's caution in her interview-based study of Chicana/Mexicana sexuality: "Using interviews to understand sexuality is problematic, as knowledge about sexuality is often 'nondiscursive,' that is, knowledge that is assumed rather than made explicit" (1997, p. 393). Within these epistemological limits, therefore, the analysis here focuses primarily on *ideals* of gendered and sexual behavior and on the responses of youth to "hegemonic masculinity" and dominant femininity within the subculture, using the framework of R. W. Connell in his rich and complex study, *Masculinities* (1995). Not only are masculinity and femininity relational concepts, but hegemonic masculinity (and femininity) also exist in relation to other kinds of embodied ideologies, producing a "gender politics within masculinity" and femininity (Connell 1995, p. 51).

Much of the emerging literature—authored almost always by women—on second-generation South Asian Americans' production of gender and sexuality focuses on intergenerational conflicts around sexual norms and the regulation of femininity in immigrant communities (Das Dasgupta 1998; Gupta 1999). While these works address important issues and illuminate underexplored areas of research, they tend to frame the issues in terms of conflicts between "tradition"—equated with South Asian cultures, immigrant parents, and sexual repressiveness and "modernity"—equated with the U.S. mainstream popular culture and sexual liberation (Ahmed 1999; Aafreen 1999; Hasnat 1998; Khan 1998). The struggles of second-generation women are often intense, and their resistance courageous, but there is a danger in reproducing critiques of South Asian patriarchy at the expense of examining U.S. sexism and its imbrication with systems of race and labor. A smaller body of critical work by feminist and queer theorists/activists challenges the well-worn trope of "culture conflict" and examines its ideological and material production (Das Dasgupta and Dasgupta 1996; Gopinath 1995a; 1995b; 1997; Ratti 1993; Shah 1994). Yet the reliance on the framework of chaste "tradition" and seductive "modernity," particularly evident in many autobiographical accounts by young South Asian American women, reveals the discursive mode that second-generation youth use to understand the contradictions of gender and sexuality and of cultural nostalgia in their lives.

The following discussion explores: (1) the emergence of this discourse in the context of regulatory practices in the family, (2) desire and idealized femininity and masculinity among Indian American youth, and (3) the intersections and disjunctures between the rhetoric of ethnic authenticity and gender and sexual ideologies.

Don't Ask, Don't Tell: Gender and Sexuality in the Family

Issues of dating, marriage, and sexuality are extremely popular and volatile topics in Indian American community periodicals and discussion forums, which almost always have at least one column or panel that focuses on these issues—not to mention the matrimonial columns in most community newspapers and, now, on Web sites that list the specifications of desire in social and bodily terms (Mukhi 1996; Jana 2000). The stories presented in articles and at conferences are generally narratives of intergenerational conflict over the appropriateness of dating or the choice of partner, practices that provoke community anxiety and scrutiny most visibly when women are involved. These stories coexist, however, with the mainstream media preoccupation with arranged marriages in the South Asian American community; the *New York Times* and the *New Yorker* have published prominent stories that attempt to understand how young South Asian Americans can forgo personal will for that of family and tradition in the choice of lifetime sexual partner (Dugger 1998; Gourevitch 1999).[2] The story fits all too neatly with Orientalized understandings of Asian cultures that sacrifice personal freedom to inexplicable but ancient traditions and collectivist control, unlike the individualist liberty of the rational, enlightened West (Said 1978). The trope of arranged marriage, however, seems to be a lens particularly reserved for South Asian Americans, perhaps because it provides the counterpoint to the image of a hypersexualized land of Kama Sutra. Public discussions of dating and marriage among second-generation Indian Americans, and their underlying erotic fantasies, are thus fraught with the politics of not only gender and sexuality but also nation, generation, and race.

Dating and marriage arouse parental anxiety because they are perceived as intimately linked with the continuity of the ethnic group and the maintenance of group boundaries (Barth 1969).[3] A study of Indian American immigrants and their children in California found that a full 95 percent of the 120 adolescents interviewed reported that they did date, but over half admitted that they preferred not to tell their parents

(Agarwal 1991). Nearly all the youth I spoke to said their parents were uncomfortable with, if not opposed to, the idea of dating, and most said they were told they could not date until a certain age, which was lower for sons than for daughters in many cases. Both youth and parents discussed dating with the underlying presumption of heterosexuality; none of the youth in this study identified as queer, although this does not mean that all of them were heterosexual. The framework within which discussions of gender and sexuality took place was definitely heteronormative, as was the case generally in student organization subcultures. I was told at a workshop on sexuality that I facilitated at NYU that no one in Shruti knew of an Indian American who was visibly "out" on campus. When I asked them to explain this strikingly atypical situation, the students reflected that the Indian American subculture on campus resembled a family and that the fear of repercussions from information leaking to the larger community would be too great for an individual to identify openly as queer. "Family" and "community" were understood by Indian American youth as sites of cultural belonging but also of regulatory power and surveillance. Second-generation youth developed strategic responses to these rules, enabling their movement across different cultural fields. They resisted these monitoring practices but also negotiated the pressures of their peer groups, creating a repertoire of logistical, linguistic, and emotional practices to deal with these social contradictions.

The pervasiveness of prohibitions on dating made the subject a defining feature of second-generation youth, an "insider code" that all could embrace, in rueful irony, regardless of class, region, or religion. Parental restrictions on dating are not exclusive to Indian American or Asian American families, but the negotiation of cultural scripts between immigrant parents and their children invokes notions of "culture" and "tradition" that are made possible by recourse to a country "elsewhere" and by a nostalgia for another time. References to the "dating rule" evoked a complex and often emotion-laden set of adolescent experiences for second-generation youth as they recalled confrontations with the different life-scripts that seemed to emerge before them. Purnima recalled, "My mom had said a long time ago that you can't date until you're sixteen. Like it even matters, you know, they just don't ever want you to, they sat me down and they just said, 'We think you're going to start dating and then you're going to be married,' and I was like, 'That's the last thing on my mind.'" For Purnima, the dating rule defined age appropriateness only in theory, because she was skeptical that her parents would let her date even when she turned sixteen. The dating norms of Purnima's peer group, however, which was largely non-Indian at the time, contradicted the sanctions of her parents, which is partly why Purnima questioned the dating rule. Age-related transitions or culturally recognized rites of passage that are pervasive across generational groups are anticipated by adolescents, who await these experiences as markers of their own entry into another developmental status (Stevens-Long 1990). At the same time, age-graded passages vary in their particularity by ethnic group, class background, and gender and take on a different meaning for every family and individual. I suggest that the strategies Indian American youth use to negotiate different expectations and meanings of dating are, in fact, their *own* rite of passage in adolescence, as is the case for other second-generation youth who learn that puberty and sexuality have charged social meanings that call for specific ways of acting and speaking.

The dating rule for Indian American youth is, in effect, a gendered double standard that is more lenient on males than females. Reena was resentful of the rules that her parents imposed on her but that did not apply equally to her older brother: "He was partying every weekend, meanwhile I'm the same age now, and it's like, 'Oh, no! You're a girl, you have to stay home.' It's like, it's really unfair, and I see all my American friends going, 'Oh, I'm going to a club, the Palladium and everything.' I have to be home by twelve . . . and it shouldn't be like that, because why should a guy get away with it, and you have to be suffering, and not having the fun." Studies of Indian immigrant families concur that parents have more conservative standards for daughters than for sons with regard to dating and premarital relationships (Agarwal 1991; Gibson 1988; Mani 1993). The men I interviewed themselves were aware that the dating and socializing rules they were expected to follow were more permissive than those for their sisters or female friends. Jay remarked, "My parents were very, I would consider, lenient with me as opposed to my sister. I think being an Indian girl would have been a lot rougher growing up [S: Oh yeah! (both laugh)] than an Indian guy, so I know I didn't get anywhere as near as harsh as my sister got it." Jay, like some of the other young men, was sympathetic to his sister's situation and acted as her ally in trying to evade their parents' sanctions. Since he had his own phone line to receive calls from his female friends, his sister's boyfriend also called on this private line to avoid angering their parents. When his sister wanted to go out on dates, Jay would tell his parents that she was accompanying him.

A few men, however, including Jay, also said they did not talk to their parents about dating and romantic interests. Some men said that although they may not have been able to talk about their girlfriends with their parents, the fact that dating was a possibility for young men was implicit in their parents' joking banter, while this was never the case for women, whose sexuality could not be taken lightly. Biju did not experience any explicit proscriptions against dating, but he said, "It's just something we don't really talk about. Like, my mom always jokes around, like, 'Oh, your girlfriend called.' I was, 'Which one?' You know, just joking around, she'll always tease me and stuff like that. And when people, certain people call a lot, they'll [his parents will] be like, 'Who's that? What's going on?' you know. I mean, it's not generally something we talk about." Like other young Indian American men, Ravi observed that his parents' discomfort with discussing his dating relationships led to an ostrichlike game of censorship, in which his parents pretended not to know what was going on and he chose not to tell them. This strategy of "don't ask, don't tell" left the topic not quite outlawed but vaguely associated with unmentionable experiences. For young men, the partitions between different cultural fields were somewhat porous, and they remained in place largely due to parental discomfort or awkwardness. Needless to say, young Indian American women did not get the proverbial wink from their fathers, nor were they teased by their mothers about their "exploits."

The strategy women used most often to deal with the denial of their sexuality was to make the boundaries between their different worlds opaque, at least in the eyes of their parents, and to shift from one bodily disposition or habitus to another while moving across cultural fields. For women involved in interracial relationships, particularly with African American men, their transgression was doubled in the eyes of parents; many second-generation youth said their parents had a hierarchy that revealed their anti-Black and anti-Muslim prejudices, preferring that their children marry a White American, who could be Christian or Jewish, or an Indian American from another regional or caste group, rather than a Muslim Indian or an African American. Young women in interracial or interreligious relationships often chose to lie about their partners rather than confront their parents' prejudices. Karen Leonard (1999, pp. 108–9) brings to light the cases of several young Indian American women who married White American partners without their parents' knowledge, for fear of hurting them, keeping the marriage secret for months or sometimes years. This strategy of nondisclosure, she suggests, is an expression of resistance by young women in response to a "strategy of power," parents' threat of abandonment or withdrawal of love as a means of controlling their daughters.

In a similar but ultimately thwarted situation, Kaushalya did not tell her parents about her African American boyfriend because she was afraid her parents would "disown" her if she were seriously involved with a Black man. She said of the no-dating sanction, "It was funny 'cause it's like, I knew it, I knew that was the rule, so I never really questioned it, I just took it for granted; I mean first of all because he was . . . because he was African American I couldn't bring him home so obviously it was no question that it was going to be a secret, . . . and it was a pretty long relationship, like it was a long time that it was kept a secret. But toward the end, I just started to hate lying to my parents, and I started to feel guilty." Having to hide part of her life from her parents felt like a betrayal, and eventually she ended the relationship, believing it could never become a long-term possibility if it did not have her parents' acceptance. Yet the secret she had held also forced her to learn how to create fictions instantly, a strategy that became habitual: "Two and a half years of my life, I was with him for two and a half years and the whole time, it was a bunch of lies. I just became the qu- [queen] . . . I could think of a lie right on the spot. . . . Even now when I don't need to lie, I just lie."

The strategy of nondisclosure comes with its price for those who share the poignant title "queen of lies"; for many of the youth I interviewed, the burden of guilt proved difficult, compounded by the disbelief of non–South Asian or non-second-generation friends who could not comprehend the need to invent fictional lives. Reena recalled her experience of having to hide her relationship from her parents, despite the fact that her boyfriend's family shared their origins in the Indian state of Gujarat: "In society in general, like, 'You mean your mother doesn't know about your boyfriend for four years?' It just struck them as odd and then there was just like, 'Oh my God, I'm doing something wrong,' and then even lying to them, because I just don't think lying should be an option because it eats you inside, it's not right, but you have to, because there is no other choice and you don't want to hurt them and you don't want to hurt yourself either."

Both men and women learned that to negotiate parental control of their sexuality and peer social rituals, they would have to switch codes and retell their lives for different audiences, developing linguistic strategies to translate cultural experiences. Vijay, for example, learned how to contain his parents' anxieties when he was quite young: "They're like, 'Why you have to go out at night? What is this going-out business?' I'm like, "Mom, 'cause everyone else goes out at night. It's *fine*, you know, all the girls are out at night.' You have to code these words. She was like, 'All right, fine. You come back,' my first curfew was twelve . . . which is quite good still." Telling his mother that it was acceptable to stay out late because girls were allowed to do so was Vijay's way of conveying that it was permissible for a boy to be out at least until midnight. Some second-generation women, and a couple of men, recalled inventing or using same-sex friends as a cover for dating, pretending that they were going to meet "Sally" at the "library" or going to the movies with a group of friends.

Second-generation youth I spoke to reinterpreted or fictionalized their lives according to culturally specific ideals because, on one level, they realized that their parents wanted to believe their children were growing up according to the cultural scripts into which they had been socialized in India. On a deeper level, the youth were perhaps responding to the tug of their parents' cultural nostalgia, their need to believe that, although they were living in the United States, some aspects of life had not changed or could at least be reined in to resemble the familiar. In a poignant short story about two second-generation South Asian women, S. Bari (1996) compares the protective boundaries maintained by immigrant parents to the "lakshman rekha," the name of the fateful line drawn in the Hindu epic the Ramayana. When the mythological heroine, Sita, is left alone, she is told to stay within the confines of a circle drawn outside her home; she steps beyond it, however, and her husband, Ram, eventually accuses her of sexual infidelity. Bari writes of the contemporary significance of this mythological boundary for immigrant parents: "In their pride and fear they had drawn what some would call a lakshman rekha around the goings and comings that constituted their lives. If they stepped outside of that circle, no one could assure their safety. Narmeen understood that when her parents crossed the ocean and found a home by the Mississippi, they had overstepped. Frightened by the bare new country, they got out their chalk and drew the protective line around their home and their minds. America was exiled to beyond" (1996, p. 217). Bari skillfully evokes the subtle affective and social factors that shape the responses of immigrants to life in a new country. The circle, she points out, is drawn to alleviate the first generation's own fears and anxieties about change and to uphold their "pride" in the face of uncertainties about their own social acceptance and material success.

Several studies point out that Indian immigrant parents revert to petrified templates of dating and sexual norms in India (Agarwal 1991; Das Dasgupta and Dasgupta 1996; Roy 1998), denying that these social mores have changed in the "home" country since the 1960s or 1970s and clinging to their amber memories more tenaciously as their children begin to challenge them. Socializing their children into these morally and culturally permissible scripts is presumably one area where immigrants feel they have some control; outside the family and ethnic community lie less familiar cultural narratives. Kathleen Stewart (1992) suggests that in some communities the practice of cultural nostalgia can actually be a form of resistance, a way of redeeming a life of struggle by recalling the past; however, in this instance it seems that nostalgia can also be a form of control. Monitoring their children's bodies may be monitoring a mirage, however, for second-generation youth learn to produce the fictions that their parents want to see and hear.

Monitored Women and Moneyed Men

The emotional stakes in producing these fictional lives for parents were much higher for women than for men because the control of female sexuality in an Indian family has a moral and cultural significance that is different from that for men. A common approach to understanding the "woman question" in Indian immigrant communities, taken by both academic analyses and popular critiques, is to point to the social meaning of female sexuality in a "traditional" Indian context. Women are believed to be the repositories of the family "izzat," or reputation, and of the family's status in the community (Gibson 1988; Wakil, Siddique, and Wakil 1981). For example, Chandrika said that while her parents did not prohibit her or her sister from dating or going to the high school prom, they were concerned about the image their daughters would have in the eyes of other Indian families, and she remarked, "This is the community, if you go out with too many boys or something, you become ruined. . . . It was an issue of my mother wanting to protect my sister from a lot of things, from idle gossip." Gossip is one of several devices used to monitor and control the sexuality of young women, as observed in Marie Gillespie's (1995) study of second-generation Punjabi British youth in London. According to traditional dictates, women are expected to be virgins at the time of marriage, which is understood as a necessary and important event sealing the status of a woman, and thus of her family, in the community. In her study of Punjabi Sikh immigrants in California, Margaret Gibson observes, "Punjabis worry in particular about their daughters' reputations. 'All our respect is in their hands,' the parents told us. A girl's indiscretions could jeopardize marriage arrangements not only for herself but for her siblings as well. A family's good name is of paramount importance in arranging a marriage, and parents expressed a heavy responsibility to keep their daughters', and thus the family's, name untarnished" (1988, p. 120).

Yet these traditional dictates about gender norms are not etched in stone but are variously interpreted and contested. Especially in a diasporic context or in a time of social or economic transition, gender ideologies previously taken for granted can be reconsidered, denaturalized, and recreated. Gendered expectations that are presumably cultural or social also have a material dimension that is highlighted by changes in the family's labor and consumption practices. I argue that to focus the analysis of the social control of Indian American women *only* on notions of "izzat" is to leave in place a particular cultural discourse about women's sexuality; this also leaves unquestioned the implicit notion of oppressive Asian "traditions" that no longer bear up to the scrutiny of the "modern," allowing the material and political practices enabled by this discourse to remain invisible. For example, the entry of Indian immigrant women into the paid workforce and the expectation that daughters should have educational credentials, such as a college degree, may be more likely in Indian families of a certain generation after migration overseas, when women's employment outside the home and higher education for daughters are perceived as necessary for class mobility (Bhachu 1988). Yet the social control of female sexuality is not always mitigated by these new labor patterns or expectations of class mobility but often comes into conflict with them, particularly in the second generation (Agarwal 1991; Hossain 1982; Wakil, Siddique, and Wakil 1981). A twenty-one-year-old woman interviewed by Priya Agarwal (1991, p. 53) voiced her frustrations: "So much is expected of us. We are expected to excel in schools and careers and still be demure and delicate, good mothers, wives, and daughter-in-laws." Echoing this dilemma, Reena spoke of her desire to go away to law school and her parents' injunction not to move away from home: "It's just, it's so frustrating because the American value is you have to be successful, you know, that's the most important thing. And then the Indian culture is, like, it's *family*, it's family, it's always family first! . . . And it's like, it's so hard, because I want to go law school and I want to be the best success I can be but I care about them more than anything . . . I would never do anything to hurt them."

Like other Indian American women, Reena struggled with her parents over the meanings of class mobility in a capitalist society and of a narrative of family cohesion that seemed to contradict this trajectory of individual success, especially in the case of young women. Manisha Roy (1998) points out that, in fact, the first generation is in the United States because they uprooted themselves and often left entire family networks behind in India, even as they argue against displacement for economic mobility when it comes to their children. Immigrant parents often become conflicted because their fundamental belief in the possibility of upward mobility through participation in a capitalist system requires the restructuring of family arrangements that worked in a different economic and social system and that they have held up as the sign of their cultural superiority as an ethnic minority.

This conflict between economic strategies and family ideology is often cast in sexual terms, shifting the focus to the sexuality of daughters and thus effectively allowing young women to feel guilty for realizing their parents' economic strategies. Reena said that underlying her parents' resistance to her moving away was the fear that she would move in with "some White boy" or non-Indian man, a transgression that loomed large over her family because Reena's female cousin had moved away to attend graduate school and was living with her Jamaican boyfriend. As Reena put it succinctly, "She's just turned into the major ho [whore] in our family . . . and that's what they automatically assume, you're going to go away, you're going to do something that we don't approve of." The anxieties about young women's sexuality and private lives are no doubt very real for immigrant parents, but they are also a readily available discourse with which conflicts about other issues, such as residential arrangements, educational investments, and occupational choices, become entangled.

For young men, the material pressures of parents were not necessarily woven into a discourse about the moral fiber or ethnic traditionalism of the community in the same way as for women. While adolescent male sexuality was not generally discussed in families, it was not used to symbolize the reputation of the family. The common narrative instead was one of class mobility through the son's expansion of the financial foundation built by the immigrant generation. Vijay, whose father was a successful business entrepreneur, said in an intense moment of self-reflection, "I'm the oldest son, so there's a big thing there, and that also comes partly from my father who's fostered this extreme, extreme, you know, pressure cooker-like mentality within me, because basically, for all practical purposes, I'm competing against my father for everything I do, I mean, he went from one to ten thousand so I have to take ten thousand times ten thousand and go to a hundred million, right?" This almost Oedipal family fable is not centered on the control of sexuality but rather on proving one's masculinity by amassing financial capital. Second-generation men I interviewed who wanted to pursue careers that are financially risky or do not pay as well were sometimes opposed by parents who felt they were jeopardizing the immigrant dream of upward class mobility. Nikhil was interested in a career in theater but said, "My mom thinks it's a passing phase; she knows how strongly I feel about it, [but] she thinks it's going to pass, she'd rather I be like a 'doctor' [Indian accent] or something, but my brother's behind me, actually, he's in medical school, so he's fulfilling my mom's dream I guess, in one aspect." Nikhil felt he was disappointing his mother by not becoming a doctor, a profession that, by marking its pronunciation with an Indian accent, he coded as embodying particularly first-generation career aspirations. Both his parents came to the United States "to escape the level of poverty" they experienced in India, and his mother, who is now a doctor, came from "an *extremely* poor family" and saw the medical profession as "*the* ultimate way for her to get out of poverty." Their sons' entry into the professional class thus represents the realization of Nikhil's parents' hopes for economic security through migration, and it is only Nikhil's brother who is seen as realizing their economic strategy to secure their entry into middle-class America.

While the class-coded expectations that parents placed on these second-generation men emphasize the traditional breadwinner role for men, women, too, experienced pressures to move into the professional class. Swapna, who was at Columbia, was torn between her passion for creative writing and her plans to do medicine: "My grandfather, before he passed away, would always stay with my mother, and he would always say, 'You, we want you to become something bigger, better than your father and mother.' Okay, their positions were comfortable, we have this great life, but they want me to become something better, and I put all my energies into writing, and it doesn't pan out and I don't hit it big, then that's going to be very hurtful for me that I didn't measure up." Yet some women I spoke to found that their parents' opposition weakened over time, or they found the resolve or rationalization within themselves to pursue their own interests. Sharmila, who was doing a double major in drama and education at NYU, said when we first met that her parents were in denial about her desire to be an actor. Sharmila auditioned for and was admitted to a summer theater workshop in Amsterdam that her parents had hoped she would not attend; however, she was determined to give her ambitions a chance and did, eventually, go to Europe. After she returned, she had a conversation with her father for the first time about her career plans and he was, to her surprise, supportive of her decision to pursue acting. Sharmila eventually starred in one of the first feature-length films produced in the United States about second-generation Indian Americans. Swapna, too, a year later, had decided not to pursue medicine but to major in English. When I spoke to Nikhil a year after our first meeting, however, he had given up his plans to study acting and had declared a major in political science. It is possible that these divergences in career trajectories had a gendered dimension and that parents might not relent as easily when it is their sons who are seriously interested in the arts or humanities; or perhaps young men themselves internalize anxieties about upward mobility. Careers in the arts are not easy for the middle or even upper middle classes to pursue, and the need for financial security is not to be taken lightly. The ways in which these anxieties or expectations about careers and capital are framed, however, reveal the gender or sexual ideologies and cultural nostalgia that immigrant parents recreate in the diaspora and that second-generation Indian Americans negotiate in their youth subculture.

Desire: Idealized Femininities and Masculinities

Central to these negotiations of gender and sexuality is the underlying current of desire: Who is desired? Who *should* be desired? How do you decide? Heterosexual desire for an Indian American partner emerges as a site where nostalgia for an authentic India is explicitly eroticized, and enters into intricate relationships with markers of "coolness." The habitus, or bodily engagement and acquisition of social conventions, that is learned in the family, immigrant community, youth subculture, or school or from the media is not simply an uncritical mimetic acquisition of the "rules of the game" in a particular cultural field. Critiquing Bourdieu's structurally deterministic view of socialization into the habitus, Butler argues that "the mimetic acquisition of a norm is at once the condition by which a certain resistance to the norm is also produced; identification will not 'work' to the extent that the norm is not fully incorporated or, indeed, incorporable. . . . [T]he question of ambivalence at the core of practical mimeticism—and hence also in the very *formation* of the subject—is left unaddressed" (1996, p. 35). The heterosexual ideals of masculinity and femininity discussed by the youth I spoke to clearly did not "work" for all or even most second-generation Indian Americans. In their ambivalence about the habitus of the "good" Indian American woman or the "responsible" Indian American man, ideals that were often inherently ambiguous or contradictory, they resisted the social norms of nostalgia or coolness that they privileged in other social contexts.

The orthodoxy of ethnic authenticity enshrined at culture shows and the subcultural capital of coolness performed at remix parties were partly dissolved, but also reinstated, by Indian American youth in their individual, private discussions about desire, dating, and marriage. While musing about what made an Indian American man or woman desirable, many questioned or contradicted the mimetic processes of reproducing Indianness, but they also revealed the building blocks of this process: the individual, subjective, or tentative enunciations or actions that constituted the basis for producing nostalgia or coolness. Building on the work of Bourdieu and also that of Maurice Merleau-

Ponty, Butler writes that "the body . . . *is* this sedimented ritual activity . . . a kind of practical activity, undeliberate and yet to some degree improvisational" (1996, p. 32). This individual layering or internalization is not always "undeliberate," for it can also involve moments of resisting the process, of choosing not to participate in the orthodoxy of nostalgia or subcultural cool. What is missing from this critique of Bourdieu, however, is the illustration of the actual, "practical" activity of both mimesis and resistance that Butler emphasizes. An analysis of such practices would support much more forcefully her notion of a performativity that resides equally in linguistic and social practices of habitus. In the rest of this chapter, I examine, first, the dominant ideal of masculinity in this youth subculture and, next, competing femininities, demonstrating how these illuminate both the metaphorical and material practices of ethnic authenticity.

Idealized Masculinity: "I'm the Man"

The dominant ideals of heterosexual masculinity among the second-generation Indian Americans I interviewed generally seemed to pivot on three major dimensions associated with subcultural capital for men: (1) the performance of subcultural popularity and embodied machismo, (2) class status and potential to join the economic elite, and (3) physical appearance. Of these three aspects of dominant masculinity, the importance of "looks" generated the most ambivalence, with both men and women observing that physical attractiveness was considered less important for men than social and economic capital. To a large extent, the idealized body types described by these second-generation Indian Americans draw on the dominant stereotypes of attractive masculinity pervading the U.S. media, that is, being tall, well-built, and, generally, fair-skinned (Connell 1995). Sunil, a young man at NYU, succinctly described the ideal body image for Indian American men: "Six-one, with muscles." Sunil also happened to be an active member of the NYU chapter of Iota Nu Delta (IND), a recently formed Indian American fraternity that was first created at the State University of New York (SUNY), Binghamton. One of IND's goals, he said, was to encourage Indian American men to focus on strengthening themselves intellectually as well as physically, so that they looked "strong, tall, muscular." To develop this physical image, he said the fraternity "promote[d] working out and becoming physically fit as well." Wondering if the inculcation of this image was in any way a response to depictions of Asian American men as feminized, I asked Sunil if the fraternity was trying to move away from any stereotypes of Indian American men. He replied, "Yeah, we don't want to be known as 7-Eleven owners any more. We want to be known as a strong community where we can do a lot for America." The emphasis on embodying masculine strength thus slips easily into the flexing of economic muscle, moving away from the immigrant model of small, entrepreneurial businesses and toward consolidation of the community's financial capital and its entry into the nation-state. Sunil's statement encapsulated many of the sometimes contradictory class aspirations and gendered ideals that emerged in discussions of Indian American masculinities.

The masculine ideal for second-generation Indian Americans is associated with the projection of a hypermasculine image that connotes toughness and authority. This macho ideal is particularly important in the Indian party scene, where it is enacted visibly in clothing style, in "attitude," and, in its most extreme form, in the outbreaks of fighting between men over perceived insults or "disrespect." Sunita emphasized the importance of a macho image: "These guys show up at the party, very into their image, you know what I mean, so that's always going to lead to fights if they're that like, they're that strong. . . . Total like, just like that macho kind of guy-thing, you know . . . yeah, just like 'I'm-the-man' kind of image, you know." Biju, himself a party promoter who worked with Indian American deejays in New York, pointed out that the preoccupation with asserting this definition of masculinity led to some of the physical violence between men at parties: "You can't step on another guy's integrity, his manhood, or whatever. So if you insult him, like, in front of him, he's going to swing a punch or whatever."

The remix party subculture has produced a new image of desirable masculinity for Indian American youth that may not have existed even in the early 1990s: the popularity associated with being a deejay. Since the parties essentially hinge on the music produced in solo performance by a deejay, who is usually a young second-generation man, these men carry a good deal of subcultural capital, as is the case in dance culture more broadly in the United States and also in Europe. (See Chapter 2.) Biju noted, "A lot of girls will go out with guys not based on looks but because he's popular, or he has certain like, qualities. . . . I know a lot of girls who say, they feel good being oh, Lil' Jay's girl, or

Young men watching a performance at the annual Diwali festival at South Street Seaport, Manhattan, 1996.

DJ Red's girl, so they have some title too then." Biju describes a patriarchal situation in which some Indian American women depend on the prestige of their boyfriends' status for their own self-worth. The deejay L'il Jay, a boyish-looking second-generation Indian American, was the subject of a lengthy article in the *New York Times* (Sengupta 1996) that focused on remix parties in New York. Reena, who used to be a "close" friend of his in high school, remarked, "I think he would be the ideal, like ideal Indian guy, . . . because there are so many guys out there that are getting into the deejay scene, before it was never like that . . . where like, you wanted to be so materialized, and you have all brand-name clothes, and be like, 'I want do this party, I'm going to throw this party!' He's just, he's gotten way up there." For Reena, part of the deejay's image rested on a material dimension, with brand-name clothes signifying subcultural capital as well as economic status. Yet Reena was also critical of the compromises that some young women were willing to make in order to be in a relationship with a popular deejay: "That's what they hold, like, 'Oh, my boyfriend's a deejay,' and stuff like that. And I think they're becoming so weak in the sense that, if the guy cheats on them, that's okay with them. And they'll keep going back, and I mean, that's not the way it should be."

Male sexual aggressiveness was particularly on display at Indian parties, where dating and sexuality underlie the visceral current that drives all club cultures. Some women complained about Indian American men being sexual "players," a masculine performance that is not at all specific to this remix youth culture. Yet this hypersexualized or macho image played into ethnic yearnings in the second generation, for Reena commented that women sometimes compromised their expectations because they felt pressured to find an Indian American man for a partner. Other women were equally vocal in their critique of dominant masculinities in this subculture and resisted the notion that a subordinate role was their inevitable lot in pairing with another Indian American.

Sharmila, for example, thought that the "bad boy" image for Indian American men had only short-term appeal: "Because the whole 'hood culture has entered Indians so much, a lot of girls are attracted to that. But that's . . . a lot of times it's temporary, when they think about long-term, they want something stable, or they'll push their boyfriend to be more stable. . . . But in the beginning girls are always attracted to the kind that are like more dangerous and more mysterious." Sharmila also suggested that the "hoody" image, drawing on hip-hop and urban Black youth culture, connotes danger and instability but also a mystique that is appealing to some women, hinting at the underlying racialization of this masculinity as excitingly "other." She points out that this masculinity is sexy, at least while youth are immersed in this subculture, because it is read as contradicting the "stability" that women presumably find attractive later. This stability is defined in terms of psychological maturity as well as financial security, as typified in the "stable" image of a "doctor." Sharmila said that the appeal of the latter enabled women to "brag" about their partner's profession, again portraying women as deriving satisfaction from men's social and economic capital. This view of stable, white-collar masculinity was offered by many men as the ideal to be aspired to in adulthood. John said, "The women go for certain type of people at the parties, and I've noticed, as they get older, they get serious with the guy who's . . . maybe not the party type of person, who's also more of a family man, and who . . . didn't go to that whole party scene."

Second-generation men were very concerned with the class ideal of masculinity that their families held up for them—more so than the women who allegedly desired this in a partner. Vijay said, "[To be]

financially [successful is] very important; professionally, very important. You can't date, like, a grunge figure or anything like that. He
might be exceptional, but he doesn't dress well, that sort of stuff matters a lot. I mean, basically, if he's a lawyer, investment banker sort of
thing, right, fine." None of the women I spoke to said that the traditional breadwinner role was what they desired in a partner; on the contrary, several were explicit in noting that they wanted an egalitarian relationship. Reena was critical of her family's emphasis on finding an
affluent husband, saying, "Now that they're looking for me, it's like, he
has to have money, and it's like, well, what's money going to get you?
Because you have money doesn't mean you have happiness."

What is interesting in this equivocal discussion of sexy and stable
masculinities is that the ideal of the upwardly-mobile Indian American
man is one that seemed to evoke ambivalence among women, yet men
felt pressured to aspire to this in the "long term." This idealized masculinity emerges not entirely from this youth subculture but largely
from the class aspirations and material concerns of families and communities. The desire for class reproduction or upward mobility is infused into the masculinity that is presumably the ideal for Indian
American men but about which several youth are deeply ambivalent.
Men sometimes say it is Indian American women who desire "stable,"
affluent, professional men, yet women themselves are not so clear that
they want this "doctor . . . wearing an Armani suit," to use Upkar's
words. A "hoody" image, connoting a dangerous, hypersexual masculinity, becomes a counterpoint to this white-collar stability, suggesting that Indian American youth are not immune to the wider racialized
stereotypes of Black and Latino men as oversexed and underachieving.
This "mysterious" masculinity is still portrayed as only a short-term alternative, a temporary spurt of macho play with "other" images, but
there seems to some degree of resistance to, or at least ambivalence
about, the white-collar masculinity that awaits Indian American men.

Upward mobility and class reproduction cannot be discussed only in
terms of educational and work credentials or family and community
support for academic achievement, as some of the sociological literature on second-generation youth would suggest, neglecting the basic
point that young people have to *want* upward mobility for it to be
materialized. While studies note that some second-generation youth
who are disillusioned with American racial stratification gravitate toward "oppositional" subcultures created by youth of color, they do not

acknowledge the ways in which these racial and class trajectories are negotiated through a gendered and sexualized habitus. Homeboys may be sexy and exciting, but can white-collar masculinity be desirable? Upward mobility that will increase the economic and social capital of an immigrant community depends on the assurance not only that the next generation will move into well-paying professions but also that they will marry and reproduce the heterosexual family structure. The transition from college to the workforce involves structural factors but also a willingness to participate in this class mobility, a subjectivity that is deeply gendered and sexualized and that is often worked out through struggles over what it mean to be "cool" or "authentic" as an Indian American man or woman.

Idealized Femininity: Fantasies of Purity

While the men I spoke with negotiated the struggle over class aspirations through different modes of masculinity, the ideals of the "hoody" player or the reliable professional were not read in terms of ethnic authenticity. Both masculinities were considered equally authentic for an Indian American man, although certainly differing in their appeal to heterosexual women. Second-generation youth, however, almost always viewed female gendered and sexual behavior along the grid of "traditionalism" versus "modernity." The contradictions in gender ideology for women mapped onto the dialectic of nostalgia and cool more overtly than for men, but the sometimes hidden class contradictions of masculinity are tied to, and perhaps even depend on, the role that women are expected to perform in fulfilling nostalgic fantasies about authentic tradition.

For women as for men, however, images of sexual desire were also entangled with racialized markers of "Whiteness" and "Blackness." Yet there was far more consensus on the physical ideal of beauty for Indian American women, represented by the triumvirate of "a thin figure, long hair, and fair skin." Many youth recognized that this emphasis on light skin color was tied not just to sexual but also to implicit racial desire, to look "near white" (Okihiro 1994); long, flowing hair, too, figures in this longing to pass as White, as evoked by the term *good hair* in the politics of Black hair style (Mercer 1987). For Indian American women, these ideals are understood as a response to both the racial hierarchies of the United States and the beauty myths of postcolonial India. The young women I spoke to analyzed these images using a transnational frame of reference for gender ideology, alluding both to the production of skin bleaches in India, such as the notorious "Fair and Lovely" cream, and to the femininity performed by actresses in the Indian film industry. Purnima linked the idealized triumvirate of body image for women in the diaspora to the "Bollywood look": "Skinny. Long hair. Um, fair. Definitely the same images of beauty that we have in India. . . . But it's funny because when I go see a guy friend a lot of them have, [laughs] like, I've seen those Madhuri Dixit [with mock breathlessness] posters in men's rooms, who are obviously, they're not looking Indian. I mean, they look, *so fair*. And they're probably North Indian and stuff but . . . I'm just, like these people do not look Asian." Madhuri Dixit was an extremely popular Indian film icon and sex symbol at the time I was doing this research, and her picture adorned the walls of several Indian American men's rooms.

The reference to (North) Indian film starlets was telling because the feminine ideal in Hindi cinema generally emphasizes light skin—and also typically oozes a sultry female sexuality. Sunita, too, noted that popular magazines from India establish a standard of beauty for second-generation youth that, ironically, promotes a "Western" look: "The perfect like Indian girl [is] . . . I'd say a kind of like Hindi film actress. I used to not think that was so true, but it is so true. Like my friends here at Columbia, they're always like drooling over all those magazines and those Indian girls in the films and all that. [The Hindi film look] is very Western, it's not like it's completely Indian." Nostalgia thus paradoxically entails a longing for a femininity that is coded as dubiously Indian, with "native" Indians flaunting looks that could pass for White. Bollywood films are only media productions, but they open up for some the contradictions of inauthenticity in the "homeland" through portrayals of a seductive, "Western-influenced" femininity.

These contradictory images conjured up by cultural nostalgia collide with the performance of "cool" style in second-generation subculture. The "clubber" image that Indian American women present at student organization meetings, South Asian student conferences, and bhangra remix parties in Manhattan generally favors sleek, body-hugging clothes; styled, flowing, and, sometimes, lightened hair; and a carefully made-up face. This club image is not particular to New York alone, and I was struck by it at at other campuses and at events attended by students from out of state, such as the annual conference of the

Desi youth on a float decorated with posters of Indian film and music stars at
the India Day parade, Manhattan, 1998.

South Asian Students' Alliance (SASA), which draws hundreds of second-generation South Asian students from colleges across the
Northeast. This conference is a mammoth social scene where many
participants say that sexual, if not romantic, encounters are very much
on the informal agenda. At the SASA conference in Philadelphia in
1996, the South Asian American women swarming in the hallways of
the plush hotel venue clearly performed the "desi club girl" look.

While men who belong to the clubgoing subculture, as well as many
who do not, dress in hip-hop style, with its signature baggy pants and
baseball caps, even Indian American women who frequent remix parties do not generally sport hip-hop attire. Manisha thought this was because a "hoody" or urban hip-hop-inspired style was seen as not feminine enough for women, and it was also interpreted as indicating
identification with African American or Latino youth. (See Chapter 2.)
She observed that a hoody look for a woman could lead to marginalization within the Indian American subculture: "I think that the guys
are actually intimidated by people like me, who sometimes dress like a
guy. I guess maybe it shows a different identity and they think that they
might not be strong enough for that . . . but the guys that are part of

the Indian cliques that dress like that, like hoody and all that, they usually go out with the girls that dress not like that." Men can flaunt hip-hop style without any questioning of their membership in this Indian American subculture, yet women are expected to embody a certain kind of ethnic affiliation through style. Manisha's wide pants and loose shirts connote an androgynous femininity or streetwise toughness that is perceived to be at odds with true Indian femininity, as Ravi points out:

> Maybe it's a little, um, sexist on my part, but there's a lot of gangsta-type girls too that come along with it [Indian party culture]. . . . But most of them are . . . true from the heart. You may think else [otherwise] outwards when you see them. But they're not, surprisingly they don't, their insides don't match the outsides that they try to create . . . if I was to see some non-Indian girl, dressed in a certain way, you know what I mean, I would say, "Oh God, whatever!" . . . [F]or the Indian girls you can say that too, but they're not like that. . . . [T]hey're not as tough as the image they try to create. I mean, then again, their roots keep 'em to where they are. I mean, they'll still be the same way when you see them in front of their parents.

Ravi believed that Indian American women who sport a "gangsta" image are simply presenting a façade that belies their authentic Indian "roots," their essential, inner Indianness, and would pass the litmus test of behaving appropriately in the presence of Indian parents. Demure femininity is the authentic mode of being "true from the heart" for Indian American women, despite their "outward" performance of popular local style. Issues of style and image for Indian American women are thus clearly harnessed to the politics of ethnic authenticity, with femininity performing a symbolic role that leaves the material negotiations of ethnic minority status to men.

This second-generation subculture seems to idealize two kinds of heterosexual femininity that contradict not only the Black-identified "gangsta girl" image but also each other, evoking the tensions between desires for nostalgia and coolness. Many women complained that the femininity considered alluring in a girlfriend was very different from that embodied by the ideal wife. Swapna voiced her frustration: "There's this whole duality that I find very interesting that what they want and what they date, what they want is really, like, heart-wrenching, they want the traditional Indian wife, it's really scary that they still want this, they want someone who doesn't smoke, who doesn't drink, . . . they want to date someone who's thin, but they want to marry someone who's curvy, like I don't understand these things." The familiar gendered double standard was read in terms of a dichotomy between tradition and modernity that was also tied to a perception of the transition from youthful sexuality to adulthood as a time of chaste "tradition." Several women, as well as some men, commented that Indian American men seemed to want date women simply because they were considered physically attractive or sexually alluring, a complaint common among college-age American women but cast in specifically cultural terms for these second-generation youth.

Some men acknowledged that the prevailing image of female desirability emphasized physical attractiveness over intelligence or assertiveness; however, they were simultaneously critical of the sexism inherent in this preference. Sunil, for instance, pointed out, "Like the guy's expected to be smart, have a good job waiting for him after he graduates. I don't see that much happening in, like as far as the woman being [smart and professional]. Then, I'd still say, yeah, it's very sexist to say they're not supposed to be smart, if they are, great, but if they're not, it doesn't matter." Yet Sunita commented that, in her view, men were sometimes ambivalent about the sexually alluring femininity performed at remix parties: "Indian guys are totally like that, they're like, I won't marry her, she's da-da-da, she's disgusting, yet they're willing to, you know, use her for something, you know what I mean, and they know that inside, that's not the girl they want, but they think that girl should be able to wait around for that." The implication here is that women whom men seem to desire for sexual relationships would sully relationships legitimated by tradition, as opposed to the chaste women idealized as marriage partners.

Many consider that these chaste or vampish femininities also mark ethnic authenticity and index the women's traditional or modern attitudes, often understood in relation to remix youth culture's temptations. John commented on the attributes of women whom Indian American men would presumably like to date in the college years:

> More Americanized and more outgoing, the parties and this and that, that type of person. But at the same time that type of person is not, [is] the stereotype, probably; if they're really into that whole party scene, and only want to go out, chances are, I don't know how they're going to take care of their families, when they come, when they're put in that position. I mean, some of them might, and I guess they're more wild and they're more

promiscuous, and you know, Indian men, now, when they're young, like
that, that's what their mind is focused on.

John contrasted this "promiscuous" American femininity with the nur-
turance and responsibility for family that he conflated with traditional
Indian womanhood: "As you get older, you want the so-called typical
Indian woman who stays home, but will take care of the family, and you
know that they'll nurture the kids the right way, be like the loving
mom, as opposed to the mom who's always shopping or always out,
leaves the kids at home, they're hungry, they make microwave food,
this and that, like that."

Women were sharply critical of this dichotomization of femininities.
Sharmila explicitly pointed out that the mapping of "Indian" onto traditionalism and "Western" onto modernity creates a deeply problematic binary:

> A lot of guys I know like very, very traditional-looking women, a lot of my
> friends, in the end, want the traditional woman . . . as in the one who has
> very traditional values. . . . I know tons of [guys who say] I just want to get
> married and have my wife be home for me and cook dinner and she'll be
> waiting at home, and she'll do this and she'll do that. . . . [P]eople don't un-
> derstand that being modern and being Western are different things, and
> they think that being modern means being Western in terms of values and
> that's not true, and I think there's a big dichotomy between people's [views].

The valuing of "traditional" femininity was noted by some as becoming more important as men approach adulthood and think about family and cultural reproduction. John reflected that his own attitudes
about marriage and family had begun to "revert more to the traditional
thing" as he grew older. He also pointed out that men who dated non-
Indian women while in college were likely to end the relationship when
they began to think seriously about marriage, because they wanted an
Indian spouse.

Yet women, too, were sometimes critical of Indian American women
who asserted their sexuality. These critiques entailed moments of contradiction for some women, who resisted the control of their bodies in
some contexts but were uneasy about the femininity that other women
performed at remix parties. Although Reena was critical of her family's
anxieties about her sexuality and her desire for independence, she described a woman she saw at an Indian party: "This girl I went to a high

school with, she's always been a ho but, just, it just surprised me that she would wear this V-neck down to here, her butt up to there, I was like . . . [expression of shock] and I could never see myself in that kind of an outfit, and she has a boyfriend, and I was just like, Oh my God!" The invoking of the virgin/whore dichotomy is complicated because Reena herself discussed the frustrations of not being able to talk to her parents about her relationships and of their assumption that independence connoted an illicit sexual relationship. Parents are often unaware of the sexualization of style at these Indian parties, so while the divide between sexuality and family life continues, the family is no longer the only source of moral judgment. Peers take on from parents the function of scrutinizing and judging gendered and sexual behavior, and their evaluations often reveal continuities with their parents' vision of Indian femininity as embodying chastity and tradition.

This contradiction has to be situated in the context of everyday experiences of moving among cultural fields that represent different bodily habituses, that are understood in national and ethnic terms. The experience of keeping issues of dating and sexuality hidden from parents was a shared one for Reena and other second-generation women; this splitting of sexual lives from family life was, in fact, a defining feature of second-generation Indianness. What was perceived as threatening or devaluing was a public flaunting of female sexuality, which was criticized for being un-Indian or "Americanized." Women's bodies perform these presumably conflicting femininities that are read as "virtuously Indian" or "vampishly American" and that evoke ambivalence among women and contradictory desires among men.

Butler points out that Bourdieu views "social conventions" as "animating the bodies which, in turn, reproduce and ritualize those conventions as practice," and she adds that "the *habitus* is formed, but it is also formative" (1996, p. 33). In dismissing but also desiring different kinds of femininity performed by second-generation women, both men and women are implicitly critiquing, but also longing for, the conventionally understood social categories that these habitus embody. Indian American youth do not simply acquiesce to the project of cultural nostalgia and their families' and community's attempts to reproduce or recreate ethnic identity. As in the case of sexy or stable masculinities, "traditional" femininity is framed as chaste, as less alluring than the seductive "Americanized" femininity of youth culture. Men and women are not, however, simply expressing their ambivalence about ethnicization and upward mobility that depend on giving up other lifestyle possibilities and bodily or cultural dispositions to which they are drawn in the present moment. These choices are also understood in terms of the meanings that the present and the future have for them. They understand these dispositions as modes of being that are presumably relinquished when they pass into adulthood. The nostalgia evoked in this subculture is also a nostalgia for a moment that youth feel is going to pass. The cultural nostalgia for a mythic India of "authentic" tradition is infused by an equally socially constructed notion of youthfulness as a time of "freedom," economic, social, and sexual (Griffin 1993; Grossberg 1992). Clearly, these young men and women already experience economic pressures and social control of their sexualities, even in adolescence, and their idealization of youthful freedom—like the nostalgia for a nonexistent India—emerges because of the constraints on this freedom. A "pure Indian culture" and a "liberated" youthfulness are both mirages for which second-generation youth have mixed desires. These femininities and masculinities and the choices they represent are more complex than the simple dichotomy of ethnicization/assimilation and the binary of "near White"/"almost Black" suggest.

Flores points out that "the problem of contemporaneity as it poses itself specifically in the study of popular culture" is "the coexistence of tradition and modernity" (2000, p. 20). The dichotomy of "Indian" and "American" is not absolute, for ultimately these second-generation youth belong to both cultural fields and demonstrate the blurred boundaries between them, as discussed in Chapter 2. The "Americanized" sexualities they critique and desire are, nevertheless, performed by Indian American women in an almost exclusively South Asian American dance culture, while "Indian" femininity is modeled for them by immigrant women in the United States or actresses in an Indian film genre that can hardly be called culturally virtuous. Yet this dichotomy of chaste tradition and promiscuous hybridity provides a discursive framework in the politics of authenticity that plays out in this second-generation youth subculture. The contradictions that this framework literally en-genders raise the questions: What is at stake in this gender ideology, and what are the social and material processes involved in its production as a framework for understanding second-generation experiences?

Conclusion

The discourse of chaste tradition and contaminated hybridity is socialized to some extent by immigrant parents in the context of moral codes
that equate Indian with "good" or "pure" and American with "culturally inferior" or "polluted." This ideology of cultural purity is infused
into the politics of nostalgia in diasporic communities, where cultural
preservation becomes tied to the reproduction of an immigrant group.
The privileging of cultural "origins" becomes a charged political issue
in debates over assimilation and multiculturalism, within but also outside immigrant communities. While resisting the nativism of anti-immigrant movements, Indian American communities of color may turn
to multiculturalist notions of cultural difference that leave unquestioned the structural inequalities of both local and global contexts, such
as the implications of economic restructuring and asymmetrical flows
of migrant labor (Kumar 2000). Doreen Massey points out that cultural nostalgia also becomes a discourse for negotiating a group's internal politics or loss of status when individuals "seek the identity of a
place by laying claim to some particular moment/location in time-
space when the definition of the area and the social relations dominant
within it were to the advantage of that particular claimant group . . . a
moment and a form where they had a power which they can thereby
justify themselves in retaking" (1994, p. 169). The politics of place is
thus also a mode for expressing or contesting relations of domination
or subordination. For the immigrant generation, nostalgia can be a way
to invoke a time when they felt themselves to be in greater control over
their children's unfolding lives or their own economic destinies—even
if, in actuality, this was not always the case in India.

One way to understand cultural nostalgia as an ideology of social reproduction is to consider the concern with purity and pollution that
runs through Hindu beliefs and caste-coded prescriptions in relation to
portrayals of overseas Indians as culturally contaminated.[4] Going overseas, for early twentieth-century Indian migrants, was literally described as traversing the black water (kala pani), with "black" signifying dirty and evoking the taint of foreign contact—a construct of
"otherness" that went beyond the domain of caste and religion (Jensen
1988). This does not mean that generations of Indian migrants across
the far-flung reaches of the Indian diaspora have not imbibed and
recreated elements of diverse cultural systems—and continue to do

so—but there is nonetheless a rhetoric about national purity that creates social hierarchies among second-generation youth and that coexists with cultural syncretism in these diasporic communities (Baumann
1996; Khan 1995; van der Veer 1997). The discourse of cultural purity
is also tied to material resources and class privilege, for it becomes a
way for members of the immigrant elite or community leaders to establish their authority in sanctioning certain versions of Indian culture
and casting others as suspiciously inauthentic, hybrid, or merely "popular" (Khandelwal 1995; Das Dasgupta and Dasgupta 1996). Yet as
Juan Flores (2000, p. 26) points out, the national culture so eagerly
"preserved" in diasporic communities is inherently, if only implicitly,
hybrid:

> The preservation and reenergizing of national traditions is most active at the
> seams of contemporary transnational formations, at the point of rupture and
> refashioning characteristic of diasporic conditions and migratory peoples,
> where an appeal to those traditions helps to provide a sense of grounding in
> place and time. The particularity characteristic of popular culture practice is
> now present not so much in some presumed untampered lineage of native
> heritage as in the very hybridization itself, in the blending and juxtaposition
> of seemingly disparate elements of divergent traditions and practices.

The moralization of ethnic identity conveyed in rankings of
pure/authentic and impure/hybrid identity is also inextricably intertwined with the sexualization of ethnicity. An analysis of the feminization of tradition, or indeed of the nation, opens up the question of what
is at stake in the gendering of authenticity. Feminist critiques of the
workings of nationalism and cultural reproduction point out that
women are often viewed as the vessels of tradition in various immigrant
and nonimmigrant communities; for example, Deniz Kandiyoti's
(1994, p. 382) comparative analysis of nationalist movements and discourses in the Middle East and South Asia focuses on their construction of "women as the symbolic repository of group identity." Floya
Anthias and Nira Yuval-Davis note that the figure of woman is often
used to symbolize the national or ethnic group, as in references to the
"nation as a loved woman"—for example, the reference to India as
"Bharat-Mata" (literally, "Mother India"). They point out that the
boundaries of the ethnic group are often defined through female sexuality, and the sexual behavior of women is often used as a litmus test for
their own ethnic authenticity and sometimes that of their children
(Anthias and Yuval-Davis 1989, p. 9).

Furthermore, when women are more closely linked than men to the responsibility of child-rearing and the socialization of new generations into the community, their behavior is subject to social control. Women's activities, including their sexual behavior, are seen as integral to this important process of cultural reproduction and hence are closely monitored (Jayawardena and de Alwis 1996; Ortner 1974). Anthias and Yuval-Davis observe that biological reproduction becomes linked to ideological reproduction: "The role of women as ideological reproducers is very often related to women being seen as the 'cultural carriers' of the group. Women are the main socializers of small children but in the case of ethnic minorities . . . they may be required to transmit the rich heritage of ethnic symbols and ways of life to other members of the ethnic group, especially the young" (1989, p. 9).

The control of women's sexual behavior as a plank of nationalist ideology is conjunctural and takes on specific meanings in different social sites and historical moments. An influential body of postcolonial and feminist scholarship has focused on the "reification of the role of women" during the colonial period in India and has pointed to the ways in which "the recovery of tradition throughout the proto-nationalist and nationalist period was always the recovery of the 'traditional' woman" (Sangari and Vaid 1989, p. 10). Lata Mani notes that "women become emblematic of tradition, and the reworking of tradition is largely conducted through debating the rights and status of women in society" (cited in Bhattacharjee 1992, p. 30).[5] In the Indian nationalist consciousness that Partha Chatterjee analyzed, "tradition" was equated with a "spiritual essence" that elevated India above "the West" in the domain of spirituality and stood in opposition to the material advancement in "science, technology, and economic organization" that characterized "modern Western civilization" (1989, p. 623). This dichotomy was significant for gendered relations during the emergence of the nationalist movement among middle-class Bengalis in the nineteenth century, according to Chatterjee, and was mapped onto a parallel binary of "the home and the world (ghar and bahir)" that was responsible for the project of cultural preservation symbolized by women: "The world is the external, the domain of the material; the home represents one's inner spiritual self, one's true identity. The world is the treacherous terrain of the pursuit of material interests. . . . It is also typically the domain of the male. The home in its essence must remain unaffected by the profane activities of the material world—and woman is its representation" (1989, p. 624). Cultural nationalism and the "formation of desired notions of spirituality and of womanhood" were key to constituting the middle class, according to Kumkum Sangari and Sudesh Vaid, for "hierarchies and patriarchies are sought to be maintained on both material and spiritual grounds" (1989, p. 10). Masculinity is always implicitly at stake in this gendering of nation or community as woman, for cultural nationalism or the experience of colonial domination comes to be understood within a patriarchal framework of recovering or surrendering the honor of women that constructs signs of "virility" or "loss of manliness" (Jayawardena and de Alwis 1996, p. xvii; De Groot 1998, p. 145).

This construction of womanhood to underwrite political and economic power has been perpetuated by present-day religious nationalism in India. Kumari Jayawardena and Malathi de Alwis argue that fundamentalist movements across South Asia invoke ideologies of ethnic or national loyalty and gain institutional power by using "women's bodies as a battlefield": "Women are seen to be the repository of tradition and their inviolability has been a powerful tool of cultural defence against modernisation and westernisation" (1996, p. xv). Their edited volume, *Embodied Violence: Communalising Women's Sexuality in South Asia*, documents the ways in which political strategies and legal decrees have been harnessed so that "fundamentalism naturalises and sacralises the family and [female] sexuality and secludes women from the public sphere" (Jayawardena and de Alwis 1996, p. ix). Similarly, Anannya Bhattacharjee has argued, in an incisive essay, that Indian American women are expected to perform the work of sustaining the private, ethnic essence of community identity in the United States while designating men as participants in the public or mainstream sphere of capitalist enterprise and state policy. (1992, pp. 31–32).

As Michelle Rosaldo pointed out, however, in her pioneering work on the anthropology of gender, it is also important to note that "domestic groups are themselves highly varied" and that the boundaries between the so-called domestic and public spheres are more rigid in some social contexts than in others (1974, p. 35). Rosaldo suggests that it is important to understand how these boundaries between "private" and "public" realms become sources of power and the strategies that women use to subvert or control their position. In post-1965 Indian American communities, Shamita Das Dasgupta and Sayantani Dasgupta suggest, the immigrant male bourgeoisie is deeply invested in the image of the model minority community and therefore in its gendered ideologies: "Construction of this exemplary public face has been dominated by the wealthy and powerful Indian male bourgeoisie who controls the community's religious, political, informational, and cultural institutions. . . . [T]he bourgeoisie created certain icons to embody the integrity of the idealized community. Primary among these icons is the image of the Asian Indian woman as chaste, modest, nurturing, obedient, and loyal" (1996, p. 228). Straying from this idealized womanhood is thus interpreted as undermining ethnic loyalty: "[A]nything that threatens to dilute this model of Indian womanhood constitutes a betrayal of all that it stands for: nation, religion, God, the spirit of India, culture, tradition, family" (Bhattacharjee 1992, p. 31).

As future mothers and wives, second-generation women are associated with the domestic sphere and with the spirituality and cultural traditionalism that it presumably embodies. Bhattacharjee points out, however, that this "private" sanctum cannot be narrowly defined to refer to just the family space. The ethnic community that gathers at social and cultural events and organizations represents a "culturally private" space that complements that of the family. Indian American community gatherings, though public, are restricted to the "extended 'family of Indians'" and hence are *also* defined as private because they are circumscribed by the community's norms and sanctions. Bhattacharjee contends, "It is in this [private] space that the immigrant bourgeoisie guards what it perceives to be the nation's cultural essence against contamination by dominant Western values. It is here that the immigrant bourgeoisie steadies itself in the face of changes in a foreign country" (1992, p. 38). These culturally coded sexual and gendered norms also shape imaginings of Indian womanhood in the second generation. Das Dasgupta and Dasgupta write, "Of central importance in the cultural schooling of community 'youth' is the careful preservation of gender roles. To this end, the 'chastity' and 'purity' of community daughters is much prized, evidenced by the unequal parental restrictions of the autonomous dating behavior of daughters, and the increased vigilance against the exogamy of girls" (1996, p. 386).

Controlling women's sexuality becomes a criterion for ethnic purity, and thus cultural and moral superiority, that reflects the anxieties about status and belonging in the immigrant generation. The second generation experiences some ambivalence about these standards for femininity, especially second-generation women who contest what they see as a double standard for sexual behavior. They are critical of the overtly sexualized image of women in the remix popular culture, which they consider part of the unseemly competition for men, and they are also uneasy about being viewed as less "authentic"/"traditional" than women from India. Some men recognize the paradoxes of these expectations of second-generation women, but the discourse of authenticity seems to overshadow their engagement with this critique. What is important to note is that while second-generation women may be confined and judged by these standards of ethnically pure femininity, they themselves participate in this scrutiny and in the evaluation of other women because, as Jayawardena and de Alwis point out, women are caught between allegiances to ethnic loyalty and resistances to oppressive gendered ideals: "This dilemma needs to be recognized as it helps us understand why some women accept their 'constructions' in order to defend their culture. . . . [W]e need to locate identities within power relations and recognize that people have multiple identities" (1996, p. xiii). It is particularly difficult for women to reject this framework of gendered cultural authenticity altogether in a context where women belong to an immigrant community that symbolically asserts its ethnic distinctiveness, for such rejection means renouncing claims to ethnic belonging according to the prevailing definitions.

Female chastity and marriage are a preoccupation of social groups across cultural contexts, one that has been linked, particularly in the work of Sherry Ortner and in other anthropological and historical analyses, to social stratification systems in which female virginity signifies the potential for higher family status through marriage, and to religious ideologies of purity that are used by the state to enforce class divisions (Chakravarti 1996; Fruzetti 1982; Ortner 1996, p. 53). Underlying some of these analyses, either implicitly or explicitly, is a symbolic framework in which women's sexuality is tied to the social order through metaphors of purity and pollution. As Rosaldo points out, "Women, as wives, mothers, witches, midwives, nuns, or whores, are defined almost exclusively in terms of their sexual functions. . . . [P]urity and pollution are ideas that apply primarily to women, who must either deny their physical bodies or circumscribe their dangerous sexuality" (1974, p. 31).[6] The notion that purity and pollution are key tropes in the attempt to define and sustain social hierarchies has been posited by Mary Douglas (1996, p. 41), who suggests that impurities are considered dangerous because they represent anomalies that presumably threaten systems of categorization. Within patrilineal and patriarchal social systems, women are on the margins; as liminal outsiders/insiders, they symbolize the danger of potential threats to the social order, particularly when the group identity is seen as vulnerable to external challenges such as the influences of a colonizing culture or new society (Bhattacharjee 1992; Goddard 1987; Mani 1993; Ortner 1996).

Culture enters this semiotic framework for discussing female sexuality through reified dichotomies of "nature" and "culture" that reinscribe gendered hierarchies (Massey 1994, p. 10). Ortner (1974) suggests that the trope of virgin/whore is tied to an underlying perception of women as closer to "nature" than men and more involved in presumably "natural" activities such as child-rearing and domestic work, as opposed to "higher-level" cultural activities such as religion, politics, and finance, associated with men. Because of these ascribed family roles and relationships with individuals that cut across social categories, women are seen as representing either the *subversion* of social categories, and so are perceived as anomalies, or the *transcendence* of those categories or relationships: "The Madonna/whore complex" is an example of "feminine symbolism, [that] far more often than masculine symbolism, manifests this propensity toward polarized ambiguity—sometimes utterly exalted, sometimes utterly debased" (Ortner 1974, p. 86).

This analysis suggests that an ambiguously classifiable femininity is seen as dangerous because it disrupts the categories of pure or contaminated identity that are used to circumscribe the ethnic community and define cultural tradition. Women who identify with an Indian American subculture but who also flaunt their sexuality are viewed with uneasiness because the crossing of boundaries produces a collective anxiety. Writing about young Chicana women who are *pachucas*, the "predecessors of *cholas* and of today's homegirls," Rosa Fregoso writes, "Boldly displaying their sexuality, pachucas refuse to be confined by domesticity. The pachuca is therefore the place that marks the limits of la familia and is also the one who introduces disorder into its essentially patriarchal project" (1999, p. 75). Women represent the boundaries of not just the family but also the ethnic group or nation, and the shifting border they epitomize is seen as threatening to the cohesiveness or distinctiveness of collective cultural or national identity (Anthias and Yuval-Davis 1989, p. 13; Jayawardena and de Alwis 1996, p. x; Goddard

1987, pp. 184–85) and to state authority and regulated citizenship (Yuval-Davis and Werbner 1999).

The anxiety about women who cross or challenge boundaries applies to other, related border phenomena, for, as geographer David Sibley writes, "mixing and non-conformity, like expressions of sexuality outside conventional bounds, create anxiety" (1995, p. 55); hybridity thus comes to represent a "heterogeneous, dangerously unstable zone" (Stallybrass and White 1986, p. 193). Feminist geographers have demonstrated the ways in which gender and sexual politics are deeply implicated in the ideologies of space and place produced in processes of migration and globalization. Massey notes that the feminization of "the local" rests on a notion of "place" as particularized, in contrast to "space," and as "a site of authenticity"; she observes, "This is a view of place which searches after a non-existent lost authenticity, which lends itself to reactionary politics, and which is utterly bound up with a particular cultural reading of something called Woman" (1994, p. 11). Sibley's argument about the politics of space and cultural regulation, as expressed in the "language of defilement," helps address the ways in which earlier generations of Indian migrants were seen as contaminated by their anomalous experience of crossing the "black water," thereby privileging the experiences of those who could afford to be secure in their sedentary, "authentic" status. These analyses are important because they expose the ways in which a particular discourse of chastity or defilement links women's bodies and social roles to ideologies of authenticity, tradition, or nation (as the discussion of remix popular culture and Indian American culture shows in Chapter 3).

It is not enough, however, only to uncover discursive or metaphorical processes that do the ideological work of linking sexuality and nationalism or ethnicity. This analysis has to be extended to include a discussion of the social and material processes that discourses of chastity or authenticity leave unaddressed. R. Radhakrishnan points to the problems that emerge "when any one politics (such as 'the woman's question') is taken up and spoken for by an-other politics (such as nationalism)"; in a situation in which nationalism becomes naturalized as the totalizing political mode of expression, "the women's question . . . is constrained to take on a nationalist expression as a prerequisite for being considered 'political'" (1992, p. 78). Looking at this question of the relation of gender to nationalism from the other end, Johanna de

Groot, writing about mid- to late-nineteenth-century Iran, observes that "terms like 'honor,' 'corruption,' 'modesty,' ... came to be deployed in the political arena to address concerns with law, social reform, constitutional politics, and the nature of foreign influence.... Even where specific issues of the treatment, role, or status of women were not under explicit political discussion, political language included gender coloring" (1998, p. 146).

These analyses point to the political possibilities that are curtailed when "woman" or "female purity" is used to stand for some other discourse, such as that of ethnic authenticity in the diaspora, or is subsumed by a discourse about some other social or ideological realm. Elspeth Probyn argues that analyses of metaphors of the nation as woman that focus only on "discursive modes" are limited: "Metaphors become part of the taken for granted trappings of nationhood.... The particularities of a discrete and historical nation is [sic] thus subsumed, its singular conditions of possibility are generalized through metaphors of gender. It is of the utmost importance that we disturb these discursive modes ... the nation as female is emptied of any material evidence of its historical production" (1999, pp. 50–51). Probyn incisively points to the need to focus on the historical and social processes that are elided in the metaphorizing of nation or ethnic community. To critique a nationalist discourse expressed through the idiom of nostalgia, as in the case of Quebec that Probyn examines, one must disturb the equivalences of "nation, femininity, and vulnerability" that are taken for granted as "ordinary" practices. Probyn proposes an approach that would focus on "the ordinary" in order to question the assumptions that it bears or the cultural work that it performs in sustaining social hierarchies. However, her analysis focuses only on Quebecois television dramas, which does not allow the very women who, Probyn argues, are displaced by this metaphorical process to be brought back into focus. The analysis remains centered on media representations that cannot be mistaken for the everyday experiences of women, even though they may bear on female fantasies or familiarity with television stars (1999, p. 52).

I would like to push these feminist and cultural studies critiques further by arguing that destabilizing the metaphor of ethnic authenticity as female chastity requires not only "moving beyond metaphorical analysis" (Probyn 1999, p. 50) and looking at the daily experiences of "ordinary" women but also examining masculinity. What is important to acknowledge in the case of Indian American remix culture in New York is that the materiality of cultural nostalgia or subcultural cool depends on the relationship between feminized authenticity and a masculinity that struggles with racialized and classed ideologies. Clearly, it is important to write women into analyses of cultural nationalism and collective nostalgia, as a body of critical feminist work has done (Kaplan, Alarcon, and Moallem 1999; Parker et al. 1992). To fulfill the promise of a feminist materialist analysis, however, it would be productive to uncover what is sometimes left implicit in these analyses, namely, masculinity and its embeddedness in material processes. The ideology of ethnic authenticity in the second generation and the cultural nostalgia that it evokes in youth cultural production rest, in part, on an Indian American masculinity that must negotiate Black/White racial binaries and model minority expectations. Women clearly wrestle with class ideals and racial imaginings of "appropriate" work or relationships as well, but their choices are framed using the ideology of ethnic authenticity and sexual modesty, as well as a metaphor of morality that is rarely used for men. Remix youth culture becomes a space in which the anticipation of heterosexual relationships between second-generation Indian Americans and the reproduction of the family's and community's boundaries are held in tension with fantasies about what a life outside a near-White middle class would be like. Black masculinity and economic instability become a counterpoint to the "traditional" heterosexual family structure and upward mobility, one that is nonetheless linked to a nostalgia for an imaginary past, yet focused on its fulfillment in an imagined future.

5

Conclusion

Critical Nostalgia and Commodified Cool

ostalgia and coolness are used by youth in the remix Indian American subculture to recreate and contest ideologies of ethnic authenticity but also to negotiate meanings of femininity and masculinity, class aspirations, and racial locations. Radhika's story in the first chapter and the experiences of other second-generation youth in New York suggest that the politics of nostalgia is a response to specific experiences of moving among different cultural fields in childhood, "going back" to India and "coming out" as ethnic in college, performing and constructing "tradition" at culture shows, and negotiating religious and secular discourses of nationalism. These individual and collective practices of nostalgia and subcultural cool are also a response to the positioning of Indian Americans and other post-1965 Indian immigrants in the United States of the late 1990s. Specifically, second-generation youth must respond to the social and economic contradictions of (1) the nostalgia of immigrant parents and the petrification of visions of India in the diaspora, (2) the tension between assimilationist and pluralist models of national identity in the United States, and (3) the context of multiculturalist identity politics and ethnic segregation on college campuses. At the same time that Indian American youth are trying to make sense of state, educational, and community discourses of race and ethnicity, they are also participating in youth subcultures and drawing on

189

the resources of popular culture to address or evade their social and material dilemmas. The desi club culture in New York offers a space in which the sounds of cultural nostalgia are remixed with the beats of urban cool, highlighting contradictions in racialization, class ideology, and sexual desire that are expressed through style or performed on the dance floor. The tensions between "nostalgia" and "cool" are in part addressed by analyses of authenticity and hybridity in anthropology and cultural studies; however, I argue that this dialectic between nostalgia and cool opens up other frames of analysis, perspectives that are perhaps submerged by the discourse of cultural purity.

The dichotomy that second-generation youth create between "pure" Indian traditions and an "inauthentic," mixed aesthetic overlooks the reality that hybridity has shaped even so-called authentic cultural traditions on the subcontinent, which has had a long history of multiple cultural influences and cross-fertilization with other cultural traditions. This perspective is summarized in Benedict Anderson's statement: "Communities are to be distinguished, not by their falsity/genuineness, but by the style in which they are imagined" (1990, p. 6). Yet, theoretical interventions notwithstanding, the concern with national or ethnic authenticity continues to be a fundamental tension in diasporic communities, as argued in Paul Gilroy's influential analysis of cultural politics in the Afro-Caribbean diaspora, *The Black Atlantic* (1993). Gilroy notes that "rhetorical strategies" are used to produce notions of "cultural insiderism" and distinctions between essentialist and hybrid cultural identities (1993, p. 83–84). He links this contestation of authentic "Black" identification to a particular modernist discourse of national identity: "In particular, this legacy conditions the continuing aspiration to acquire a supposedly authentic, natural, and stable 'rooted' identity. This invariant identity is in turn the premise of a thinking 'racial' self that is both socialized and unified by its connection with other kindred souls encountered usually, though not always, within the fortified frontiers of those discrete ethnic cultures which also happen to coincide with the contours of a sovereign nation state that guarantees their continuity" (Gilroy 1993, pp. 30–31).

Ethnic or national authenticity is also sought by those who are living outside the boundaries of their ancestral nation-state, a diasporic condition in which Gilroy is centrally interested, observing: "The invocation of tradition may itself be a distinct, though covert, response to the destabilizing flux of the post-contemporary world" (1993, p. 101). In the case of second-generation Indian Americans, this turn to "tradition" is not at all covert; rather, it seems to be necessarily on display. The construction of tradition is not just *performative*, displayed at culture shows and community events, but also *discursive*, occurring on the level of rhetoric and in conversation. Indian American youth asserted notions of authentic ethnicity most readily in their discourse about identity—instantiating Gilroy's notion of rhetorical strategies of cultural insiderism—and in orchestrated performances of popular or classical Indian culture that demonstrate symbolic ethnicity.

Gilroy is critical of the reification of identity and the hierarchies it creates, but he is also wary of perspectives that emphasize cultural fusion and hybridity, arguing that both positions are, in a sense, essentializing. "Ontologically" essentialist visions may present an "absolutist conception of ethnic cultures," but "strategic" alternatives may celebrate internal differences without acknowledging the "lingering power of specifically radicalized forms of power and subordination" (Gilroy 1993, pp. 31–32). Each perspective, he concludes, has its limitations, but there has been no attempt to mediate between the two positions. We need to transcend the dichotomy of hybrid versus essential identities and move away from the assumption that this is a motif uniquely characteristic of particular groups, such as immigrant communities or youth cultures (Amit-Talai 1995). Gilroy furthermore argues that the very notion of hybridity leads back to the idea of purity, and he states forcefully, "Who the f___ wants purity? The idea of hybridity, of intermixture, presupposes two anterior purities. . . . I think there isn't any . . . anterior purity . . . that's why I try not to use the word hybrid. . . . Cultural production is not like mixing cocktails" (cited in Hutnyk 1999/2000, p. 39).

The trouble is that people do indeed "want purity." While there have been theoretical attempts to step back from a preoccupation with notions of essentialism or hybridity, another group of cultural theorists has called attention to the contradictions apparent "on the ground." They argue that cultural essentializations continue to demand analytical attention, if only through a revised framework, for they fulfill a certain function in people's lives. Stuart Hall (1996, p. 443), commenting on the "end of the innocent notion of the essential black subject" in Britain, offers a notion of "new ethnicities" that, though somewhat abstract, is more cautiously envisioned and situated in the need for an antiracist politics. He emphasizes that a shift in cultural politics or in racial terminologies does not imply a complete substitution of the old political order, for the circumstances that gave rise to earlier models do not change so quickly. Essentialized notions of Black identity in Britain were co-opted by tokenist multicultural projects and racist policies that asserted the incommensurability of difference; however, Hall argues, this label need not be "permanently colonized" (1996, p. 446). A "non-coercive and more diverse conception of ethnicity" would be based on a reconceptualized notion of difference as "positional, conditional, and conjunctural" but also as facilitating "struggle and resistance" (1996, p. 447).

Gayatri Spivak has emphasized that it might be necessary to take "the risk of essence" for the sake of political strategy in a particular historical context, arguing that the critique of essentialism must acknowledge the "*strategic* use of a positivist essentialism in a scrupulously visible political interest" (1993, p. 3). Building on this acknowledgment of strategic essentialisms, Pnina Werbner argues that "the people we study essentialise their imagined communities in order to mobilise for action. . . . [A]nti-essentialist arguments . . . fail to recognise the importance for participants in moral debates of an imaginative belief in the reality of such achieved solidarities" (1997, p. 230). Werbner's distinction between "objectified" representations that are necessary for imagining "moral and aesthetic communities" and "reified" essentialisms that are "pernicious" and linked to "ethnocentrism or racism" (1997, p. 229) is perhaps overdrawn, for there is always a danger that even strategic self-objectifications of ethnic identity lead to ethnocentric or racialist practices of exclusion and rejection, as is apparent in the orthodoxies of the Indian American youth subculture that is the focus of this book. In a similar vein, Richard Fox (1996) argues for a distinction between essentializations that depends on their use in practice: between those that are empowering and "affirmative" for their subjects and others that are debilitating and "pejorative." This approach may be summed up by Diane Fuss's statement: "There is no essence to essentialism" (cited in Werbner 1997, p. 226). Fox, however, does not clearly define these categories, and the labeling of essentializations as positively or negatively valued raises a host of questions about who would be authorized to make this judgment of empowerment or hindrance, and how; but it is worth noting the more general point that "essentialisms are neither historically static nor the testamentary property of only one group. The boundaries of power that an essentialism once demarcated can be redrawn by the purposeful actions of people as they work with these essentialisms in everyday life" (Fox 1996, p. 40).

In the realm of cultural production, Dorinne Kondo (1996) uses the notion of a positive or strategic nostalgia to defend theater by Asian American playwrights that recreates an "authentic" Asian American sensibility. Kondo remains critical of exoticizing representations but argues that there is a strategic place for cultural productions that idealize a cultural "home." Rather than dismiss such constructions as "aesthetically and politically retrograde," she suggests, "We must ask who is creating this nostalgic 'home,' for whom, and for what purpose. . . . Perhaps at this particular historical moment one kind of political intervention would subvert precisely in its verisimilitude, in its 'authentic' representation of a 'reality' of marginal peoples in ways not captured in dominant cultural representations. Perhaps, in these instances, it is precisely the realism of the narrative that is politically effective" (Kondo 1996, p. 109). It is possible to see the cultural productions Kondo discusses as staging a *strategic nostalgia*, or a nostalgia used to counter hegemonic narratives that erase or distort the experiences of Asian Americans or of marginalized peoples in the United States (Stewart 1992). Yet it must be noted that Kondo's analysis focuses on cultural productions that erase exoticisms and portray second- and third-generation Asian American experiences in relation to questions of multiple loyalties for "marginal peoples." These representations do not attempt to mimic or Orientalize an "authentic" ancestral culture, as do the culture shows staged by the South Asian student organizations in this study. If anything, Kondo suggests that some diasporic cultural productions, such as representations of *sansei* (third-generation Japanese American) experiences, essentialize a *hybrid* experience, which may at first seem paradoxical. These performances are strategically authenticating, recreating "intentional" rather than "organic" hybrids, to use Werbner's distinction. (See Chapter 3.) The point is not to produce yet another conceptual hierarchy to rank these constructions of ethnic identity but to acknowledge how theoretical discourse may ignore the different kinds of political imperatives that youth bring to constructions of authenticity, and their sometimes contradictory implications.

Yo, desis in the house! (Courtesy of
Srinivas Kuruganti)

Critical Nostalgia

Desire, in the cultural politics of the diaspora, is closely intertwined
with the collective yearning for an authentic tradition or pure place of
origin. Yet the politics of nostalgia and cultural purity create a system
of moral distinctions that marginalizes those who do not demonstrate
particular markers of cultural nationalism, as is evidenced by the testi-
monies of Radhika and other second-generation youth. It is also important to note, however, the ways in which Indian American men and
women critique this ideology of authenticity and challenge dichotomies of pure/impure ethnicity through the complexity of their

everyday practices. Second-generation youth participate in, even help produce, performances of culture that simultaneously remix elements of "tradition" and "modernity," "the authentic" and "the hybrid." While many Indian American youth categorize remix popular culture as culturally diluted and inferior to "pure" artistic traditions, in their daily lives they participate in activities that evidence a range of cultural influences. Going to classes on a multiethnic campus, wearing hip-hop gear, participating in sports, working at a part-time job—all these are examples of activities that cannot be easily used to symbolize pure Indianness. Deborah Battaglia (1999) astutely suggests that social actors engage in a "process of social ambiguation, making moving targets of themselves as they move out of identities and create new categories between spaces."

Rather than opting for an abstract, largely theoretical notion of "third space" or "third time-space" (Bhabha 1990; Lavie and Swedenburg 1996) that seems to be concretized only with difficulty, it would be useful to draw conclusions from observing the complexities enacted in daily practice (Ortner 1994). The experiences of Indian American youth call for a theory of identity in cultural practice that transcends old binaries of essentialization and hybridity, while still being able to encompass both possibilities as aspects of the lived realities of social actors. Second-generation youth, indeed all individuals, are able to draw on models of personhood that are based on stability and authenticity of cultural elements in some situations and to embrace identities that emphasize fluidity and multiplicity at other moments. This perspective draws on Jeanette Mageo's (1995, pp. 282–83) conceptualization of "dialogic cohesiveness" among the dimensions of self highlighted in the "ontological premises" of a particular culture, as well as elements of "self" that appear to be excluded from those premises. On the level of identity, then, individuals draw on, as well as co-create, different elements of cultural premises at various moments in their lives, asserting stability as well as flux.

A similar approach that transcends conceptual dichotomies can be used to rethink notions of subcultural resistance or cultural capitulation, in the shadow of the Birmingham school's emphasis on working-class populism and the Frankfurt school's critique of mass culture. Roger Lancaster critiques the binary framework of resistance/conformity that emerges in most analyses of performativity: "An interpretive performance, an analytical technology, hums its familiar noise:

parody or praise, subversion or intensification, deviation or norms, re-sistant or enabling, play or serious. . . . But what if a dramatic moment *en cours* is overwhelmed by nuance and ambiguity?" (1997, p. 568). As demonstrated in the discussion of racially coded style at remix parties, the political imaginaries of Black-identified desi youth remain ambigu-ous, deflecting the question of "near Black" or "almost White" as they grapple with the implications of their class position and the racialized anxieties of their parents. For men, too, class and material status is often understood through a discourse of masculinity, which is variously seen as "cool" and dangerous or as stable and professional. Women, however, do the work of embodying promiscuous hybridity or nostal-gic tradition, which continues to be in tension with the material and racial positionings of Indian American youth.

The ambiguity that women represent in their sullying of categories of authenticity and hybridity also suggests a rethinking of the meaning of "resistance" in order to capture these nuances of individual and col-lective ambivalence. As Nicholas Dirks observes, "In denaturalizing order, we must also denaturalize power, attending to its own fissures and dispersals. In turn, we should not see resistance as pure counter-part to power, for there are dangers in reifying our concepts of strug-gle. But if order can be seen as an effect of power rather than its con-dition, then resistance, too, can be freed from the (teleological) requirement that it establish a new order in order to be recognized as significant" (1994, p. 501). Mediating the either/or of the subver-sion/conformity trap of popular culture analyses need not, however, be an easy theoretical escape.[1] An emphasis on ambiguity situated in the dialectics of nostalgia and subcultural cool does not necessarily imply a transcendence of the political and social conflicts in which these prac-tices are embedded; there remain conflicts, erasures, and silences that are deeply problematic, as the critical comments of these youth sug-gest. Assertions of authenticity, of sexual surveillance, of racial distanc-ing, and of subcultural orthodoxies still remain, and cannot be glossed over with an analytical sleight of hand.

Phil Cohen's insightful analysis of moral panics centered on youth could well be applied to the preoccupation with ethnic authenticity, as he points to "the scapegoating mechanisms whereby youth is made to represent a whole series of conflicts which originate elsewhere in soci-ety, for example, in the class structure. In this view the youth question is by definition diversionary, deflecting public attention and resources away from what can and should be changed (political and economic conditions) and towards something which is essentially unchangeable (adolescent behaviour)" (1997, p. 192). So also ideologies of ethnic (and sexual) purity provide a discourse through which issues of racialization, class mobility, and citizenship are negotiated, and sometimes evaded or deflected, as is apparent in discussions of remix popular culture. For example, the intense parental concern with young women's sexuality and accounts of intergenerational conflict provide a framework within which to address other issues, such as women's entry into the workforce, future professionalization, and residential arrangements; significant class concerns are embedded in these conflicts that are ostensibly focused on sexuality, and underwrite the ideology of ethnic authenticity. Indian American femininities and masculinities are performed through a habitus that represents different racial alignments and work possibilities and that also shapes these racial and class ideologies.

One way to intervene in the ideological impasse of pitting nostalgia, as retrograde and fictive, against "cool," as contemporary and consumerist, is to view both as part of a mutually encompassing dialectic in which nostalgia is embedded in cool and vice versa. Rather than thinking about nostalgia and cool as a binary, as two sides of a cassette-tape that has to be flipped over so it can only play one side at an given moment, it would be more appropriate to shift the metaphor to turntable technology and think of these cultural complexes as samples of sounds drawn from diverse sonic traditions, layered one over the other, entering the mix at unexpected moments, and transforming one another through scratches and breaks. Moreover, both practices of nostalgia and cool are realized through processes of material and cultural consumption. Youth consume—and produce—commodities such as music and fashion in ways that show that their desire for these cultural products and their investments, affective and material, in nostalgia and cool overlap in complex and sometimes ambivalent ways. These desires and investments are part of the processes of self-making for young consumers and citizens. As Daniel Miller points out, consumption is a "moral project," built on the possibilities that commodities offer to reimagine cultural ideologies, such as those of "self" and "other": "Consumption is simply a process of objectification—that is, a use of goods and services in which the object or activity becomes simultaneously a practice in the world and a form in which we construct our understandings in the world" (1995, p. 30). Not only does the New York desi youth subculture demonstrate that nostalgia is as much about the future—the lives that youth imagine—as it is about the past, but it also offers the possibility of remaking the ambient sounds of cool in the present, of envisioning a "critical nostalgia."

Dot.nostalgia

This understanding of nostalgia as simultaneously allowing for cultural and materialist critique was brought home to me when this remix youth culture became emblematic of a style that has become main-stream as turn-of-the-millennium "Indo-chic." Madonna's pseudo-Indian dance performance with henna-painted hands in 1998, and ap-pearances by other White female music stars, such as Gwen Stefani, wearing bindis on their brows or dressing in saris, heralded a new, late capitalist Orientalization of India in the United States and Europe. The fashion and entertainment industries have refashioned henna as "temporary tattoos," and sometimes as a women's ritual that appeals to New Age feminist or body art subcultures in the United States, while bindis are recreated as "body glitter" for "tribal ravers" at "Goa trance" or global techno dance parties, inspired by fantasies of the Indian hip-pie haven as mystical paradise (Fernandes 2000). In the late 1990s in New York City, it seemed that sari borders and Indian motifs began to appear everywhere—on women's clothes, embellishing skirts, jeans, and halter tops; at clothing stores; and in street markets. This new ver-sion of "ethnic cool" flooded the city, culminating in the "Bollywood fashion" window display at Macy's Broadway store in the summer of 2000.

Young South Asian Americans, I have found, are deeply ambivalent about this mainstreaming of what was once a style performed only within desi youth culture or only by other desis. Markers worn by South Asian women that have been read as signs of "tradition," "oth-erness," or, in the case of the violent attacks by the Dotbusters, unas-similable "dotheads" are now packaged and sold to make White femi-ninity "exotic." I argue elsewhere that this cross-cultural consumption is a counterpoint to the adoption of hip-hop style by desi youth, for the diffusion of Indo-chic is almost always framed as a White/Asian cross-ing and provokes intense debates about cultural "appropriation" and ownership (Maira 2000a). The underlying practices of economic ap-propriation, Third World labor, and transnational capital, however, are

Youth Solidarity Summer participants at India Day parade, Manhattan, 1998.

masked by the discourse of cultural ownership and the "true" meaning of henna or bindis. Anti-Asian racism, incidents of police brutality, and racial assaults on young men of color in New York underscore that racial boundaries are invested with deep emotional meaning and also bodily experiences of racialized rejection and violence. The young desi women that I interviewed in Massachusetts, who had grown up in different locations in the South Asian diaspora, expressed an uneasiness about seeing the markers of their ethnic "authenticity" cross racial boundaries, but they were simultaneously able to link this consumption of Indo-chic to global economic restructuring, American multinational profits, and U.S. racism. This moment of mainstreaming remix style has provoked a critical nostalgia: desi youth can take pleasure in body art, remix styles, and vivid colors that evoke "home"—if only an imagined one—while still engaging in a critique of the material processes that make it possible for cheap Asian labor to produce these commodities for American fashion designers and "body art" entrepreneurs.

This critical nostalgia is something I grapple with in my own life and in my work with a program for youth of South Asian descent that has created a space for young desis to rethink what it means to be "authentically" South Asian in North America. Youth Solidarity Summer, a weeklong program held annually in New York, has drawn college-age youth from the United States and Canada who are engaged in a range

of projects linked to feminist movements, queer activism, labor organization, environmentalism, and art. It offers desi youth a way to respond to ideologies of authenticity that exclude those who are disloyal
to narrow visions of who is really "South Asian" and to learn that being
progressive or radical is not opposed to being South Asian or Asian
American, as model minority stereotypes of docile immigrants suggest.
My work in helping build Youth Solidarity Summer in the first few
years was a response, at some level, to the frustrations and also the passionate questioning of Radhika, Chandrika, Jay, Manisha, Biju, and the
other youth I spoke to (whose names have been changed here). The intense enjoyment, but also discomfort, that they felt at desi remix parties and my own (critically nostalgic?) pleasure in bhangra music and
dance drew me to this youth subculture. Remix popular culture continues to evolve and shift, so that the music and spaces I have written
about here represent a particular moment in the mid-1990s when desi
parties had just begun to emerge in mainstream public culture.

Cultural Studies, Ethnic Studies, and Materialist Ethnography

This book is an attempt to intervene in debates about cultural theory
and methodology in cultural studies, anthropology, and Asian American studies, particularly in the area of youth culture studies. The terrain of culture is always the site for negotiations of ideology and struggles for power, a premise that cultural anthropologists and cultural
studies theorists have worked with for years and that cultural critics in
Asian American studies have begun to highlight as well, largely in the
realm of theoretical and textual analysis.[2] Questions of methodology
and disciplinarity are linked, on more than one level, to the problem of
essentialism that Ellen Rooney describes as a "blind spot that won't go
away" in cultural criticism (1996, p. 7). Spivak, for example, asks:

> Is essentialism a code word for a feeling for the empirical, sometimes? . . .
> Why is the thought of the social free of essences? To worry about such dis-
> tinctions too much might keep us from infiltrating the knowledge venture of
> imperialism, which was absolutely spectacular and which still holds institu-
> tional power—the establishment of anthropology, comparative literature, . . .
> et cetera. . . . If one establishes an interdisciplinary space which does not en-
> gage with this most important arena (a silent, unemphatic arena) of warring
> power in the disciplines themselves . . . antiessentialism versus essentialism
> can prove a red herring. (1993, p. 8)

The implication is that, rather than battle only over essentialisms and antiessentialisms, it is more critical to fight for the strategic importance of cultural studies or ethnic studies or feminist studies as political and intellectual projects. This is especially true as these interdisciplinary or transdisciplinary programs are swept up by processes of institutionalization as well as downsizing in the U.S. academy (Pfister 1996).

Spivak's own critique, however, acknowledges that the linkage of essentialism to empiricism and of antiessentialism to social constructionism is limiting and politically counterproductive; for example, the tension between "difference" and "solidarity" within feminist or race-based movements has produced critiques of essentialized categories of "woman" and "experience" but also a recognition of the need for a common platform for political mobilization (hooks 1997; Kaplan 1996; Lorde 1997; Massey 1994; Ortner 1996; Rooney 1996). Addressing these debates, McRobbie emphasizes the need to reconcile what she calls "the three Es: the empirical, the ethnographic, the experiential" with the "anti-Es: anti-essentialism, post-structuralism, psychoanalysis" (1999, pp. 75–78); like other theorists, she sees the need to conjoin a humanist and politically relevant materialist analysis with an understanding of representation and discourse in constituting experience and disciplining subjects. The task is not simply to mediate between two warring camps but to recognize that the very perception of opposition between "Es" and "anti-Es" is part of the larger process of disciplining knowledge in the academy. Disciplinary imperialism is tied to national and economic imperialism, in Spivak's view, through institutionalized "knowledge ventures" such as area studies and comparative studies, against which cultural studies presumably works while allowing itself at strategic moments to take the "risk of essence."

Cultural studies clearly cannot lose sight of either relations of cultural production—what Lawrence Grossberg (1996, p. 50) calls "radical contextualism"—or of the nuances of lived experience; I agree with those who argue that it needs to combine both to produce a "materialist ethnography" (Kirschner 1998). American cultural studies theorists, including Grossberg himself, have been criticized for neglecting "the sense of culture as practice, form, and institution" and for formalizing "questions of power" that seem divorced from everyday experience and from social and political movements (O'Connor 1996, p. 191; Stuart Hall, cited in Pfister 1996, p. 291). A materialist ethnographic project should address weaknesses in cultural studies approaches that critics argue are a legacy of the historical emergence of American cultural studies in the field of communication, which has been primarily concerned with semiotic analyses of mass media "texts" or reception by audiences abstracted from their local contexts (Grossberg 1996, p. 141). This re-creation of cultural studies on the opposite side of the ocean from Birmingham led to a reliance on the now "discredited, linear model of communication: sender, messenger, receiver" (Grossberg 1996, p. 140). Mapping onto Stuart Hall's "encoding/decoding" model —analysis of processes of production, decoding of texts, and ethnographies of consumption in specific interpretive communities—the problem is not that these three aspects are not important to consider together but that cultural studies analyses rarely have done so, according to Grossberg. Instead, this model served to leave intact the disciplinary division of labor between political economy, literary criticism, and cultural anthropology in the U.S. academy.

In addition, the U.S. academy—particularly humanities fields and slightly less so the social sciences—lacks the incentives to do the kind of collective academic work that characterized earlier British cultural studies projects "embedded in a Left political culture" (O'Connor 1996, p. 191); not to mention the persistent reification of disciplinary boundaries in academic departments despite a rhetoric valorizing interdisciplinarity. Both of these structural forces undermine attempts to legitimate Asian American studies in the academy or to do interdisciplinary or transdisciplinary work linked to a progressive cultural critique. The academic job-market crunch and the increasing reliance on part-time academic labor in the 1990s have also worked in favor of disciplinary imperialism, as institutions trim down to "bread and butter" subject matter and graduate students and adjuncts realize they must not only publish or perish but also "discipline or vanish," to rework Ellen Rooney's telling phrase (1996). This is not to idealize or overstate the legacy of the Birmingham school, or the context of production of British cultural studies more generally, but to point to the ways in which questions about the lived experience of youth have fallen between disciplinary boundaries or have been abandoned to those perhaps less interested in the political meanings of everyday life and popular culture.

Asian American studies, while ostensibly an interdisciplinary project, reproduces these disciplinary divisions of academic labor, due to the particular ways in which ethnic studies programs are housed in universities and curricula are institutionalized. Cultural studies, however, is a project that is obviously aligned with the intellectual and political interests of many in Asian American studies, women's studies, queer studies, and other ethnic studies projects who entered these fields looking for a way to transcend disciplinary boundaries and to generate a critical body of knowledge to aid in the social and material struggles of the post–Civil Rights, late capitalist era in the United States. My hope is that disciplinary border crossers or refugees can collectively seize the potential fluidity of our disciplinary transgressions and use it to strengthen a more radical cultural studies.

Appendix
Notes on Research Methods

Contacting Research Participants

My contact with Indian American youth in New York happened in a number of ways, some planned and others spontaneous, and led to several warm, mutually supportive relationships. I began my research with a pilot study in Boston and Cambridge in 1995–96, where I interviewed six second-generation Indian American college students. Compared to my findings in the Boston area at the time, I became aware that certain dimensions of second-generation Indian American experiences were particular to New York and to a large, metropolitan, multiethnic setting, such as the popularity of parties hosted by Indian American deejays at different clubs and the adoption of hip-hop style.

Contacting students on college campuses in Manhattan was initially difficult because universities do not release students' telephone numbers, and I had to use a variety of strategies to get in touch with Indian American students. Ultimately, the deep desire of many youth to help document second-generation experiences, as they often emphasized to me, drove many of them to help me and to ask their friends to participate as well. Speaking only to members of Indian/South Asian campus organizations runs the risk of self-selection, so I also drew on students' personal contacts, although naturally youth often referred me to friends who had similar viewpoints. In addition to scheduled interviews I had many informal conversations with other Indian American students at campus events, student conferences, social gatherings, and community functions, conversations that I have been having for several years.

Students at Hunter College, as well as at NYU, seemed to belong to ethnically segregated social groups, a fact that was very visible as I walked through the hallways at Hunter or at the Loeb Student Center at NYU, where South Asian (or only Indian) American students could be seen hanging out in clusters. Indian American students on these campuses also belonged to larger social networks of Indian American youth that stretched across college boundaries. Indian American youth at NYU, for example, referred me to students at Pace University, a commuter campus that had a newly formed "Indo-American" society. Both of the students I spoke to from Pace, however, thought that the hectic schedules of commuter students made it difficult to create an Indian American student community centered on campus life; not co-incidentally, both of these students met with me at NYU.

To my surprise, unlike South Asian student organizations in the Boston area, the New York groups did not cosponsor social, cultural, or political events across campuses or make any systematic effort to share information about events at other institutions. Ironically, in a few instances I found myself bearing news of events from one campus to another, for most students had no idea was happening on the other side of town. The one exception seemed to be in the arena of Indian remix parties, which is why this is such an important social space and focus of this study. (It was not until almost a year after my research, however, that I heard for the first time of a student-organized party that was officially publicized by both NYU and Columbia.)

Another striking aspect of my research was that I found it much easier to get in touch with women than with men. Part of this was undoubtedly the effect of the snowball sampling technique, for students referred me to their friends and social networks were often gender-segregated. Nevertheless, it was intriguing to me that women were much more willing than men, and often quite eager, to recommend their friends to participate in the study and, furthermore, that some of them wanted to be interviewed in pairs or groups rather than individually, thus introducing me to even more women. None of the men requested a group interview, a difference that may have been gendered and rooted in different ideas about friendship, disclosure, and discussion or may simply have been a product of chance. That my "key informants" at Columbia and Hunter were women, however, was interesting and, in my view, not coincidental. There was sometimes a tinge of awkwardness when I engaged in discussions with young men about issues of dating and physical attractiveness, and it is possible that the men tailored their remarks about gender roles to their conversation with me, an Indian American woman; nevertheless, it was illuminating to find out what they would want a woman to hear. With women, I had many empathic and intense conversations, particularly on the topic of relationships with parents and gendered double standards, reflecting the pervasiveness of this concern among second-generation women.

Interviews and Observations

I did in-depth interviews with twenty-four Indian American college students, ten men and fourteen women, ranging in age from seventeen to twenty-one. Ten of the interviewees were students at New York University (NYU), seven at Columbia, five at Hunter College, and two at Pace University. I also did two focus-group discussions, one with five male students or graduates of NYU and one with six first-year women students at NYU. The names of all of the students were changed for use in this book. Intensive, open-ended interviews with a small sample allowed greater depth and contextualization than could be obtained in shorter, standardized interviews and made it possible to situate the findings in individual life histories and the evolving trajectory of identity development. In conjunction with the interviews, I participated in ongoing observations of events and activities, such as South Asian student organization meetings on campus, culture shows, community events, social gatherings, and off-campus parties. Student organizations also invited me to become involved in their programs, for example, doing a fiction reading at NYU that addressed questions of dating and sexual stereotypes among Indian Americans, an event that became reflexively intertwined with the research project. These moments gave the students yet another context in which I could be positioned and offered me opportunities to interact with students as they went about the business of creating an Indian American community on their campus. To get feedback on my emerging analysis from the youth I interviewed, I mailed them copies of the interview transcripts, though very few responded with any comments. I also shared my preliminary thoughts at a roundtable discussion organized by the Asian/Pacific/American Studies program at NYU; one of the students present at the discussion resonated so strongly with the issues I presented that she asked to be part of the study as well.

The Politics of Doing Research

Researcher responsibility and community gatekeeping were ongoing issues that I wrestled with as I did my fieldwork—yet another dimension of this ethnographic rite of passage that forced me to think about the political implications of my work. Initially, I met with some resistance from individuals in the local Indian American community that seemed to stem from suspicions of an academic interloper exploiting members of "the community," but this waned over time as my work was better understood. The distrust of researchers is perhaps warranted, and was acute among those who were beginning to tire of the flurry of media and academic interest in South Asian Americans and youth culture at that moment in New York. Furthermore, the growth and increased heterogeneity of the Indian American population in New York has been accompanied in the last five or six years by a rise in the number and visibility of community organizations that serve the Indian and South Asian American community, as well as a drawing of boundaries around guarded areas of community turf. In addition, there has been a certain hardening of borders between "the community" and "the academy," and rigid moral positions attached to the divide may obscure the ambiguities of authority, privilege, and representation. Ethnic studies researchers are sometimes particularly susceptible to the romance of "community" as a source of moral redemption or a site of inherently progressive politics, glossing over the contradictory relations of power within communities and the role of anti-intellectualism in preserving the status quo. Issues of accountability and loyalty are complex and not always clear-cut, which is why I think it is important to discuss these experiences more openly and think deeply about the politics of research in relation to the notion of "community."

I found myself situated in multiple community contexts and involved in creating different notions of community at various moments during my stay in New York. The most stimulating of these moments was a summer youth program that I helped organize in 1997. Youth Solidarity Summer offered workshops on South Asian history, identity, politics, and community activism to youth of South Asian origin from the United States and Canada. I mention this program here because I learned a great deal from my conversations and relationships with the student participants and the other organizers, whose insights and experiences helped me think more critically about the politics of community, research, and solidarity and about my own positionality. It is to them that I owe my optimism that a theory and practice of youth culture critique can be integrated.

Notes

1. In Maira and Srikanth 1996, p. 276.

2. South Asia encompasses Bangladesh, Bhutan, India, the Maldives, Nepal, Pakistan, and Sri Lanka.

3. The reason for this significant regional preponderance lies in a complex intersection of factors such as colonization, population pressure, transnational labor recruitment, and chain migration. High population density in central Punjab coupled with inheritance laws that fragmented land into equal shares left many men in debt, driving them to seek other sources of income (Leonard 1992). Since many of these men hailed from so-called martial castes, military and police service under the British government was considered a viable alternative and later proved a stepping-stone to overseas labor. Sikhs stationed in Hong Kong, China, and Southeast Asia were then recruited by agents to work in Canada, and they sent news of employment opportunities back to other men who set out for the port of Calcutta, whence they sailed to Hong Kong en route to North America (Hess 1976; Leonard, 1992).

4. In an instance of painful irony, the bindi has been recreated in the late 1990s as an exoticized fashion item in mainstream popular culture. The link to the often-forgotten Dotbusters incident was powerfully made in *Dothead*, a video installation by Swati Khurana and Shefali Mehta, shown at the Diasporadics festival, New York, 1999.

5. Punjab is a state in North India (and also extends to neighboring Pakistan, having been divided by the partition of the subcontinent in 1947); Sikhs are members of an Indian religious group.

6. One young man who participated in the study revealed after we met that he had come here at age thirteen and hence was perhaps technically in the "1.5 generation" cohort, sharing some experiences associated with both of these sometimes blurry categories. Definitions of second-generation classification vary in the literature; Waters (1994) notes that the "classic" definition refers to those born in the United States of immigrant parents but uses the term more broadly in her own study to include both U.S.- and foreign-born youth. Rumbaut (1994) suggests that

those born outside the United States but who emigrate before twelve years of age belong to the "1.5 generation," while others extend this term to include those who emigrate in late adolescence or young adulthood. Portes and Zhou (1993) use the term to include both the U.S.-born and those who arrived before age twelve. My adoption of Waters's more fluid definition is an attempt to acknowledge that cut-off ages are somewhat arbitrary and do not reflect the subjective nature of ethnic identification. Furthermore, it is more important to acknowledge that exposure to multiple spheres of socialization in childhood (e.g., in American schools and in the home), coupled with a recent family history of immigration, is a defining feature of second-generation identity.

7. Several youth, however, had a different interpretation of the term *second-generation*, as do many people outside the field of immigration or diaspora studies, for they used it to refer to the second *U.S.-born* generation and thus assumed that they actually represented the first generation. The discrepancy between technical and popular usage of the term thus caused some confusion and led to clarifications of terminology at the opening of several interviews. The generational term was not one that informants felt strongly about, for they were more interested in telling their stories about what it meant to grow up in an immigrant family in the United States. I continued to use the term *second-generation* rather than the popular label *first-generation* because it shifts away from the determining criterion of nativity and allows the immigrant generation to be considered first-generation Indian Americans, rather than erasing this history from the trajectory of the group in the United States. The use of "second-generation" also draws attention to the fact that there is a visible and growing population of Indian descent, particularly on the East Coast, that does not have the same history of migration as do Indian descendants in California, where there are Indian American communities that are three generations old.

8. For example, a preliminary study finds that working- and lower-middle-class Indian immigrants in Lowell, Massachusetts, have (re)created religious and cultural organizations. Furthermore, strategies used by previous generations of immigrants who managed multiple allegiances and who participated in global labor markets are finally being recognized (Gerstle 1996).

9. Neil Mehta (Oberlin College, Class of 1998), "Dancing the Walk: An Indian New Yorker's Story," Internet posting, source unknown.

Chapter 2

The title of this chapter echoes the title of Somini Sengupta's (1996) in-depth article on desi parties in New York, "To be young, Indian, and hip." My thanks to her for being a critical interlocutor as I did the research for this chapter.

1. Bhangra music traditionally involves three instruments: the dhol and dholki (drums) and the thumri (a stringed instrument). The lyrics traditionally celebrate the beauty of Punjab, village life, and women.

2. Films include *Gimme Something to Dance To* (dir. Tejaswani Ganti, New York City, 1995) and *Desi Dub* (dir. Swati Khurana and Leith Murgai, New York City, 1997). A full-page article in the *New York Times* by Somini Sengupta (1996) noted

the large contingent of second-generation South Asian youth who are "rooted in hip-hop and Hindi pop" of the "music and club scene." The article sparked much debate among South Asian American youth in the city, many of whom were confronted with a public representation of their subculture in the mainstream media for the first time.

3. Traditionally, powdered dots, and more commonly today, small felt or plastic designs, worn by women between the eyebrows.

4. Popular culture has been variously defined according to the particular theoretical perspectives and political proclivities of different schools of thought. The Frankfurt school theorists viewed popular culture as the product of industries supporting the capitalist status quo; certain Marxist political economy perspectives consider it a form of dominant ideology; and cultural populists focus on consumer subversion through popular culture (Strinati 1995, p. xviii). Several theorists attempt to synthesize the insights of these various traditions, to acknowledge the strategic potential of consumers but also systems of production and power (e.g., Flores 2000; Kelley 1997; Lipsitz 1994; Rose 1994a).

5. Sarah Thornton (1997b, p. 3) traces the intellectual genealogy of British subcultural studies of the 1970s to two earlier schools of thought: the Chicago school of sociology, which was interested in the particularity of urban life as manifested in "subcultures," and the Frankfurt school's Marxist theory of mass society. Both perspectives were fused in the Birmingham tradition, which focused on the "relationship of subcultures to media, commerce, and mass culture."

6. While participants in this Indian American subculture in New York were much more likely to speak of sharing a "culture" or of learning about their "culture" than to use the term *subculture* explicitly, the word *scene* in their everyday parlance—as in "the Indian party scene"—refers to what the Birmingham theorists would call a subculture. Needless to say, desi youth were well aware of the collectivity indexed by the notion of a subculture and discussed at length the distinctiveness of social life organized around Indian remix music or parties.

7. A similar argument is made by McRobbie about the origins of jungle music, or drum 'n' bass, in the United Kingdom; she states, "Drum 'n' bass is a working-class and a black culture built on the virtual non-existence of an alternative labour market for young unqualified males in London" (1999, p. 155).

8. For more on the notion of schemas, see Strauss and Quinn 1994.

9. The name Mutiny in fact refers to *Ghadar*, the newspaper and network of radical independence fighters created by Indian immigrants on the West Coast in the early twentieth century (Jensen 1988).

10. In turning to hip-hop to challenge representations of Asian American masculinity, Wang points out that these rappers reinscribe a "hegemonic ideology" of "ideal masculinity and sexuality" that rests on a stereotypical notion of "the authentic black subject in hip hop" and that ultimately uses an "idealized white masculinity" as its normalizing frame of reference (1997, pp. 14–15, 17).

11. An example of Asian American youth cultural production using hip-hop to resolve the perception of racial ambiguity while asserting solidarity with youth of color is the progressive "zine" *Native Tongh*, by the hip-hop-identified MaddBuddha, whose credo is "A yellow shade in a black and white world." Key Kool, a Japanese

American hip-hop artist, expressed a similar view at the plenary session of the conference "FreeZone," on Asian/Pacific/American youth culture, held at New York University in 2000; he argued that rather than speak of Asian American hip-hop, which implies that hip-hop is ethnic specific, he preferred to speak of Asian Americans *in* hip-hop, a common language and youth movement. For other examples of Asian American musicians in hip-hop taking similar positions, see Wang 1997.

12. In 1922, the Supreme Court decided that Takao Ozawa, a Japanese immigrant, was not Caucasian and hence was ineligible for citizenship. From 1906 to 1923, the courts struggled with how to racially classify Asians and Arabs and how to define the ambiguous term *White*, granting naturalization rights to some Indian immigrants in opposition to the arguments of government attorneys that Indians were neither "White" nor "Caucasian." At least sixty-nine Indians were naturalized between 1908 and 1922, but definitions of their racial classification were based on amorphous and often contradictory anthropological, geographical, and popular understandings of race, reflecting the debates of the time (Jensen 1988).

13. Strictly speaking, the ideology of authenticity erected in this subculture is not doxic, for it is self-consciously performed rather than self-evident and implicit and so represents an orthodox order, in Bourdieu's analysis (1977/1994, p. 160).

Chapter 3

1. The FIA buckled under pressure, after several years of well-publicized protests by SALGA, and the queer organization was allowed to march in the India Day parade in 2000.

2. The Indian American or South Asian American case obviously is complicated because the subcontinent was partitioned, in the aftermath of colonialism, along lines of religion, which cut across regional and linguistic communities that had long lived together and that now existed on both sides of national boundaries, as in Punjab/Pakistan and Bengal/Bangladesh. Migrants from these divided regions, on arriving in the United States, often have a new opportunity to come into contact with immigrants from the other side of the border and to rediscover shared histories and cultures that have been elided on the subcontinent. Many first-generation Indian Americans, however, are still resistant to pan–South Asian coalitions because they carry with them the nationalistic antagonisms and memories of conflict from their home countries, as do other Asian immigrants to the United States (Espiritu 1992). It is their children, then, who (re)imagine a pan–South Asian identity that attempts to unify the second generation across national boundaries.

3. "Ritual" is used here in the fundamental sense of a cultural practice that mediates between "enduring cultural structures and the current situation" and that expresses but also recreates and challenges social identities embedded in sociopolitical contexts (Bell 1997, p. 79; Dirks 1994).

4. *India Today: North American Special*, June 15, 1996, pp. 60c–60d.

5. Two Indian American women studying at Brown University went on a very different kind of train journey through India in 1997. Called the Azad Bharat Rail Yatra (Independent India Rail Journey), this tour was organized to commemorate the fiftieth anniversary of India's independence and designed to teach both resident

and overseas Indian youth about contemporary Indian social and political issues. One of the women noted, however, that no attention was paid to "women's issues," suggesting that once again this travel experience was designed to create a particular construction of India, one with which this woman could not completely engage.

6. Increasing differentiation of ethnic stimuli and experiences and awareness of the implications of ethnic and cultural difference may lead to a period of transition in ethnic identity development, followed by the elaboration and crystallization of attitudes toward ethnic identity and, finally, integration of a new construction of identity.

7. Contradicting Gans's argument, however, research on middle- to upper-middle-class Indian immigrants suggests that even while they are integrated into mainstream educational and occupational sectors of American society, they still rely on ethnic institutions for their social and cultural life (Hossain 1982; Khandelwal 1995). As Gibson (1988) points out, they display a strategic "accommodation without assimilation." Upward mobility and ethnic identification are not mutually exclusive for these immigrants, as proponents of the "straight (or bumpy) line" assimilationist theory have suggested.

8. From M. Taussig, *Mimesis and Alterity: A Particular History of the Senses* (New York: Routledge, 1993), p. 233.

9. Columbia University did not allow the release of numbers of students by ethnic group, and Hunter College did not have these statistics. Since I did not speak to the presidents of student organizations on these two campuses, I did not have any estimates, but my conjecture from talking to other informants is that the number of members were somewhere between those of NYU and Pace University.

10. See Amitava Kumar and Sanjeev Chatterjee's documentary film *Pure Chutney* for a provocative and poetic reflection on the politics of purity among communities of Indian origin in Trinidad (http://www.purechutney.com).

11. The HSC is an explicitly transnational organization that targets Indian youth in the diaspora, with a Global Hindu Youth Activities Network of youth organizations in the UK, Trinidad, South Africa, Fiji, Malaysia, and Singapore and a Global Hindu Electronic Network providing information on Hindu heritage and history.

12. These assertions of the VHP and HSC have been publicized and contested by Indian American activists and intellectuals who support secularism in South Asia. In 1996, when the HSC chapter at MIT in Cambridge, Massachusetts, hosted a conference on Indian women's issues, a public controversy erupted over HSC's stance on the status of women and its relation to the patriarchal notions in the "Hindutva" ideology of VHP leaders.

Chapter 4

1. Indian immigrants' own racial prejudices reportedly discouraged intermarriages with Black women, although there were a few early instances of African American brides (Leonard 1992).

2. The *New York Times* story was part of a series of articles, "Here and There: The Pull of Tradition," while the *New Yorker* article was subtitled "Can tradition make a young woman happy?"

3. Statistics on out-marriage are difficult to obtain for second-generation Indian Americans, since this is a population that is largely comprised of adolescents and young adults, with the exception of older immigrant communities in areas such as California. Within this population, a growing segment of Indian Americans have recently married; however data on marriage trends is not available as yet. Furthermore, existing studies of Asian American marriage patterns have not always presented statistics for Asian Americans, but impressionistic analyses report a professed inclination toward out-marriage at least among middle- and upper-middle-class Indian American women (Das Dasgupta and Dasgupta 1996).

4. Vibha Chandra (1997, p. 163) contends that the hierarchy of purity and pollution connoted by caste status influences views of migration in Indian diasporas: "At the turn of the present century, Indian attitude towards migration depended on caste status. For the upper castes, migration was forbidden because it was a polluting enterprise; however, migration held no stigma for the lower castes because they were [*sic*] born contaminated." Certain groups who could migrate, however, used the economic benefits of overseas business enterprises to enhance their caste status, as in the case of the Patidar caste from Gujarat, which dominated migration from India to East Africa in the early decades of the twentieth century (Chandra 1997, p. 169).

5. This authentic tradition, according to Lata Mani (1986; 1987) was itself produced by colonialist discourse; "it was colonialist discourse that, by assuming the hegemony of Brahmanical religious texts, the complete submission of all Hindus to the dictates of the texts, defined the tradition that was to be criticized and reformed" (cited in Chatterjee 1989, p. 623).

6. So, for example, Lila Abu-Lughod's ethnography of an Egyptian Bedouin tribe finds that female sexuality is considered a threat to the social order and associated with "polluting" functions, such as menstruation and reproduction, because it is seen as contradicting the values of autonomy, honor, and religious piety enshrined by social conventions (1986, p. 148). Similarly, Fruzetti's study (1982) of marriage and women's rituals in rural West Bengal suggests that a bride must be a virgin in order to guarantee the purity of lineage and, furthermore, that women and the women's domain of the household are considered most vulnerable to pollution.

Chapter 5

1. Thanks to Randall Knoper for provoking some of the ideas here.

2. For anthropological and cultural studies approaches, see Clarke et al. 1976; Dirks 1994; Ortner 1994; Stallybrass and White 1986; and Willis 1977. For a literary approach, see Lowe 1996.

References

Aafreen, S. 1999. In search of self. Pp. 50–57 in *Emerging voices: South Asian American women redefine self, family, and community*, edited by S. Gupta. New Delhi: Sage.

Abu-Lughod, L. 1986. *Veiled sentiments: Honor and poetry in a Bedouin society*. Berkeley: University of California Press.

Advani, A. G. 1997. Against the tide: Reflections on organizing New York City's South Asian taxicab drivers. Pp. 215–22 in *Making more waves: New writing by Asian American women*, edited by E. H. Kim, L. V. Villanueva, and Asian Women United of California. Boston: Beacon Press.

Agarwal, P. 1991. *Passage from India: Post-1965 Indian immigrants and their children: Conflicts, concerns, and solutions*. Palos Verdes: Yuvati.

Agha, S. A. 1991. *A nostalgist's map of America*. New York: W. W. Norton.

Ahmed, K. 1999. Adolescent development for South Asian American girls. Pp. 37–49 in *Emerging voices: South Asian American women redefine self, family, and community*, edited by S. Gupta. New Delhi: Sage.

Alba, R., and V. Nee. 1997. Rethinking assimilation theory for a new generation of immigrants. *International Migration Review* 31(4): 826–874.

Allport, G. 1954. *The nature of prejudice*. Boston: Beacon Press.

Alvarez, J. 1991. *How the Garcia girls lost their accents*. New York: Plume.

Amit-Talai, V. 1995. The 'multi' cultural of youth. Pp. 223–33 in *Youth cultures: A cross-cultural perspective*, edited by V. Amit-Talai and H. Wulff. London: Routledge.

Anderson, B. 1983. *Imagined communities: Reflections on the origin and spread of nationalism*. New York: Verso (1991 edition).

Anderson, K., and D. C. Jack. 1991. Learning to listen: Interview techniques and analyses. Pp. 11–26 in *Women's words: The feminist practice of oral history*, edited by S. B. Gluck and D. Patai. New York: Routledge.

Anthias, F., and N. Yuval-Davis. 1989. Introduction. Pp. 1–15 in *Woman, Nation, State*, edited by F. Anthias and N. Yuval-Davis. New York: St. Martin's Press.

Appadurai, A. 1996. Disjuncture and difference in the global cultural economy. Pp. 27–47 in *Modernity at large: Cultural dimensions of globalization*. Minneapolis: University of Minnesota Press.

217

Aronson, D. 1976. Ethnicity as a cultural system: An introductory essay. Pp. 9–19 in *Ethnicity in the Americas*, edited by F. Henry. The Hague: Mouton.

Ashcraft, N. 1989. The clash of traditions: Asian-Indian immigrants in crisis. *Studies in Third World Societies* 38: 53–70.

Back, L. 1994. *X amount of sat sri akal: Apache Indian, reggae music and intermezzo culture*. South Asia Seminar Series, ICCCR, Universities of Manchester and Keele, United Kingdom.

Bacon, J. 1996. *Lifelines: Community, family, and assimilation among Asian Indian immigrants*. New York: Oxford University Press.

Bakhtin, M. M. 1981. Discourse in the novel. Pp. 259–422 in *The Dialogic Imagination: Four Essays by M. M. Bakhtin*, translated by C. Emerson and M. Holquist. Austin: University of Texas Press.

Banerjea, K., and P. Banerjea. 1996. Psyche and soul: A view from the 'South.' Pp. 105–24 in *Dis-Orienting rhythms: The politics of the new Asian dance music*, edited by S. Sharma, J. Hutnyk, and A. Sharma. London: Zed Press.

Bari, S. 1996. The lakshman rekha: A fable. Pp. 214–24 in *Contours of the heart: South Asians map North America*, edited by S. Maira and R. Srikanth. New York: Asian American Writers' Workshop.

Barth, F., ed. 1969. *Ethnic groups and boundaries: The social organization of cultural difference*. Boston: Little, Brown.

Basch, L., N. Glick Schiller, and C. Szanton Blanc, eds. 1994. *Nations unbound: Transnational projects, postcolonial predicaments, and deterritorialized nation-states*. Amsterdam: Gordon and Breach.

Battaglia, D. 1999. Comment at panel "Time out of Place: The Temporalities of Diaspora." 98th Annual Meeting of the American Anthropological Association, Chicago, November.

Baumann, G. 1996. *Contesting culture: Discourses of identity in multi-ethnic London*. Cambridge: Cambridge University Press.

Bell, C. 1997. *Ritual: Perspectives and dimensions*. New York: Oxford University Press.

Bhabha, H. 1990. Interview with Homi Bhabha: The third space. Pp. 207–21 in *Identity: Community, culture, difference*, edited by Jonathon Rutherford. London: Lawrence and Wishart.

———. 1994. *The location of culture*. London: Routledge.

Bhachu, P. 1988. *Apni marzi kardhi* home and work: Sikh women in Britain. Pp. 76–102 in *Enterprising women: Ethnicity, economy, and gender relations*, edited by S. Westwood and P. Bhachu. London: Routledge.

———. 1996. The multiple landscapes of transnational Asian women in the diaspora. In *Re-situating identities: The politics of race, ethnicity, and culture*, edited by V. Amit-Talai and C. Knowles. Peterborough, Ontario: Broadview.

Bhardwaj, S. M., and N. M. Rao. 1990. Asian Indians in the United States: A geographic appraisal. Pp. 197–217 in *South Asians overseas: Migration and ethnicity*, edited by C. Clarke, C. Peach, and S. Vertovec. Cambridge: Cambridge University Press.

Bhattacharjee, A. 1992. The habit of ex-nomination: Nation, woman, and the Indian immigrant bourgeoisie. *Public Culture* 5(1): 19–44.

————. 1997. The public/private mirage: Mapping homes and undomesticating violence work in the South Asian immigrant community. Pp. 308–29 in *Feminist genealogies, colonial legacies, democratic futures*, edited by M. J. Alexander and C. T. Mohanty. New York: Routledge.

Bourdieu, P. 1977/1994. Structures, habitus, power: Basis for a theory of symbolic power. Pp. 155–99 in *Culture/power/history: A reader in contemporary social theory*, edited by N. Dirks, G. Eley, and S. Ortner. Princeton: Princeton University Press.

Bourdieu, P. 1984. *Distinction: A social critique of the judgement of taste*, translated by R. Nice. Cambridge: Harvard University Press.

Brooks-Gunn, J., and E. O. Reiter. 1990. The role of pubertal processes. Pp. 16–53 in *At the threshold: The developing adolescent*, edited by S. S. Feldman and G. R. Elliott. Cambridge: Harvard University Press.

Brow, J. 1990. Notes on community, hegemony, and the uses of the past. *Anthropology Quarterly* 63(1): 1–6.

Brown, L. M., and C. Gilligan. 1992. *Meeting at the crossroads*. New York: Ballantine.

Brown, R. H. 1989a. The migrating self: Persons and polities in the process of modernization. *Studies in Third World Societies* 39: 1–11.

————. 1989b. Self and Polity in India and the United States: Some Philosophical Reflections and Field Observations. *Studies in Third World Societies* 38: 1–25.

Bruner, E. M. 1996. Tourism in the Balinese borderzone. Pp. 157–179 in *Displacement, diaspora, and geographies of identity*, edited by S. Lavie and T. Swedenburg. Durham and London: Duke University Press.

Butler, J. 1990. *Gender trouble: Feminism and the subversion of identity*. New York and London: Routledge.

————. 1996. Performativity's social magic. Pp. 29–47 in *The social and political body*, edited by T. R. Schatzki and W. Natter. New York: Guildford Press.

Caplan, P. 1987. Introduction. Pp. 1–30 in *The cultural construction of sexuality*, edited by P. Caplan. London: Tavistock.

Chakravarti, U. 1996. The myth of 'patriots' and 'traitors': Pandita Ramabai, Brahmanical patriarchy, and militant Hindu nationalism. Pp. 190–239 in *Embodied violence: Communalising women's sexuality in South Asia*, edited by K. Jayawardena and M. de Alwis. Atlantic Highlands, NJ and London: Zed Books.

Chandra, V. P. 1997. Remigration: The return of the prodigals—An analysis of the impact of cycles of migration and remigration on caste mobility. *International Migration Review* 31: 162–70.

Chatterjee, P. 1989. Colonialism, nationalism, and colonialized women: The contest in India. *American Ethnologist* 16(4): 622–33.

Christenson, P. G., and D. F. Roberts. *It's not only rock & roll: Popular music in the lives of adolescents*. Cresskill, NJ: Hampton Press, 1998.

Clarke, J., S. Hall, T. Jefferson, and B. Roberts. 1976. Subcultures, cultures, and class. Pp. 9–79 in *Resistance through rituals: Youth subcultures in post-war Britain*, edited by S. Hall and T. Jefferson. London: Hutchinson, in association with the Centre for Contemporary Cultural Studies, University of Birmingham.

Clifford, J. 1986a. On ethnographic allegory. Pp. 98–121 in *Writing culture: The poetics and politics of ethnography*, edited by J. Clifford and G. Marcus. Berkeley: University of California Press.

———. 1986b. Partial truths. Pp. 1–26 in *Writing culture: The poetics and politics of ethnography*, edited by J. Clifford and G. Marcus. Berkeley: University of California Press.

———. 1997. Diasporas. Pp. 283–90 in *The ethnicity reader: Nationalism, multiculturalism, and migration*, edited by M. Guibernau and J. Rex. Cambridge: Polity Press.

Cohen, P. 1997. *Rethinking the youth question: Education, labour, and cultural studies.* Durham: Duke University Press.

Cohen, S. 1997. Symbols of trouble. Pp. 149–62 in *The subcultures reader*, edited by K. Gelder and S. Thornton. London: Routledge.

Connell, R. W. 1995. *Masculinities*. Berkeley: University of California Press.

D'Andrade, R. 1984. Cultural meaning systems. Pp. 88–119 in *Culture theory: Essays of mind, self, and emotion*, edited by R. A. Shweder and R. A. LeVine. New York: Cambridge University Press.

———. 1992. Schemas and motivation. Pp. 23–44 in *Human motives and cultural models*, edited by R. D'Andrade and C. Strauss. Cambridge: Cambridge University Press.

Daniels, R. 1989. *History of Indian immigration to the United States: An interpretive essay.* New York: The Asia Society.

Das Dasgupta, S. Ed. 1998. *A patchwork shawl: Chronicles of South Asian women in America.* New Brunswick: Rutgers University Press.

Das Dasgupta, S., and S. Dasgupta. 1996. Women in exile: Gender relations in the Asian Indian community. Pp. 381–400 in *Contours of the heart: South Asians map North America*, edited by S. Maira and R. Srikanth. New York: Asian American Writers' Workshop.

Dasgupta, S. 1989. *On the trail of an uncertain dream: Asian Indian immigrant experience in America.* New York: AMS.

Davé, S., et al. 2000. "De-privileging Positions: Indian Americans, South Asian Americans, and the Politics of Asian American Studies." *Journal of Asian American Studies*, 3(1): 67–100.

de Certeau, M. 1984. *The practice of everyday life.* Berkeley: University of California Press.

de Groot, J. 1998. Coexisting and conflicting identities: Women and nationalisms in twentieth-century Iran. Pp. 139–65 in *Nation, empire, colony: Historicizing gender and race*, edited by R. Pierson and N. Chaudhuri. Bloomington: Indiana University Press.

Desai, P. N., and G. V. Coelho. 1980. Indian immigrants in America: Some cultural aspects of psychological adaptation. Pp. 363–86 in *The new ethnics: Asian Indians in the United States*, edited by P. Saran and E. Eames. New York: Praeger.

De Vos, G. A. 1978. Selective permeability and reference group sanctioning: Psychocultural continuities in role degradation. Pp. 7–24 in *Major social issues*, edited by M. Yinger and S. Cutler. New York: Free Press.

————. 1982. Ethnic pluralism: Conflict and accommodation. Pp. 5–41 in *Ethnic identity: Cultural continuity and change*, edited by G. De Vos and L. Romanucci-Ross. Chicago: University of Chicago Press.

————. 1990. Conflict and accommodation in ethnic interaction. Pp. 204–45 in *Status inequality: The self in culture*, edited by G. A. De Vos and M. Suárez-Orozco. Newbury Park: Sage.

di Leonardo, M., and R. N. Lancaster. 1997. Introduction: Embodied meanings, carnal practices. Pp. 1–10 in *The gender/sexuality reader: Culture, history, political economy*, edited by R. N. Lancaster and M. di Leonardo. New York: Routledge.

Dirks, N. 1994. Ritual and resistance: Subversion as a social fact. Pp. 483–503 in *Culture/power/history: A reader in contemporary social theory*, edited by N. Dirks, G. Ely, and S. Ortner. Princeton: Princeton University Press.

Dominguez, V. 2000. For a politics of love and rescue. *Cultural Anthropology* 15(3): 361–93.

Douglas, M. 1966. *Purity and danger: An analysis of the concepts of pollution and taboo*. London: Routledge.

Drew, J. 1989. Modes of marginality: Sociological reflections on the worldwide Indian diaspora. *Studies in Third World Societies* 39: 81–96.

Dugger, C. 1998. In India, an arranged marriage of two worlds. *New York Times*, July 20, A1, B6–B7.

Duncombe, S. 1988. Let's all be alienated together: Zines and the making of underground community. Pp. 427–51 in *Generations of youth: Youth cultures and history in twentieth-century America*, edited by J. Austin and M. Willard. New York: New York University Press.

Durham, M. G. 1999. Effing the Ineffable: U.S. media and images of Asian femininity. Pp. 75–92 in *Asian Pacific American Genders and Sexualities*, edited by T. K. Nakayama. Tempe, Ariz.: Arizona State University.

Eckert, P. 1989. *Jocks and burnouts: Social categories and identity in the high school*. New York: Teachers College Press.

Epstein, J. S. 1998. Introduction: Generation X, youth culture, and identity. Pp. 1–23 in *Youth culture: Identity in a postmodern world*, edited by J. Epstein. Malden, MA: Blackwell.

Erikson, E. H. 1968. *Identity: Youth and crisis*. New York and London: W. W. Norton and Company (1994 edition).

Esser, D. et al. 1999. Reorganizing organizing: Immigrant labor in North America —Interview with New York Taxi Workers' Alliance. *Amerasia (Special Issue— Satyagraha in America: The political culture of South Asians in the U.S.* Eds. Biju Mathew and Vijay Prashad) 25(3): 171–181.

Espiritu, Y. L. 1992. *Asian American panethnicity: Bridging institutions and identities*. Philadelphia: Temple University Press.

Feld, S. 1988. Notes on world beat. *Public Culture Bulletin* 1(1): 31–37.

Fernandes, N. 2000. Goa trance. *Man's World*, June.

Fernandez, M., and W. T. Liu. 1989. Asian Indians in the United States: Economic, educational, and family profiles from the 1980 census. *Studies in Third World Societies* 38: 149–79.

Fernández-Kelly, P., and R. Schauffler. 1994. Divided fates: Immigrant children in a restructured U.S. economy. *International Migration Review* 28(4): 662–689.

Fischer, M. 1986. Ethnicity and the post-modern arts of memory. Pp. 194–233 in *Writing culture: The poetics and politics of ethnography*, edited by J. Clifford and G. Marcus. Berkeley: University of California Press.

Fisher, M. P. 1980. *The Indians of New York City: A study of immigrants from India*. New Delhi: Heritage.

Flores, J. 2000. *From bomba to hip hop, 2000*. New York: Columbia University Press.

Fox, R. G. 1996. Gandhi and feminized nationalism in India. Pp. 37–49 in *Women out of place: The gender of agency and the race of nationality*, edited by B. Williams. New York: Routledge.

Fregoso, R. L. 1999. Re-imagining Chicana urban identities in the public sphere, cool chuca style. Pp. 72–91 in *Between woman and nation: Nationalisms, transnational feminisms, and the state*, edited by C. Kaplan, N. Alarcon, and M. Moallem. Durham: Duke University Press.

Frith, S. 1992. The cultural study of popular music. Pp. 174–86 in *Cultural studies*, edited by L. Grossberg, C. Nelson, and P. A. Treichler. New York: Routledge.

Frith, S. 1997. Formalism, realism, and leisure: The case of punk. Pp. 163–174 in *The subcultures reader*, edited by K. Gelder and S. Thornton. London: Routledge.

Fruzetti, L. 1982. *The gift of a virgin: Women, marriage, and ritual in a Bengali society*. New Brunswick: Rutgers University Press.

Galang, M. E. 1996. *Her wild American self*. Minneapolis: Coffee House Press.

Gans, H. 1979. Symbolic ethnicity: The future of ethnic groups and cultures in America. *Ethnic and Racial Studies* 2(1): 1–20.

———. 1992. Second-generation decline: Scenarios for the economic and ethnic futures of the post-1965 American immigrants. *Ethnic and Racial Studies* 15(2): 173–92.

Garcia, C. 1992. *Dreaming in Cuban*. New York: Ballantine.

Gelder, K. 1997. Introduction to part three. Pp. 145–48 in *The subcultures reader*, edited by K. Gelder and S. Thornton. New York: Routledge.

George, N. 1998. *Hip hop America*. New York: Penguin.

George, R. M. 1997. "From expatriate aristocrat to immigrant nobody": South Asian racial strategies in the Southern California context. *Diaspora* 6(1): 31–60.

Ghosh, A. 1989. The diaspora in Indian culture. *Public Culture* 2(1): 73–78.

Gibson, M. A. 1988. *Accommodation without assimilation: Sikh immigrants in an American high school*. Ithaca: Cornell University Press.

Gibson, M. A., and P. K. Bhachu. 1991. The dynamics of educational decision making: A comparative study of Sikhs in Britain and the United States. Pp. 63–95 in *Minority status and schooling: A comparative study of immigrant and involuntary minorities*, edited by M. A. Gibson and J. U. Ogbu. New York: Garland.

Gillespie, M. 1995. *Television, ethnicity, and cultural change*. London, New York: Routledge.

Gilroy, P. 1993. *The black Atlantic: Modernity and double consciousness*. Cambridge: Harvard University Press.

Giroux, H. A. 1996. White panic and the racial coding of violence, and Racism and the aesthetic of hyper-real violence: Pulp Fiction and other visual Tragedies. Pp. 27–54 and 55–88 in *Fugitive cultures: Race, violence, and youth*. New York: Routledge.

Glazer, N. & Moynihan, D. P. 1963. *Beyond the melting pot: the Negroes, Puerto Ricans, Jews, Italians, and Irish of New York City*. Cambridge, Mass: M.I.T. Press and Harvard University Press.

Glazer, N., and D. P. Moynihan. 1975. *Ethnicity: Theory and experience*. Cambridge: Harvard University Press.

Goddard, V. 1987. Honour and shame: The control of women's sexuality and group identity in Naples. Pp. 166–92 in *The cultural construction of sexuality*, edited by P. Caplan. London: Tavistock.

Goodstein, L. 1998. At camps, young U.S. Sikhs cling to heritage. *New York Times*, July 18, A1–A7.

Gopinath, G. 1995a. "Bombay, U.K., Yuba City": Bhangra music and the engendering of diaspora. *Diaspora* 4(3): 303–21.

———. 1995b. Notes on a queer South Asian planet: Gayatri Gopinath on queer transnational cultures. *Rungh: A South Asian Quarterly of Culture, Comment & Criticism* 3(3): 9–10.

———. 1997. Nostalgia, desire, diaspora: South Asian sexualities in motion. *Positions: East Asia Cultures Critique* 5(2): 468–89.

Gourevitch, P. 1999. A husband for Dil: Can tradition make a young woman happy? *New Yorker*, February 22–March 1, pp. 78, 80, 93–94, 98–102.

Grasmuck, S., and P. Pessar. 1991. *Between two islands: Dominican international migration*. Berkeley: University of California Press.

Greeley, A. 1974. *Ethnicity in the United States: A preliminary reconnaissance*. New York: John Wiley.

Grewal, I., and C. Kaplan. 1994. Introduction: Transnational feminist practices and questions of postmodernity. Pp. 1–33 in *Scattered hegemonies: Postmodernity and transnational feminist practices*, edited by I. Grewal and C. Kaplan. Minneapolis: University of Minnesota Press.

Griffin, C. 1993. *Representations of youth: The study of youth and adolescence in Britain and America*. Cambridge: Polity Press.

Grimberg, S., and D. Friedman, directors. 1997. *Miss India, Georgia*. Videocassette, 56 min. Urban Life Productions.

Grossberg, L. 1992. *We gotta get out of this place: Popular conservatism and popular culture*. New York: Routledge.

———. 1996. Toward a genealogy of the state of cultural studies: The discipline of communication and the reception of cultural studies in the United States. Pp. 131–69 in *Disciplinarity and dissent in cultural studies*, edited by C. Nelson and D. P. Gaonkar. New York: Routledge.

Grover, S. 1996. The malady back home hurts the diaspora too. *Communalism Combat* (November): 20–21.

Guibernau, M., and J. Rex. 1997. Introduction: The growing importance of the concept of ethnicity. Pp. 1–11 in *The ethnicity reader: Nationalism, multiculturalism, and migration*, edited by M. Guibernau and J. Rex. Cambridge: Polity Press.

Gupta, A. 1998. At the crossroads: College activism and its impact on Asian American identity formation. Pp. 127–145 in *A part, yet apart: South Asians in Asian America*, edited by L. D. Shankar and R. Srikanth. Philadelphia: Temple University Press.

Gupta, A., and J. Ferguson. 1997. After "peoples and cultures." Pp. 1–29 in *Culture, power, place: Explorations in critical anthropology*, edited by A. Gupta and J. Ferguson. Durham: Duke University Press.

Gupta, S., ed. 1999. *Emerging voices: South Asian American women redefine self, family, and community*. New Delhi: Sage.

Hale, S. 1991. Feminist process and self-criticism: Interviewing Sudanese women. Pp. 121–36 in *Women's words: The feminist practice of oral history*, edited by S. Gluck and D. Patai. New York: Routledge.

Hall, K. 1995. "There's a time to act English and a time to act Indian": The politics of identity among British-Sikh teenagers. Pp. 243–264 in *Children and the politics of culture*, edited by S. Stephens. Princeton, NJ: Princeton University Press.

Hall, P. A. 1997. African American music: Dynamics of appropriation and innovation. Pp. 31–51 in *Borrowed power: Essays on cultural appropriation*, edited by B. Ziff and P. V. Rao. New Brunswick: Rutgers University Press.

Hall, S. 1990. Cultural identity and diaspora. Pp. 222–237 in *Identity: Community, culture, difference*, edited by Jonathan Rutherford. London: Lawrence and Wishart.

Hall, S. 1997. The local and the global: Globalization and ethnicity. Pp. 173–187 in *The local and the global: Globalization and ethnicity*, edited by A. McClintock, A. Mufti, and E. Shohat. Minneapolis: University of Minnesota Press.

Hall, S. 1996. New ethnicities. Pp. 441–49 in *Stuart Hall: Critical dialogues in cultural studies*, edited by D. Morley and K. H. Chen.

Hannerz, U. 1996. *Transnational connections: Culture, people, places*. London and New York: Routledge.

Hardt, M., and A. Negri. 2000. *Empire*. Cambridge, Mass.: Harvard University Press.

Harvey, D. 1989. *The condition of postmodernity*. Cambridge, Mass.: Blackwell.

Hasnat, N. 1998. Being "Amreekan": Fried chicken versus chicken tikka. Pp. 33–45 in *A patchwork shawl: Chronicles of South Asian women in America*, edited by S. Das Dasgupta. New Brunswick: Rutgers University Press.

Hastrup, K., and K. Olwig. 1997. Introduction. Pp. 1–14 in *Siting culture: The shifting anthropological object*, edited by K. Olwig and K. Hastrup. London: Routledge.

Hebdige, D. 1979. *Subculture: The Meaning of Style*. London: Methuen.

Heller, M. 1987. The role of language in the formation of ethnic identity. Pp. 180–200 in *Children's ethnic socialization: Pluralism and development*, edited by J. S. Phinney and M. J. Rotheram. Newbury Park: Sage.

Helweg, A., and U. Helweg. 1990. *An immigrant success story: East Indians in America*. Philadelphia: University of Pennsylvania Press.

Hess, G. 1976. The forgotten Asian American: The East Indian community in the United States, Pp. 157–177 in *The Asian American: The historical experience*, edited by N. Hundley, Jr. Santa Barbara, CA: Clio Books.

Hing, B. H. 1993. *Making and remaking Asian America through immigration policy, 1850–1990*. Stanford: Stanford University Press.

Hirschman, C. 1994. Problems and prospects of studying immigrant adaptation from the 1990 population census: From generational comparisons to the process of "becoming American." *International Migration Review* 28(4): 690–713.

Hoch, Danny. *Jails, Hospitals, and Hip Hop*. Videotape of performance courtesy of New WORLD Theater, University of Massachusetts, Amherst.

Hong, J., and P. G. Min. 1999. *Ethnic attachment among second generation Korean adolescents*. Amerasia Journal 25(1): 165–178.

hooks, b. 1997. Sisterhood: Political solidarity between women. Pp. 396–411 in *Dangerous liaisons: Gender, nation, and postcolonial perspectives*, edited by A. McClintock, A. Mufti, and S. Shohat. Minneapolis: University of Minnesota Press.

Hossain, M. 1982. South Asians in Southern California: A sociological study of immigrants from India, Pakistan, and Bangladesh. *South Asia Bulletin* 2(1): 74–83.

Hutnyk, J. 1999/2000. Hybridity saves: Authenticity and/or the critique of appropriation. *Amerasia Journal* 25(3): 39–58.

Ivy, M. 1998. Mourning the Japanese thing. Pp. 93–118 in *In Near Ruins: Cultural Theory at the End of the Century*, ed. Nicholas Dirks. Minneapolis: University of Minnesota Press.

Jain, U. R. 1989. *The Gujaratis of San Francisco*. New York: AMS.

Jana, R. 2000. Arranged marriages, minus the parents. *New York Times: Circuits*, August 17, G1, G10.

Jayawardena, K., and M. de Alwis. 1996. Introduction. Pp. ix–xxiv in *Embodied violence: Communalising women's sexuality in South Asia*, edited by K. Jayawardena and M. de Alwis. London: Zed Books.

Jen, G. 1996. *Mona in the promised land*. New York: Alfred A. Knopf.

Jensen, J. 1988. *Passage from India: Asian Indian immigrants in North America*. New Haven: Yale University Press.

Jessor, R. 1996. Ethnographic methods in contemporary perspective. Pp. 1–14 in *Ethnography and human development*, edited by R. Jessor, A. Colby, and R. A. Shweder. Chicago: University of Chicago Press.

Jones, E. E., and S. J. Korchin. 1982. Minority mental health: Perspectives. Pp. 3–36 in *Minority mental health*, edited by E. E. Jones and S. J. Korchin. New York: Praeger.

Kalita, S. M. 1999. Discovering India: An Asian American goes in search of her roots. *Asianweek*, May 20, pp. 15–17.

Kanaganayakam, C. 1995. *Configurations of exile: South Asian writers and their world*. Toronto: TSAR.

Kandiyoti, D. 1994. Identity and its discontents: Women and the nation. Pp. 376–91 in *Colonial discourse and post-colonial theory*, edited by P. Williams and L. Chrisman. New York: Columbia University Press.

Kaplan, C. 1996. Postmodern geographies: Feminist politics of location. Pp. 143–187 in *Questions of travel*. Durham: Duke University Press.

Kaplan, C., N. Alarcon, and M. Moallem, eds. 1999. *Between woman and nation: Nationalisms, transnational feminisms, and the state*. Durham: Duke University Press.

Katchadourian, H. 1990. Sexuality. Pp. 330–51 in *At the threshold: The developing adolescent*, edited by S. S. Feldman and G. R. Elliott. Cambridge: Harvard University Press.

Keating, D. P. 1990. Adolescent thinking. Pp. 54–89 in *At the threshold: The developing adolescent*, edited by S. S. Feldman and G. R. Elliott. Cambridge, Mass.: Harvard University Press.

Kelley, R. D. G. 1997. *Yo' mama's disfunktional! Fighting the culture wars in urban America*. Boston: Beacon Press.

Kelley, R. 1999. People in me. *ColorLines* 1(3): 5–7.

Khagram, S., M. Desai, and J. Varughese. 2001. Seen, rich, but unheard? The politics of Asian Indians in the United States. Pp. 258–284 in *Asian Americans and politics: Perspectives, experiences, prospects*, edited by G. H. Chang. Washington, D.C.: Woodrow Wilson Press.

Khan, A. 1995. Homeland, motherland: Authenticity, legitimacy, and ideologies of place among Muslims in Trinidad. Pp. 93–131 in *Nation and migration: The politics of space in the South Asian diaspora*, edited by P. van der Veer. Philadelphia: University of Pennsylvania Press.

Khan, S. 1998. Sexual exiles. Pp. 62–72 in *A patchwork shawl: Chronicles of South Asian women in America*, edited by S. Das Dasgupta. New Brunswick: Rutgers University Press.

Khandelwal, M. S. 1995. Indian immigrants in Queens, New York City: Patterns of spatial concentration and distribution, 1965–1990. Pp. 178–96 in *Nation and migration: The politics of space in the South Asian diaspora*, edited by P. van der Veer. Philadelphia: University of Pennsylvania Press.

Kibria, N. 1993. *Family tightrope: The changing lives of Vietnamese Americans*. Princeton: Princeton University Press.

———. 1999. College and notions of "Asian American": Second generation Chinese and Korean Americans negotiate race and identity. *Amerasia Journal* 25(1): 29–51.

Kim, K. C., and W. M. Hurh. 1993. Beyond assimilation and pluralism: Syncretic sociocultural adaptation of Korean immigrants in the U.S. *Ethnic and Racial Studies* 16(4): 696–713.

Kirschner, T. 1998. Studying rock: Towards a materialist ethnography. Pp. 247–68 in *Mapping the beat: Popular music and contemporary theory*, edited by T. Swiss, J. Sloop, and A. Herman. Malden, MA: Blackwell.

Kitano, H. H. 1980. *Race relations*. Englewood Cliffs, NJ: Prentice-Hall.

Kleinfeld, N. R. 2000. Guarding the borders of the hip-hop nation: In the 'hood and in the burbz, white money feeds rap. True believers fear selling out. *New York Times*, July 6, A1, A18–A19.

Knauft, B. 1996. *Genealogies for the present in cultural anthropology*. New York: Routledge.

Kondo, D. 1995. Bad girls: Theater, women of color, and the politics of representation. Pp. 49–64 in *Women writing culture*, edited by R. Behar and D. A. Gordon. Berkeley: University of California Press.

———. 1996. The narrative production of "home," community, and political identity in Asian American theater. Pp. 97–117 in *Displacement, diaspora, and geogra-*

phies of identity, edited by S. Lavie and T. Swedenburg. Durham: Duke University Press.

Kumar, A. 2000. *Passport photos.* Berkeley: University of California Press.

LaFeber, W. 1999. *Michael Jordan and the new global capitalism.* New York: W. W. Norton.

Lancaster, R. 1997. Guto's performance: Notes on the transvestism of everyday life. Pp. 559–74 in *The gender/sexuality reader,* edited by R. Lancaster and M. di Leonardo. New York: Routledge.

Lancaster, R., and M. di Leonardo, eds. 1997. *The gender/sexuality reader.* New York: Routledge.

Lavie, S., and T. Swedenburg. 1996. Introduction. Pp. 1–25 in *Displacement, diaspora, and geographies of identity,* edited by S. Lavie and T. Swedenburg. Durham: Duke University Press.

Leblanc, L. 1999. *Pretty in punk: Girls' gender resistance in a boys' subculture.* New Brunswick: Rutgers University Press.

Lee, C. R. 1995. *Native speaker.* New York: Riverhead Books.

Lee, S. 1996. *Unraveling the "model minority" stereotype: Listening to Asian American youth.* New York: Teachers College Press, Columbia University.

Leonard, K. I. 1992. *Making ethnic choices: California's Punjabi Mexican Americans.* Philadelphia: Temple University Press.

———. 1997. *The South Asian Americans.* Westport, Conn.: Greenwood Press.

———. 1999. The management of desire: Sexuality and marriage for young South Asian women in America. Pp. 107–119 in *Emerging voices: South Asian American women redefine self, family, and community,* edited by S. Gupta. New Delhi: Sage.

Lessinger, J. 1995. *From the Ganges to the Hudson: Indian immigrants in New York City.* Boston: Allyn and Bacon.

Lipsitz, G. 1994. *Dangerous crossroads: Popular music, postmodernism, and the poetics of place.* London: Verso.

Little India Business Directory. 1997–1998. Reading, PA: Little India Publications.

Lorde, A. 1997. Age, race, class, and sex: Women redefining difference. Pp. 374–80 in *Dangerous liaisons: Gender, nation, and postcolonial perspectives,* edited by A. McClintock, A. Mufti, and S. Shohat. Minneapolis: University of Minnesota Press.

Lowe, L. 1996. *Immigrant acts: On Asian American cultural politics.* Durham: Duke University Press.

Mageo, J. M. 1995. The reconfiguring self. *American Anthropologist* 97(2): 282–96.

Mahler, S. J. 1995. *American dreaming: Immigrant life on the margins.* Princeton, NJ: Princeton University Press.

Maira, S. 1995. Ethnic identity development of second-generation Indian American adolescents: A literature review. Unpublished qualifying paper, Harvard Graduate School of Education.

———. 1998. Desis reprazent: Bhangra remix and hip hop in New York City. *Post-Colonial Studies,* special issue edited by John Hutnyk and Virinder Kalra, 1(3): 357–70.

————. 1999. The politics of "cool": Indian American youth culture in New York City. Pp. 177–193 in *The geography of encounters : Asians in the Americas,* edited by R. Rustomji-Kerns, R. Srikanth, and L. Strobel. Boulder, CO: Rowman & Littlefield.

————. 2000a. Henna and hip hop: The politics of cultural production and the work of cultural studies. *Journal of Asian American Studies* 3(3): 329–69.

————. 2000b. Ideologies of authenticity: Youth, nationalism, and diaspora. *Amerasia Journal—Satyagraha in America: The Political Culture of South Asian Americans,* special issue edited by Vijay Prashad and Biju Mathew, 25(3): 139–49.

Maira, S., and P. Levitt. 1997. Variations on transnationalism: Preliminary lessons from Gujarati immigrant experiences in Massachusetts. Paper presented at symposium on "Globalization and South Asia," 26th Annual Conference on South Asia, University of Wisconsin, Madison.

Maira, S., and R. Srikanth, eds. 1996. *Contours of the heart: South Asians map North America.* New York: Asian American Writers' Workshop.

Malkii, L. H. 1995. *Purity and exile: Violence, memory, and national cosmology among Hutu refugees in Tanzania.* Chicago: University of Chicago Press.

Mani, L. 1986. The production of an official discourse on sati in early nineteenth-century Bengal. *Economic and Political Weekly: Review of Women's Studies* (April): 32–40.

————. 1987. Contentious traditions: The debate on sati in colonial India. *Cultural Critique* 7: 119–56.

————. 1993. Gender, class, and cultural conflict: Indu Krishnan's *Knowing her place.* Pp. 32–36 in *Our feet walk the sky: Women of the South Asian diaspora,* edited by the Women of South Asia Descent Collective. San Francisco: Aunt Lute Books.

Marcus, G. 1998. Anthropology on the move. Pp. 3–29 in *Ethnography through thick and thin.* Princeton: Princeton University Press.

Massey, D. 1994. *Space, place, and gender.* Minneapolis: University of Minnesota Press.

Mathew, B., and V. Prashad. 1996. The saffron dollar: *Pehle paisa, phir bhagwan. Himal South Asia* (September): 38–42.

Mazumdar, S. 1982. Punjabi immigration to California in the context of capitalist development. *South Asia Bulletin* 2(1): 19–28.

————. 1989. Racist responses to racism: The Aryan myth and South Asians in the United States. *South Asia Bulletin* 9(1): 47–55.

McAllister, C. 1996. Authenticity and Guatemala's Maya queen. Pp. 105–24 in *Beauty queens and the global stage: Gender, contests, and power,* edited by C. Cohen, R. Wilk, & B. Stoeltje. New York: Routledge.

McRobbie, A. 1991. *Feminism and youth culture: From Jackie to Just Seventeen.* London: Macmillan.

————. 1994. New times in cultural studies. Pp. 24–43 in *Postmodernism and popular culture.* London: Routledge.

————. 1999. *In the culture society: Art, fashion, and popular music.* London: Routledge.

————, ed. 1997. *Back to reality: Social experience and cultural studies.* Manchester: Manchester University Press.

Mead M. 1961. *Coming of age in Samoa.* 3d ed. New York: William Morrow.

Meer, A. 1994. *Bombay talkie.* New York: High Risk Books.

Mehta, G. 1979. *Karma cola: Marketing the mystic East.* New York: Simon and Schuster.

Melnick, J. 1996. R 'n' B skeletons in the closet: The men of doo wop. *Minnesota Review* 47: 217–29.

Melwani, L. 1995. Voyage of rediscovery. *Little India* 5(6): 10–23.

Melwani, L. 1996. Living on the edge. *India Today: North American Special,* May 15: 60b–60c.

Mercer, K. 1987. Black hair/style politics. *New Formations* 3: 33–54.

Miller, B. 1995. Precepts and practices: Researching identity formation among Indian Hindu adolescents in the United States. Pp. 71–85 in *Cultural practices as contexts for development,* edited by J. J. Goodnow and P. J. Miller. San Francisco: Jossey-Bass.

Miller, D. 1995. Consumption as the Vanguard of History. Pp. 1–57 in *Acknowledging Consumption: A Review of New Studies,* edited by Daniel Miller. London: Routledge.

Minoura, Y. 1992. A sensitive period for the incorporation of a cultural meaning system: A study of Japanese children growing up in the United States. *Ethos* 20(3): 304–39.

Mishler, E. G. 1986. *Research interviewing: Context and narrative.* Cambridge: Harvard University Press.

———. 1996. Missing persons: Recovering developmental stories/histories. Pp. 73–99 in *Ethnography and human development,* edited by R. Jessor, A. Colby, and R. A. Shweder. Chicago: University of Chicago Press.

Misir, D. N. 1996. The murder of Navroze Mody: Race, violence, and the search for order. *Amerasia* 22(2): 55–75.

Miss India, Georgia. 1997. Prod. and dir. Daniel Friedman and Sharon Grimberg, 56 min., Urban Life Productions, videocassette.

Mohanty, C. T. 1997. Under Western eyes: Feminist scholarship and colonial discourses. Pp. 255–77 in *Dangerous liaisons: Gender, nation, and postcolonial perspectives,* edited by A. McClintock, A. Mufti, and S. Shohat. Minneapolis: University of Minnesota Press.

Moffatt, M. 1989. *Coming of age in New Jersey: College and American culture.* New Brunswick: Rutgers University Press.

Mollenkopf, J., and M. Castells, eds. 1991. *Dual city: Restructuring New York.* New York: Russell Sage Foundation.

Morrison, T. 1994. On the backs of Blacks. Pp. 97–100 in *Arguing immigration,* edited by N. Mills. New York: Touchstone.

Mukhi, S. M. 1996. Guess who's coming to dinner. *Little India* 6(5): 49–54.

———. 2000. *Doing the desi thing: Performing Indianness in New York City.* New York: Garland.

Narayan, K. 1993. How native is a "native" anthropologist? *American Anthropologist* 95(3): 671–86.

Nonini, D., and A. Ong. 1997. Chinese transnationalism as an alternative modernity. Pp. 3–33 in *Ungrounded empires: The cultural politics of modern Chinese transnationalism,* edited by A. Ong and D. Nonini. New York: Routledge.

Novak, M. 1971. *The rise of the unmeltable ethnics: Politics and culture in the seventies.* New York: Macmillan.

Nunez, S. 1995. *A feather on the breath of God.* New York: HarperCollins.

O'Connor, A. 1996. The problem of American cultural studies. Pp. 187–196 in *What is cultural studies? A reader,* edited by John Storey. London and New York: Arnold.

Ogbu, J. 1978. *Minority education and caste: The American system in cross-cultural perspective.* New York: Academic Press.

Okihiro, G. 1994. Is yellow black or white? Pp. 31–63 in *Margins and mainstreams: Asians in American history and culture.* Seattle: University of Washington Press.

Olwig, K. 1997. Cultural sites: Sustaining a home in a deterritorialized world. Pp. 17–38 in *Siting culture: The shifting anthropological object,* edited by K. Hastrup and K. Olwig. London: Routledge.

Omi, M., and H. Winant. 1994. *Racial formation in the United States: From the 1960s to the 1990s.* 2d ed. New York: Routledge.

Ong, A. 1999. *Flexible citizenship: The cultural logics of transnationality.* Durham: Duke University Press.

Ortner, S. B. 1974. Is female to male as nature is to culture? Pp. 67–87 in *Woman, culture, and society,* edited by M. Rosaldo and L. Lamphere. Stanford: Stanford University Press.

———. 1991. Reading America: Preliminary notes on class and culture. Pp. 163–89 in *Recapturing anthropology: Working in the present,* edited by R. Fox. Santa Fe: School of American Research Press.

———. 1994. Theory in anthropology since the sixties. Pp. 372–411 in *Culture/power/history,* edited by N. Dirks, G. Ely, and S. Ortner. Princeton: Princeton University Press.

———. 1996. *Making gender: The politics and erotics of culture.* Boston: Beacon Press.

Osajima, K. 1988. Asian Americans as the model minority: An analysis of the popular press image in the 1960s and 1980s. Pp. 165–74 in *Reflections on shattered windows: Promises and prospects for Asian American studies,* edited by G. Okihiro et al. Pullman: Washington State University Press.

Pais, A. 2000. A cry for help. *India Today International,* May 8, pp. 40c–40d.

Palumbo-Liu, D. 1999. *Asian/American: Historical crossings of a racial frontier.* Stanford: Stanford University Press.

Park, K. 1999. "I really do feel I'm 1.5": The construction of self and community by young Korean Americans." *Amerasia Journal* 25(1): 139–63.

Parker, A., M. Russo, D. Sommer, and P. Yaeger, eds. 1992. Introduction. Pp. 1–18 in *Nationalisms and sexualities,* edited by A. Parker et al. New York: Routledge.

Patterson, O. 1977. *Ethnic chauvinism: The reactionary impulse.* New York: Stein & Day.

Perkins, W. E. 1996. The rap attack: An introduction. Pp. 1–45 in *Droppin' science: Critical essays on rap music and hip hop culture,* edited by W. E. Perkins. Philadelphia: Temple University Press.

Perlman, J., and R. Waldinger. 1997. Second generation decline? Children of immigrants, past and present—A reconsideration. *International Migration Review* 31(4): 893–922.

Pfister, J. 1996. The Americanization of cultural studies. Pp. 287–99 in *What is cultural studies?* edited by J. Storey. London: Arnold.

Pini, M. 1997. Women and the early British rave scene. Pp. 152–69 in *Back to reality? Social experience and cultural studies,* edited by A. McRobbie. Manchester: Manchester University Press.

Portes, A., ed. 1994. The new second generation. Special issue of *International Migration Review* 28(4).

———. 1995. Transnational communities: Their emergence and significance in the contemporary world system. The Johns Hopkins University Program in Comparative and International Development Working Paper Series, No. 16. Baltimore: Johns Hopkins University.

———. 1997. Immigration theory for a new century: Some problems and opportunities. *International Migration Review* 31(4): 799–825.

Portes, A., and M. Zhou. 1993. The new second generation: Segmented assimilation and its variants among post-1965 immigrant youth. *Annals of the American Academy of Political and Social Science* 530: 74–98.

Prashad, V. 1996. Desh: The contradictions of 'homeland.' Pp. 225–36 in *Contours of the heart: South Asians map North America,* edited by S. Maira and R. Srikanth. New York: Asian American Writers' Workshop.

———. 2000. *The karma of brown folk.* Minneapolis: University of Minnesota.

Probyn, Elspeth. 1999. Bloody metaphors and other allegories of the ordinary. Pp. 47–62 in *Between woman and nation: Nationalisms, transnational feminisms, and the state,* edited by C. Kaplan, N. Alarcon, and M. Moallem. Durham: Duke University Press.

Puri, J. 1999. *Woman, body, desire in post-colonial India: Narrating gender and sexuality.* New York: Routledge.

Radhakrishnan, R. 1992. Nationalism, gender, and the narrative of identity. Pp. 77–95 in *Nationalisms and sexualities,* edited by A. Parker et al. New York: Routledge.

Rajagopal, A. 1998. Being Hindu in the diaspora. *SAMAR (South Asian Magazine for Action and Reflection)* (9): 15–21.

Ramirez, M., III. 1984. Assessing and understanding biculturalism-multiculturalism in Mexican-American adults. Pp. 77–94 in *Chicano Psychology,* edited by J. L. Martinez Jr. and R. H. Mendoza. 2d ed. Orlando: Academic Press.

Ramirez, M., III, B. G. Cox, and A. Castaneda. 1977. *The psychodynamics of biculturalism.* Prepared for Organizational Effectiveness Research Programs, Office of Naval Research. Santa Cruz, CA: Systems and Evaluations in Education.

Ratti, R., ed. 1993. *A lotus of another color: An unfolding of the South Asian gay and lesbian experience.* Boston: Alyson.

Roediger, D. 1998. What to make of Wiggers: A work in progress. Pp. 358–366 in *Generations of Youth: Youth cultures and history in twentieth-century America,* edited by J. Austin and M. N. Willard. New York: New York University Press.

Rogers, A. 1991. A feminist poetics of psychotherapy. Pp. 33–53 in *Women, girls, and psychotherapy: Reframing resistance,* edited by C. Gilligan, A. Rogers, and D. Tolman. Binghamton, NY: Harrington Park Press.

———. 1992. Marguerite Sechehaye and Renee: A feminist reading of two accounts of a treatment. *Qualitative Studies in Education* 5(3): 245–51.

Roland, A. 1989. The Indian self: Reflections in the mirror of American life. *Studies in Third World Societies* 38: 43–52.

Rooney, E. 1996. Discipline and vanish: Feminism, the resistance to theory, and the politics of cultural studies. Pp. 208–220 in *What is cultural studies?* edited by J. Storey. London: Arnold.

Roosens, E. 1989. *Creating ethnicity: The process of ethnogenesis.* Newbury Park: Sage.

Rosaldo, M. 1974. Woman, culture, and society: A theoretical overview. Pp. 17–42 in *Woman, culture, and society,* edited by M. Rosaldo and L. Lamphere. Stanford: Stanford University Press.

Rosaldo, M., and L. Lamphere. 1974. Introduction. Pp. 1–16 in *Woman, culture, and society,* edited by M. Rosaldo and L. Lamphere. Stanford: Stanford University Press.

Rosaldo, R. 1997. Cultural citizenship, inequality, and multiculturalism. Pp. 27–38 in *Latino cultural citizenship: Claiming identity, space, and rights,* edited by W. F. Flores and R. Benmayor. Boston: Beacon Press.

Rose, T. 1994a. *Black noise: Rap music and black culture in contemporary America.* Hanover, NH: Wesleyan/University Press of New England.

———. 1994b. A style nobody can deal with: Politics, style and the postindustrial city in hip hop. Pp. 71–88 in *Microphone fiends: Youth music and youth culture,* edited by A. Ross and T. Rose. New York: Routledge.

Rosenthal, D. A. 1987. Ethnic identity development in adolescents. Pp. 156–79 in *Children's ethnic socialization: Pluralism and development,* edited by J. S. Phinney and M. J. Rotheram, eds. Newbury Park: Sage.

Ross, A. 1994. Tribalism in effect. Pp. 284–299 in *On Fashion,* edited by S. Benstock and S. Ferriss. New Brunswick, NJ: Rutgers University Press.

Ross, E., and R. Rapp. 1997. Sex and society: A research note from social history and anthropology. Pp. 153–68 in *The gender/sexuality reader: Culture, history, political economy,* edited by R. N. Lancaster and M. di Leonardo. New York: Routledge.

Rotheram, M. J., and J. S. Phinney. 1987. Introduction: Definitions and perspectives in the study of children's ethnic socialization. Pp. 10–28 in *Children's ethnic socialization: Pluralism and development,* edited by J. S. Phinney and M. J. Rotheram. Newbury Park: Sage.

Rouse, R. 1992. Making sense of settlement: Class transformation, cultural struggle, and transnationalism among Mexican migrants in the United States. In *Towards a transnational perspective on migration: Race, class, ethnicity, and nationalism reconsidered,* edited by N. Glick Schiller, L. Basch, and C. Szanton Blanc. New York: New York Academy of Sciences.

Roy, M. 1998. Mothers and daughters in Indian American families: A failed communication. Pp. 97–110 in *A patchwork shawl: Chronicles of South Asian women in America,* edited by S. Das Dasgupta. New Brunswick: Rutgers University Press.

Royce, A. P. 1982. *Ethnic identity: Strategies of diversity.* Bloomington: Indiana University Press.

Rumbaut, R. G. 1994. The crucible within: Ethnic identity, self-esteem, and segmented assimilation among children of immigrants. *International Migration Review* 8(4): 748–93.

Russell, J. 1992. Race and reflexivity: The Black Other in contemporary Japanese Mass culture. Pp. 296–318 in *Rereading cultural anthropology*, edited by G. Marcus. Durham: Duke University Press.

Said, E. 1978. *Orientalism*. New York: Vintage.

Safran, W. 1991. Diasporas in modern societies: Myths of homeland and return. *Diaspora* 1(1): 83–99.

Sangari, K., and S. Vaid. 1989. Introduction. Pp. 1–26 in *Recasting women: Essays in colonial history*, edited by K. Sangari and S. Vaid. New Delhi: Kali for Women.

Sansone, L. 1995. The making of a Black youth culture: Lower-class young men of Surinamese origin in Amsterdam. Pp. 114–143 in *Youth Cultures: A Cross-Cultural Perspective*, edited by V. Amit-Talai and H. Wulff. London: Routledge.

Saran, P. 1985. *The Asian Indian experience in the United States*. Cambridge: Schenkman.

Saran, P., and E. Eames, eds. 1980. *The new ethnics: Asian Indians in the United States*. New York: Praeger.

Sardiello, R. 1998. Identity and status stratification in Deadhead subculture. Pp. 118–47 in *Youth culture: Identity in a postmodern world*, edited by J. Epstein. Malden, MA: Blackwell, 1998.

Scheer, R. 2000. No defense: How the *New York Times* convicted Wen Ho Lee. *The Nation*, October 23, pp. 11–20.

Schwartz, T. 1982. Cultural totemism: Ethnic identity, primitive and modern. Pp. 106–131 in *Ethnic identities: Cultural continuities and change*, edited by G. De Vos and L. Romanucci-Ross. Chicago: University of Chicago Press.

Sengupta, S. 1996. To be young, Indian and hip: Hip-hop meets Hindi pop as a new generation of South Asians finds its own groove. *New York Times*, June 30, section 13: "The City," p. 1.

———. 1997. Groups plan protest at India Day parade: Gay organizers barred from celebration. *New York Times*, August 17, "Metro."

———. 1998. United ethnically, and by an assault. *New York Times*, October 7, "Metro," p. B1.

Serafica, F. C. 1990. Counseling Asian-American parents: A cultural-developmental approach. Pp. 222–44 in *Mental health of ethnic minorities*, edited by F. C. Serafica, A. I. Schwebel, R. K. Russell, P. D. Isaac, and L. B. Myers. New York: Praeger.

Shah, S. 1994. Presenting the blue goddess: Toward a national, pan-Asian feminist agenda. Pp. 147–158 in *The state of Asian America: Activism and resistance in the 1990s*, edited by K. Aguilar-San Juan. Boston: South End Press.

Shankar, L. D., and R. Srikanth. 1998. *A part yet apart: South Asians in Asian America*. Philadelphia: Temple University Press.

Sharma, A. 1996. Sounds Oriental: The (im)possibility of theorizing Asian musical cultures. Pp. 15–31 in *Dis-Orienting rhythms: The politics of the new Asian dance music*, edited by S. Sharma, J. Hutnyk, and A. Sharma. London: Zed Press.

Sharma, N. 1998. Identities un-rapping race: The role of hip-hop in the identity formation of second generation Indian Americans. Paper presented at the Annual Conference on South Asia, University of Wisconsin, Madison. October.

Sharma, S. 1996. Noisy Asians or 'Asian noise'? Pp. 32–55 in *Dis-Orienting rhythms: The politics of the new Asian dance music*, edited by S. Sharma, J. Hutnyk, and A. Sharma. London: Zed Press.

Sharma, S., J. Hutnyk, and A. Sharma. 1996. Introduction. Pp. 32–57 in *Dis-Orienting rhythms: The politics of the new Asian dance music*, edited by S. Sharma, J. Hutnyk, and A. Sharma. London: Zed Press.

Shukla, S. 1997. Building diaspora and nation: The 1991 'Cultural Festival of India.' *Cultural Studies* 11(2): 269–315.

Sibley, D. 1995. *Geographies of exclusion: Society and difference in the West*. London: Routledge.

Singh, A. 1996. African Americans and the new immigrants. Pp. 93–110 in *Between the lines: South Asians and postcoloniality*, edited by D. Bahri and M. Vasudeva. Philadelphia: Temple University Press.

Skoggard, I. 1998. Transnational commodity flows and the global phenomenon of the brand. Pp. 57–70 in *Consuming fashion: Adorning the transnational body*, edited by A. Brydon and S. Niessen. Oxford: Berg.

Spivak, G. C. 1993. *Outside in the teaching machine*. New York: Routledge.

Stacey, J. 1991. Can there be a feminist ethnography? Pp. 111–119 in *Women's words: The feminist practice of oral history*, edited by S. Gluck and D. Patai. New York: Routledge.

Stallybrass, P., and A. White. 1986. *The politics and poetics of transgression*. Ithaca: Cornell University Press.

Steinberg, S. 1981. *The ethnic myth: Race, ethnicity, and class in America*. Boston: Beacon Press.

Stevens-Long, J. 1990. Adult development: Theories past and future. Pp. 125–69 in *New dimensions in adult development*, edited by R. A. Nemiroff and C. A. Colarusso. New York: Basic Books.

Stewart, K. 1992. Nostalgia: A polemic. Pp. 252–66 in *Re-reading cultural anthropology*, edited by G. E. Marcus. Durham: Duke University Press.

Stokes, M. 1994. Introduction: Ethnicity, Identity, and Music. Pp. 1–27 in *Ethnicity, Identity, and Music*, edited by M. Stokes. Oxford, U.K.: Berg.

Strauss, C. 1995. Late capitalism, postmodernism, and the "fragmented" self. Paper presented at the Human Development and Psychology Colloquium, Harvard Graduate School of Education, Cambridge, Massachusetts.

Strauss, C., and N. Quinn. 1994. A cognitive/cultural psychology. Pp. 284–300 in *Assessing cultural anthropology*, edited by R. Borofsky. New York: McGraw-Hill.

Straw, W. 1997. Sizing up record collections: Gender and connoisseurship in rock music culture. Pp. 3–16 in *Sexing the groove: Popular music and gender*, edited by S. Whitely. London: Routledge.

Strinati, D. 1995. *An introduction to theories of popular culture*. London: Routledge.

Suárez-Orozco, C., and M. Suárez-Orozco. (1995). *Transformations: Migration, family life, and achievement motivation among Latino adolescents*. Stanford: Stanford University Press.

Suárez-Orozco, M. 1995. The need for strangers: Proposition 187 and the immigration malaise. *Multicultural Review* (4)2: 17–58.

Sue, S., and J. K. Morishima. 1982. Cultural perspectives on mental health issues. Pp. 1–12 in *The mental health of Asian-Americans*, edited by S. Sue and J. K. Morishima. San Francisco: Jossey-Bass.

Sutton, C. 1992. Some thoughts on gendering and internationalizing our thinking about transnational migrations. Pp. 241–49 in *Towards a transnational perspective on migration: Race, class, ethnicity, and nationalism reconsidered*, edited by N. Glick Shiller, L. Basch, and C. Szanton Blanc. New York: New York Academy of Sciences.

Suzuki, B. H. 1995. Education and the socialization of Asian Americans: A revisionist analysis of the "model minority" thesis. Pp. 113–132 in *The Asian American educational experience: A sourcebook for teachers and students*, edited by D. T. Nakanishi and T. Y. Nishida. New York and London: Routledge.

Takaki, R. 1989a. *India in the West: South Asians in America*. New York: Chelsea House.

———. 1989b. *Strangers from a different shore: A history of Asian Americans*. New York: Penguin.

Taylor, C. 1992. *Multiculturalism and the politics of recognition: An essay with commentary by Amy Gutmann*, edited by A. Gutmann. Princeton, NJ: Princeton University Press.

Taylor, T. 1997. *Global pop: World music, world markets*. New York: Routledge.

Thai, H. C. 1999. "Splitting things in half is so white!": Conceptions of family life and friendship and the formation of ethnic identity among second generation Vietnamese Americans. *Amerasia Journal* 25(1): 53–88.

Thornton, S. (1996). *Club Cultures*. Cambridge: Polity Press.

Thornton, S. 1997a. The social logic of subcultural capital. Pp. 200–209 in *The subcultures reader*, edited by K. Gelder and S. Thornton. New York: Routledge.

———. 1997b. General introduction. Pp. 1–15 in *The subcultures reader*, edited by K. Gelder and S. Thornton. New York: Routledge.

Ting-Toomey, S. 1981. Ethnic identity and close friendship in Chinese-American college students. *International Journal of Intercultural Relations* 5: 383–406.

Torney-Purta, J. 1990. Youth in relation to social institutions. Pp. 457–477 in *At the threshold: The developing adolescent*, edited by S. S. Feldman and G. R. Elliott. Cambridge, Mass.: Harvard University Press.

Touré. 1997. Members Only. *New York Times Magazine*, October 19, pp. 98–99.

Tuan, M. 1999. On Asian American ice queens and multigenerational Asian ethnics. *Amerasia* 25(1): 181–86.

Turner, G. *British cultural studies: An introduction*. 2d ed. London: Routledge, 1996.

Turner, V. 1967. *The forest of symbols: Aspects of Ndembu ritual*. Ithaca: Cornell University Press.

———. 1987. *The anthropology of performance*. New York: Performing Arts Journal Publications, 1987.

U.S. Census Bureau. 1993. *We the Americans: Asians*. U.S. Department of Commerce, Economics and Statistics Administration, Washington, D.C.

van der Veer, P. 1994. Hindu nationalism and the discourse of modernity: The Vishva Hindu Parishad. Pp. 653–69 in *Accounting for fundamentalisms: The dynamic character of movement*, edited by M. Marty and R. Scott Appleby. Chicago: University of Chicago Press.

———. 1997. 'The enigma of arrival': Hybridity and authenticity in the global space. Pp. 90–105 in *Debating cultural hybridity: Multi-cultural identities and the politics of racism*, edited by P. Werbner and T. Modood. London: Zed Books.

van Gennep, A. 1960. *The rites of passage*, translated by M. Vizedom and G. Caffee. Chicago: University of Chicago Press.

Visweswaran, K. 1993. Predicaments of the hyphen. Pp. 301–12 in *Our feet walk the sky: Women of the South Asian diaspora*, edited by the Women of South Asia Descent Collective. San Francisco: Aunt Lute Books.

———. 1997. Diaspora by design: Flexible citizenship and South Asians in U.S. racial formations. *Diaspora* 6(1): 5–29.

Visweswaran, K., and A. Mir. 1999/2000. On the politics of community in South Asian American studies. *Amerasia Journal—Satyagraha in America* 25(3): 97–108.

Wakil, S. P., C. M. Siddique, and F. A. Wakil. 1981. Between two cultures: A study in socialization of children of immigrants. *Journal of Marriage and the Family* 43(4): 929–40.

Wang, O. 1997. *Big yellow knuckles: The cultural politics of Asian American hip hop.* Paper presented at the annual meeting of the Association for Asian American Studies, Seattle, April.

Waters, M. 1990. *Ethnic options: Choosing identities in America*. Berkeley: University of California Press.

———. 1994. Ethnic and racial identities of second-generation Black immigrants in New York City. *International Migration Review* 28(4): 795–820.

Wei, W. 1993. *The Asian American movement*. Philadelphia: Temple University Press.

Werbner, P. 1997. Introduction: The dialectics of cultural hybridity. Pp. 1–26 in *Debating cultural hybridity: Multi-cultural identities and the politics of anti-racism*, edited by P. Werbner and T. Modood. London: Zed Books.

Werbner, P., and N. Yuval-Davis. 1999. Introduction: Women and the new discourse of citizenship. Pp. 1–38 in *Women, citizenship and difference*, edited by N. Yuval-Davis and P. Werbner. London and New York: Zed Books.

Westkott, M. 1990. Feminist criticism of the social sciences. Pp. 58–68 in *Feminist research methods*, edited by J. Nielsen. Boulder, CO: Westview Press.

Westwood, S. 1995. Gendering diaspora: Space, politics, and South Asian masculinities in Britain. Pp. 197–221 in *Nation and migration: The politics of space in the South Asian diaspora*, edited by P. van der Veer. Philadelphia: University of Pennsylvania Press.

Whitely, S. 1997. Introduction. Pp. xiii–xxxvi in *Sexing the groove: Popular music and gender*, edited by S. Whitely. London: Routledge.

Williams, M. 1989. Ladies on the line: Punjabi cannery workers in central California. Pp. 148–59 in *Making waves: An anthology of writings by and about Asian American women*, edited by Asian Women United of California. Boston: Beacon Press.

Williams, R. 1977. *Marxism and literature*. Oxford: Oxford University Press.

Williams, R. B. 1989. Negotiating the tradition: Religious organizations and Gujarati group identity in the United States. *Studies in Third World Societies* 39: 25–38.

Willis, Paul. 1977. *Learning to labor: How working-class kids get working-class jobs*. New York: Columbia University Press (Morningside edition, 1981).

Wong, S. 1995. *American knees*. New York: Scribner's.

Yang, F. 1999. ABC and XYZ: Religious, ethnic and racial identities of the new second generation Chinese in Christian churches. *Amerasia Journal* 25(1): 89–114.

Yinger, J. M. 1994. *Ethnicity: Source of strength? Source of conflict?* Albany: State University of New York Press.

Zavella, P. 1997. "Playing with fire": The gendered construction of Chicana/ Mexicana sexuality. Pp. 392–408 in *The gender/sexuality reader: Culture, history, political economy*, edited by R. N. Lancaster and M. di Leonardo. New York: Routledge.

Zhou, M. 1997. Segmented assimilation: Issues, controversies, and recent research on the new second generation. *International Migration Review* 31(4): 975–1008.

Zhou, M., and C. L. Bankston. 1994. Social capital and the adaptation of the second generation: The case of Vietnamese youth in New Orleans. *International Migration Review* 28(4): 821–45.

Zhou, M., and C. L. Bankston. 1998. *Growing up American: How Vietnamese Children Adapt to Life in the United States*. New York: Russell Sage Foundation.

Index

239